M000315504

THE POLITICAL CLASSROOM

Helping students develop their ability to deliberate political questions is an essential component of democratic education, but introducing political issues into the classroom is pedagogically challenging and raises ethical dilemmas for teachers. Diana E. Hess and Paula McAvoy argue that teachers will make better professional judgments about these issues if they aim toward creating "political classrooms," which engage students in deliberations about questions that ask, "How should we live together?"

Based on the findings from a large, mixed-method study about discussions of political issues within high school classrooms, *The Political Classroom* presents in-depth and engaging cases of teacher practice. Paying particular attention to how political polarization and social inequality affect classroom dynamics, Hess and McAvoy promote a coherent plan for providing students with a nonpartisan political education and for improving the quality of classroom deliberations.

Diana E. Hess is Senior Vice President of the Spencer Foundation and Professor of Social Studies Education at the University of Wisconsin–Madison, USA.

Paula McAvoy is a philosopher of education and an Associate Program Officer of the Spencer Foundation, USA.

The Critical Social Thought Series

**Edited by Michael W. Apple,
University of Wisconsin–Madison**

Contradictions of Control: School Structure and School Knowledge
Linda M. McNeil

Working Class without Work: High School Students in a De-industrializing Society
Lois Weis

Social Analysis of Education: After the New Sociology
Philip Wexler

Capitalist Schools: Explanation and Ethics in Radical Studies of Schooling
Daniel P. Liston

Getting Smart: Feminist Research and Pedagogy with/in the Postmodern
Patti Lather

Teacher Education and the Social Conditions of Schooling
Daniel P. Liston and Kenneth M. Zeichner

Race, Identity, and Representation in Education
Warren Crichlow and Cameron McCarthy, editors

Public Schools That Work: Creating Community
Gregory A. Smith, editor

Power and Method: Political Activism and Educational Research
Andrew Gitlin, editor

Critical Ethnography in Educational Research: A Theoretical and Practical Guide
Phil Francis Carspecken

The Uses of Culture: Education and the Limits of Ethnic Affiliation
Cameron McCarthy

Education, Power, and Personal Biography: Dialogues with Critical Educators
Carlos Alberto Torres, editor

Contradictions of School Reform: Educational Costs of Standardized Testing
Linda M. McNeil

Act Your Age! A Cultural Construction of Adolescence
Nancy Lesko

Tough Fronts: The Impact of Street Culture on Schooling
L. Janelle Dance

J. DeaRy

Political Spectacle and the Fate of American Schools
Mary Lee Smith with Walter Heinecke, Linda Miller-Kahn, and Patricia F. Jarvis

Rethinking Scientific Literacy
Wolff-Michael Roth and Angela Calabrese Barton

High Stakes Education: Inequality, Globalization, and Urban School Reform
Pauline Lipman

Learning to Labor in New Times
Nadine Dolby and Greg Dimitriadis, editors

Working Method: Research and Social Justice
Lois Weis and Michelle Fine

Class Reunion: The Remaking of the American White Working Class
Lois Weis

Race, Identity, and Representation in Education, Second Edition
Cameron McCarthy, Warren Crichlow, Greg Dimitriadis, and Nadine Dolby

Radical Possibilities: Public Policy, Urban Education, and a New Social Movement
Jean Anyon

Could It Be Otherwise? Parents and the Inequities of Public School Choice
Lois André-Bechely

Reading and Writing the World with Mathematics
Eric Gustein

Market Movements: African American Involvement in School Voucher Reform
Thomas C. Pedroni

Rightist Multiculturalism: Core Lessons on Neoconservative School Reform
Kristen L. Buras

Unequal By Design: High-Stakes Testing and the Standardization of Inequality
Wayne Au

Black Literate Lives: Historical and Contemporary Perspectives
Maisha T. Fisher

Hidden Markets: The New Education Privatization
Patricia Burch

Critical Perspectives on bell hooks
Maria del Guadalupe Davidson and George Yancy, editors

Advocacy Leadership: Toward a Post-Reform Agenda in Education
Gary L. Anderson

Race, Whiteness, and Education
Zeus Leonardo

Controversy in the Classroom: The Democratic Power of Discussion
Diana E. Hess

The New Political Economy of Urban Education: Neoliberalism, Race, and the Right to the City
Pauline Lipman

Critical Curriculum Studies: Education, Consciousness, and the Politics of Knowing
Wayne Au

Learning to Liberate: Community-Based Solutions to the Crisis in Urban Education
Vajra Watson

Critical Pedagogy and Social Change: Critical Analysis on the Language of Possibilitiy
Seehwa Cho

Educating Activist Allies: Social Justice Pedagogy with the Suburban and Urban Elite
Katy Swalwell

The Political Classroom: Evidence and Ethics in Democratic Education
Diana E. Hess and Paula McAvoy

THE POLITICAL CLASSROOM

Evidence and Ethics in Democratic Education

Diana E. Hess and Paula McAvoy

Routledge
Taylor & Francis Group

NEW YORK AND LONDON

First published 2015
by Routledge
711 Third Avenue, New York, NY 10017

Simultaneously published in the UK
by Routledge
2 Park Square, Milton Park, Abingdon, Oxon OX14 4RN

Routledge is an imprint of the Taylor & Francis Group, an informa business

Library of Congress Cataloging-in-Publication Data
Hess, Diana E.
  The political classroom : evidence and ethics in democratic education /
Diana E. Hess, Paula McAvoy.
    pages cm. — (Critical social thought)
  1. Education—Curricula—Political aspects—United States.
2. Democracy and education—United States. 3. Academic freedom—
United States. I. McAvoy, Paula. II. Title.
  LC89.H44 2014
  379.73—dc23
  2014022767

ISBN: 978-0-415-88098-5 (hbk)
ISBN: 978-0-415-88099-2 (pbk)
ISBN: 978-1-315-73887-1 (ebk)

Typeset in Bembo
by Apex CoVantage, LLC

We dedicate this book to the 35 teachers and their students who participated in the *Discussion of Controversial Political Issues Study* from 2005–2009.

CONTENTS

List of Figures and Tables	*xi*
Series Editor Introduction, Michael W. Apple	*xiii*
Acknowledgments	*xvii*
1 Introduction to the Political Classroom	1

PART I
Context, Evidence, and Aims   **17**

2 The Political Classroom in Context	19
3 Evidence From the Political Classroom	45
4 Educational Aims and the Political Classroom	70

PART II
Cases of Practice   **83**

5 Adams High: A Case of Inclusive Participation	85
6 Mr. Kushner: A Case of Political Friendship	109
7 Mr. Walters: A Case of Bounded Autonomy	132

PART III
Professional Judgment   **153**

Introduction to Part III   155

8   The Ethics of Framing and Selecting Issues   158

9   The Ethics of Withholding and Disclosing
    Political Views   182

10 Supporting the Political Classroom   204

Afterword, Harry Brighouse   *213*
Appendix   *217*
References   *233*
Index   *241*

FIGURES AND TABLES

Figures

1.1	Framework for Professional Judgment	12
2.1	Students' 2004 Presidential Preferences by State	39
2.2	Students' 2008 Presidential Preferences by State	40
4.1	Framework for Professional Judgment	73
8.1	Framework for Professional Judgment	155

Tables

2.1	Washington High School: Distribution of Students in Top Two Tracks by SES	29
2.2	Demographic Differences by Generation	31
2.3	Ideological Differences by Generation	32
2.4	Ideological Variance Among Millennials	33
2.5	Study Sample by State	35
2.6	Participants and Study Stages	35
2.7	Study Sample and Public High School Demographics in Three States	36
2.8	Media Consumption by Students in the Study in 2005, 2007, and 2009	41
3.1	Number of Teachers, Students, and Schools by Classroom Type	48
3.2	Classroom Practice Effects Observed at Post-Survey	59
3.3	Follow-Up Cluster Labels and Profiles	64
3.4	Cluster Mean Scores for Outcomes Used in Clustering	65
5.1	The Simulation at a Glance	90

7.1	Like-Minded Schools	136
7.2	Learning in Like-Minded Schools	149
8.1	Aims of the Political Classroom	156
8.2	Types of Issues	161
8.3	Settled Empirical and Political Issues	162
8.4	Open Empirical and Political Issues	163
A.1	Race and Ethnicity of Students by Wave	220
A.2	Socioeconomic Characteristics of Students by Wave	220
A.3	Post-Course Survey Comparison: Classroom Discussion	221
A.4	Post-Course Survey Comparison: News and Political Talk Outcomes	222
A.5	Post-Course Survey Comparison: Knowledge and Interest	224
A.6	Post-Course Survey Comparison: Political Participation	225
A.7	Like-Minded and Politically Diverse School Sample by Wave	227
A.8	Teacher and Student Views on Disclosure	228

SERIES EDITOR INTRODUCTION

One of the most significant questions that we can ask about schooling is whether education can change society. In the midst of the conflicts and inequalities that now characterize so many nations, can schools be part of the process in which a society becomes more democratic, more respectful of its people, more responsive, and more committed to equality? Generations of writers, including myself, have offered answers to what is clearly a complex set of issues surrounding this question (Apple, 2013). This complexity—and the educational, ethical, and political debates involved in answering the question—should not surprise us. After all, there has never been total agreement on what education is for, who should control it, what should be taught, and even who should be involved in asking and answering these questions (Apple, 2014).

While there have always been substantive disagreements over these issues, these conflicts have become even more volatile now. At the time of this writing, news reports are filled with stories of increasing political polarization in the United States. Positions are supposedly hardening. This is due to many things, including: the increasing racial and class segregation in where people live; an economy in crisis and growing economic inequality; the ideological segmentation of the media that does indeed give more choices, but also has the effect of cocooning people so that they experience only that with which they already agree; the strategies by politically and economically dominant groups to use racial fears and fear of the "Other" to maintain their power; a political culture in which getting elected often means not antagonizing in any way the conservative ideological base of the most extreme factions of one's party; and many more things.

But no matter what the causes, it is clear that we are living through one of those periods in United States history, and the histories of other nations as well, when economic, political, cultural, and religious conflicts are powerfully present. This makes the questions of whether education has a role to play in preparing students to live in a world where conflicts and controversies are ever present, and in helping to produce a more democratic civic culture even more salient. In *The Political Classroom*, Diana Hess and Paula McAvoy respond to this with a resounding *yes*, calling for a schooling process that is expressly aimed at creating such a culture.

In her influential previous book, *Controversy in the Classroom* (Hess, 2009), Diana Hess provided us with a detailed and powerful argument for the centrality of curricula and teaching involving controversial issues. Her analysis of classrooms engaged in this and her articulate defense of theories, policies, and practices that support this made that book a significant intervention into the debates over what should go on in classrooms if we are concerned with maintaining a democratic culture in schools and the larger society.

The call for schools to participate in building a robust civic culture that exemplifies deliberative forms of democracy places schools and their curricula in a very difficult, yet very important, position. Let us be honest. Schools, and especially public schools, are not immune to the tendencies I noted in the first paragraphs of this introduction.

The attacks on the very nature of the public sphere have become pronounced. For all too many people, public is by definition "bad" and private is by definition "good." Schools, teachers, and curricula increasingly have taken center stage in the social and ideological conflicts that permeate this society, sometimes as proxies for larger concerns but at other times as an institution that represents the dangers in our society and indeed what kind of society we want in the future (Apple, 2006).

Furthermore, like the rest of society, schools have become more segregated by class and race, and this transformation has had very real effects on the kinds of issues that schools and classrooms take up. Making this situation even more difficult, at the same time the measure of a good student, a good teacher, a good curriculum, and indeed an entire school is reduced to one thing—increased scores on achievement tests. This is an act of what might best be thought of as "collective amnesia." We forget the many things that an education worthy of its name should do. Instead, we reduce the function of education to one's ability to perform well on one thing on one day. This ignores the fact that a democratic polity needs active citizens who are willing and able to continue the ongoing vast experiment of building a just and responsive society that works for all of us.

In this collective amnesia, for all too many people, students are not only valued by their scores on tests, but they also are simply seen as future workers. In this perspective, the primary goal of schooling should be preparation of students for jobs. While not unimportant, this too is deeply problematic. This too is where *The Political Classroom* enters. As Diana Hess and Paula McAvoy powerfully argue in this compelling book, one of the most important functions of schooling is indeed to prepare students for participation in a vibrant democracy, to sort through arguments, to have evidence for their claims.

Much of the volume is grounded in one of the most detailed examinations we have ever had of what actually happens in schools. It gets us inside many different kinds of schools, both public and private, both religious and secular, both affluent and not. In the process, Hess and McAvoy jointly construct a picture of what teachers did and why they did it when teachers confronted in honest ways the controversies of this society. They show us how different students experience what they did and why. And they go further by following up on students after they left high school to see what difference their experiences made and why.

Bringing together an impressive range of theoretical, political, and educational material, *The Political Classroom* insightfully illuminates how ideological diversity or the lack of such diversity mattered in classrooms and how the intense tracking that often is present in many schools meant that students were surrounded by those who were very similar in terms of class backgrounds. Yet at the same time, other schools worked very hard to have more diverse student populations in their classrooms in order to stimulate the kinds of discussions and deliberations that enable students to respectfully engage with each other over some of the most controversial issues that divide the nation.

One of the main elements of the book is the importance of teachers, especially in a time when it is so hard to have substantive discussions that reflect the cleavages that characterize this society, such as those involving immigration policy, abortion, and similar things. There are important skills involved in successfully teaching in a way that deals with these issues. This too is an important point. These skills and the values attached to them don't occur overnight. They take years to develop. Because of this, Hess and McAvoy's book is also a response to those groups who see teaching as "easy," as something that doesn't require much thought and experience. Exactly the opposite is true. Civic-minded teaching is not something that can be scripted and learned in a short period of time. Nor is it only one thing, one set of skills that all teachers must follow. As the authors show, creating a democratic civic culture requires immense skill, patience, and courage—and a consistent reflexiveness about what is appropriate for teachers to do. And as they also demonstrate, the best examples of this in action also have time and space for teacher collaboration, time and space for teachers to work together.

This is something that is increasingly being lost as we value schools and teaching either only by the production of test scores or as simply reducible to the preparation for jobs, even though many of these jobs unfortunately actually don't require a high level of knowledge and skills, no matter what the rhetoric of major school reformers seem to be saying. And it is just as powerfully lost as we increasingly and all too uncritically assume that the techniques and ideologies that dominate the corporate world should be brought to the center of the world of education (see, for example, Berliner & Glass, 2014; Katz & Rose, 2013; Lipman, 2011; Ravitch, 2013).

There are better examples of thoughtful schooling that increase the range of skills and values that students learn and that also respect educators for the difficult work that they do in communities and schools (Apple & Beane, 2007; Watson, 2012). In her earlier volume, Diana Hess clearly demonstrated what can happen when we take these and other examples seriously. In *The Political Classroom*, Hess and McAvoy take us much further, and in doing so, they have produced a volume that helps all of us counteract the collective amnesia that is so very damaging to education right now.

It often seems trite to say things such as, "This is an important book." But let me go even further. *The Political Classroom* is a crucial book. Rich in detail about real classrooms, real students, and real teachers and guided by a deep commitment to the place of schooling in a robust democracy, it offers us not only a worrisome analysis about what is happening when we lose sight of some of the most crucial goals of schooling. It does much more. It provides us with tools and examples to understand why there is real hope for the future.

Michael W. Apple

John Bascom Professor of Curriculum and Instruction

and

Educational Policy Studies

University of Wisconsin, Madison

References

Apple, M. W. (2006). *Educating the "right" way: Markets, standards, God, and inequality* (2nd ed.). New York, NY: Routledge.

Apple, M. W. (2013). *Can education change society?* New York, NY: Routledge.

Apple, M. W. (2014). *Official knowledge: Democratic education in a conservative age* (3rd ed.). New York, NY: Routledge.

Apple, M. W. & Beane, J. A. (Eds.) (2007). *Democratic schools: Lessons in powerful education* (2nd ed.). Portsmouth, NH: Heinemann.

Berliner, D. & Glass, G. (2014). *50 Myths & lies that threaten America's public schools.* New York, NY: Teachers College Press.

Hess, D. (2009). *Controversy in the classroom: The democratic power of discussion.* New York, NY: Routledge.

Katz, M. & Rose, D. (2013). *Public education under siege.* Philadelphia, PA: University of Pennsylvania Press.

Lipman, P. (2011). *The new political economy of urban education: Neoliberalism, race, and the right to the city.* New York, NY: Routledge.

Ravitch, D. (2013). *Reign of error: The hoax of privatization and the danger to America's public schools.* New York, NY: Knopf.

Watson, V. (2012). *Learning to liberate: Community-based solutions to the crisis in urban education.* New York, NY: Routledge.

ACKNOWLEDGMENTS

We thank Michael Apple and Catherine Bernard for their support of this book. Their sage advice, constant encouragement, and patience were absolutely crucial during a writing process that took longer than we anticipated. We also thank Harry Brighouse, who encouraged us to bring ethics into conversation with the empirical evidence and was instrumental in helping us plan three deliberations of philosophers, social scientists, and educators that shaped our thinking. Throughout the writing process, Harry has offered us good advice and lots of moral support.

This book is based on a study that included 21 teachers in 35 schools and 1,001 of their students. We thank the teachers for opening their classroom doors to us and graciously sharing their time so we could understand their practice and how they thought about what happened in these classes—and we are also appreciative of the students, many of whom participated in multiple interviews over four years. Four outstanding non-profit organizations were also involved in the study: the Choices for the 21st Century Education Program at Brown University (and their state partners, the Illinois Humanities Council, and the Center for the Study of Global Change at Indiana University at Bloomington) and the Constitutional Rights Foundation Chicago. We thank their staffs for providing access to the multi-school deliberation forums that are discussed in Chapter 10. In particular, we wish to thank the executive directors: Susan Graseck of the Choices Program, Carolyn Pereira of the Constitutional Rights Foundation Chicago (who retired in 2011), and her successor, Nisan Chavkin.

In the early planning for the study, we were assisted by three civic education researchers and scholars whose work we so admire: Walter Parker at the University of Washington, Seattle; Joe Kahne from Mills College; and Wendy Richardson. Their advice about the conceptual framework and methods for the study steered us in a productive direction.

The study was housed at the Wisconsin Center for Education Research for a number of years. We appreciate the support we received from Adam Gamoran, Kay Schultz, and the administrative team at WCER. John Smithson spent innumerable hours crafting statistical models that helped us make sense of a sprawling and complex data set, and we are in his debt. The University of Wisconsin Survey Center helped us develop and then very ably executed the two sets of phone interviews after the students had left high school—one in 2007 and the other in 2009. Their staff did an excellent job.

Since planning for the study began in 2004, a number of graduate students have been instrumental in its success. First and foremost, we thank Louis Ganzler, who worked with Diana to craft the study and collect and analyze the data in the first two years. Louis wrote a superb dissertation on the study, focusing on Adams High School, the school that we showcase in Chapter 5. In addition, we thank Jeremy Stoddard, Wayne Au, Melani Winter, Ru Dawley-Carr, Shawna Rosenzweig, Sam Roecker, Alison Turner, Taehan Kim, Casey Meehan, Mike Kopish, Sarbani Chakraborty, and Sara Matthews for their assistance collecting and analyzing the data.

During the 2009–2010 academic year, we used a small grant from the Spencer Foundation to host three deliberations about the ethical dilemmas raised by the data. Harry Brighouse helped us conceptualize and organize these, and they were attended by Simone Schweber, Anthony Laden, Donald Downs, Kathryn Walsh, Robert Streiffer, Blain Neufeld, Peter Levine, Ann Cudd, Blain Neufeld, Kyla Ebels-Duggan, Larry Blum, Victoria DeFrancesco Soto, Walter Parker, Sigal Ben-Porath, Stacey Lee, Gloria Ladson-Billings, Jaime Ahlberg, Shannon Reiter, Ru Dawley-Carr, Quentin Wheeler-Bell, Shawna Rosenzweig, and Gina Schouten. We thank all of them for contributing to these rich and interesting conversations.

A number of other talented statisticians analyzed the data and worked with us to make sense of what claims we could make and which we could not. In particular, Kei Kawashima-Ginsberg has been working with us for several years and did an excellent job. We learned so much from her. We also want to thank Maya Lopuch, Teahan Kim, and Hyunseo Hwang for their work analyzing the survey data.

As we were drafting chapters, a number of readers provided helpful advice that enormously improved the quality of the writing. Thank you to Katy Swalwell, Lauren Gatti, Harry Brighouse, Matthew Ferkany, Bennett Singer, Keith Barton, Joe Kahne, Simone Schweber, Michael Feuer, Cara Gallagher, Christel Payne, Adam Nelson, Shawn Healy, Dee Runaas, Colin Ong-Dean, Ellen Middaugh, and Evan DuFaux.

Throughout the study, we have presented papers at various conferences, including the American Educational Research Association (AERA), the Association for Practical and Professional Ethics (APPE), the American Political Science Association (APSA), the College and University Faculty Association (CUFA), and the Philosophy of Education Association Great Britain (PESGB). We are grateful for everything we learned from the anonymous reviewers and our discussants.

For funding the study, we thank the Center for Information & Research in Civic Learning and Engagement (CIRCLE), the Carnegie Corporation of New

York, the McCormick Foundation, Brown University, the Graduate School of the University of Wisconsin-Madison, the Gibb Democracy Education Fund, and the Spencer Foundation. While we were writing the book, Diana took a leave from UW-Madison to join the Spencer Foundation as its Senior Vice President, and Paula took a leave from Illinois State University to come to Spencer as an Associate Program Officer. We can't begin to adequately thank Mike McPherson, the President of the Spencer Foundation, the staff, and the Board of Directors for the support they have given to this project. In particular, we thank Gladys Reyes, Research Associate at the Spencer Foundation, for her tireless, good humored, and utterly professional work as we turned drafts into a completed manuscript.

In addition to all those mentioned above, Paula would like to thank her parents, Ruth McAvoy and the late Ken McAvoy, for being excellent models of political and civic engagement. The evening news was a sacred hour in our home, and while we were taught the importance of staying informed, I'm very appreciative that they allowed their children to discover their political views on their own. My sisters, Karla and Pam, and their families have also been incredibly supportive and curious about this project. A special thanks goes to my brother Greg McAvoy and sister-in-law Susan Bickford, the family's political science consultants, for providing help whenever we needed it. I would also like to thank Michael Wilson, Seth Donnelly, Lynda Haworth, Claudia Loo, Bill McClintock, Natasha Crum and the students at Foothill Middle College, who made teaching a joy for ten years. I've also have a fabulous social support group, many of whom have already been named above: Lauren Gatti, Katie Elliott, Garrett Smith, Julie and David Minikel-Lacocque, Shannon and Stephen Vakil, Connie North, Stacy Otto, Jo-Lee Wishner and family, and the members of the BFL. Amato Nocera has been an amazing listener, reader, and source of laughter and cocktails in this process, and I am so grateful for his partnership. Finally, in 2006, Diana Hess asked if I'd take on some hourly work in the early stages of this study, and that role grew until eventually it became "We should write a book." I cannot thank her enough for bringing me into this adventure and for so generously turning her study into our study.

In addition, Diana thanks the following for the many ways in which they provided encouragement, nurture, and friendship throughout the years she worked on this project: her siblings (Sue and Chris) and their partners and children, Lisa O'Brien, Dawnene Hassett, Barbara Miller, John and Jaye Zola, Bebs Chorak, Susan Griffin, Maria Marquardt, Martha Merilos, Gary Coleman, the late Norma Wright, Ted McConnell, Michelle Herczog, Alan Lockwood, and Cathy O'Sullivan. Also, a huge thank you to Nicole Barksdale for doing such a great job juggling competing demands—always with grace, incredible skill, and good humor. Finally, this project demanded deliberation at every stage. Since Paula joined the team in 2006, I have learned so much from her through constant deliberations about empirical and philosophical questions. Paula's deep understanding of teaching, democratic theory, philosophy of education, and the enormous data set we accumulated, coupled with her fine writing skills, make this project so much better than it would have been otherwise. Thank you, Paula.

Notwithstanding the wonderful assistance, support, and advice we have received from all those we acknowledge here, we are responsible for any errors of fact or interpretation in this book. Lastly, the views and interpretations expressed here do not represent those of the Spencer Foundation, the University of Wisconsin–Madison, or any of the organizations that helped fund the research.

1

INTRODUCTION TO THE POLITICAL CLASSROOM

The 2009 school year opened amid a firestorm of political controversy. As the nation's students and teachers prepared to return to their classrooms, newly elected President Barack Obama announced that he would address the country's schoolchildren on the first day of school. According to a White House press release, President Obama's speech was intended to be motivational and "to challenge students to set goals, work hard and stay in school" (U.S. Department of Education, 2009). Although President Obama was not the first president to address schoolchildren—President George H. W. Bush had delivered a similar live speech on radio and television in 1991—some Republican politicians, parents, cable-news commentators, talk-radio hosts, and bloggers voiced strong opposition to the speech. The *New York Times* reported that, despite assurances from the White House that the speech would be "nonpartisan," some parents "were concerned because the speech had not been screened for political content" (McKinley & Dillon, 2009, para. 3). Brett Curtis, a parent in Texas, explained why he kept his three children home that day: "The thing that concerned me most about it was it seemed like a direct channel from the president of the United States into the classroom, to my child" (McKinley & Dillon, 2009, para. 4). He continued, "I don't want our schools turned over to some socialist movement," a comment that alluded to the highly contentious debate about the Affordable Care Act that was playing out at the same time (McKinley & Dillon, 2009, para. 4). Others felt that the president's speech was appropriate classroom content and that "telling children they should not hear out the president of the United States, even if their parents dislike his policies, sends the wrong message—that one should not listen to someone with whom you disagree" (McKinley & Dillon, 2009, para. 20). Though the controversy intensified, President Obama delivered the address as planned at a Virginia high school; it was streamed live on the White House website, and schools were invited to show the speech to students. While some parents kept their children home to avoid screenings, others demanded that their child's school provide an alternative activity.[1]

President Bush's 1991 speech to students also elicited criticism from political opponents—primarily for using $26,750 in public money for the event—though the issue received far less play in the media. At that time, some Democrats argued that it was unethical for the president to direct a speech at the nation's schoolchildren. Congressman Richard Gephardt of Missouri voiced a sharp critique: "The Department of Education should not be producing paid political advertising for the president; it should be helping us to produce smarter students" (Cooper & Pianin, 1991, p. A14). Republican Congressman Newt Gingrich of Georgia defended President Bush's speech, asking, "Why is it political for the president of the United States to discuss education? It was done at a nonpolitical site and was beamed to a nonpolitical audience" (Cooper & Pianin, 1991, A14).[2]

The controversy over these presidential speeches highlights enduring dilemmas in education: Are schools, as Congressman Gingrich contends, "nonpolitical sites," or are they political spaces? Are students members of a "nonpolitical audience," or are they members of the democratic public? And, can schools be political spaces without also being labeled "partisan"? These questions emanate from the continually contested relationship between the institution of schools, public and private, and the larger democratic society. Understanding this relationship sheds light on the role that schools should play in preparing young people for political life. For some, classrooms should be insulated from the political world. For others, educational institutions have a responsibility to prepare young people for political engagement. But even among people who agree that schools should educate toward democratic participation, there are disagreements about where the boundary between the schoolhouse and the public sphere should be drawn.

In the United States, one of the earliest and most instructive examples of this tension occurred during the Common School Movement, when public-school reformer Horace Mann appointed Unitarian minister and abolitionist Samuel J. May as principal of one of Massachusetts' first teacher-training schools. One evening in 1843, May gathered the young women in his charge and brought them to an abolitionist meeting—a decision that resulted in one father removing his daughter from the school. Mann sent a concerned letter to May, expressing regret that the school "lost a very fine girl from one of their most respectable families" and urging May to consider such potential consequences in the future (Mann, 1865, p. 170). In the letter exchange that followed, May defended his actions by arguing that many students already were abolitionists *or were made so by Father Pierce* [a teacher at the school]" (Mann, 1865, p. 170, [emphasis original]). Growing increasingly frustrated, Mann retorted that such teaching was akin to religious proselytizing. The teacher, Mann wrote, "had no right to make them so, any more than he had to make them Unitarians," and using the school in this way "is obviously a violation of [State and investors'] trust" (Mann, 1865, p. 170).

Both the presidential speeches and the reaction to May's abolitionist excursion demonstrate ways in which schools are influenced by the broader political and social climate. In the 1830s, just as the Common School Movement was gaining momentum, anti-slavery forces fractured into those who supported a gradualist approach to ending slavery and those, like May, who adopted the more radical view that emancipation should be immediate. Mann, who was also an abolitionist, worried that if public schools were perceived as being pro-abolitionist, it would undermine the progress that had been made toward establishing universal (though racially segregated) public education.[3] In particular, he feared that May's active involvement in the abolitionist movement would provide fuel for Common School opponents in the state legislature and discourage needed investment by the "rich men" of Massachusetts (Mann, 1865, p. 172). In her biography of Horace Mann written in 1865, his wife, Mary Tyler Peabody Mann, recalled that her husband had deep respect for May in part because he was "so profound a hater of slavery," but she defended Mann's rebuke of him during a time so polarized "that no public interest was safe that was associated with the desire to do away with chattel slavery!" (p. 168).

In the more recent example, the political climate played a role in the public's response to the presidential speeches. While President Bush's speech incited a mild political reproach by congressional Democrats, President Obama's speech resulted in a vitriolic backlash. The different reactions reflect the increasingly polarized (and racialized) political climate that has made it harder for politicians and neighbors to talk with those who disagree with them about important policy issues—a phenomenon that results in public distrust of politicians and public institutions such as schools. The cause of this polarization is a complicated story of social, political, and economic change that we address in Chapter 2, but we note here that there is a close relationship between the extent of political polarization that exists in a particular time and the amount of controversy over how schools should prepare students for the political world.

The complicated relationship between schools and the larger political context creates ethical challenges for teachers and administrators. In the Antebellum Era, proponents of the anti-slavery movement likely disagreed about whether May should have taken his students to the abolitionist meeting. Some undoubtedly thought that ending slavery should take priority over the Common School Movement. Others probably argued that an education that did not encourage students to take a stand on the most important moral question of the time was not fulfilling its mission. Still others might have agreed with Mann that taking sides on a controversial political issue violated the trust of the public, students, and parents. Or they may have believed that Mann's pragmatic approach was necessary to further the cause of free education for all. The disagreement between Mann and May revolved around the question of whether it was appropriate for schools to try to influence the political views of teachers in training, who in turn could exert that same influence on their own students. More recently, in response to public pressure, school administrators made different judgments about President Obama's speech: Some chose to cancel school-wide viewing of the address, while most went ahead and showed the speech as scheduled. Others allowed teachers to decide if they would show the speech in their classrooms, while some schools allowed students to opt out. Making assessments about who used good professional judgment in these cases is difficult and requires one to be clear about what is meant by "political" and about what one believes are the purposes of schools in a democratic society. Helping teachers, parents, administrators, and students (and even political pundits) think through the relationship between schools and democratic society—and examining some of the ethical dilemmas that necessarily arise when teachers decide to include controversial political issues in the curriculum—are the purposes of this book.

The Political Classroom

We argue that schools are, and ought to be, political sites. In this context, we use the term "political" as it applies to the role of citizens within a democracy: *We are being political when we are democratically making decisions about questions that ask, "How should we live together?"* By extension, the *political classroom* is one that helps students develop their ability to deliberate political questions. When teachers engage students in discussions about what rules ought to be adopted by a class, they are teaching them to think politically. Similarly, when teachers ask students to research and discuss a current public controversy, such as, "Should same-sex marriage be legally recognized?," they are engaging in politics.

It is important to distinguish this conception of politics from the concern of parents and teachers that schools should not be *partisan* institutions. That is, to use public schools for the benefit or advancement of a particular political party's or politician's agenda would be an over-reach of state power. But schools (public and private) nevertheless are charged with preparing young people for life in a democracy, and to strip classrooms of any political content whatsoever would be an abdication of that responsibility. Moreover, the precise nature of what counts as promoting a partisan agenda is a matter of intense contestation—especially in times of political polarization. This brings us to what we call the "political education paradox," which frames much of what we discuss in this book. Simply put, it contrasts the need to provide students with a nonpartisan political education on the one hand with the need to prepare them to participate in the actual, highly partisan political community on the other. Part of the ethical challenge of teaching about politics is determining where political education ends and partisan proselytizing begins.

At the same time, we are not saying that schools are, or should be, politically neutral institutions. In fact, the political classroom is undergirded by values that promote a particular view of democratic life and so cannot be considered neutral. In *Controversy in the Classroom,* Diana Hess (2009) argues that political discussions are an essential part of learning to live in a democracy. Mastering the ability to talk across political and ideological differences helps create an informed citizenry—an essential component of a democratic society—by teaching students to weigh evidence, consider competing views, form an opinion, articulate that opinion, and respond to those who disagree. This conception of politics has its theoretical roots in the principles of deliberative democracy. In this theory, a policy or government is considered "legitimate" when the decision-making process is open to public deliberation. Much like John Dewey's (1916/2004) view of "democracy as a way of life," deliberative theorists argue that when the public discusses policy, knowledge is expanded, self-interest is diminished, and the result is a policy that a community or polity can *legitimately* expect members to follow. Amy Gutmann and Dennis Thompson (1996) argue that this process is primarily about "reason-giving." They explain:

> We define deliberative democracy as a form of government in which free and equal citizens (and their representatives) justify decisions in a process in which they give one another reasons that are mutually acceptable and generally accessible, with the aim of reaching conclusions that are binding in the present on all citizens but open to challenge in the future.
>
> (p. 7)

Similarly, proponents of the political classroom seek to teach young people to see each other as political equals and to inculcate them into the practice of reason-giving and considering how their views and behaviors affect others.

This type of democratic education requires students to talk in particular ways about particular kinds of questions. That is, students need to discuss and deliberate questions for which there are multiple and competing views—what Hess (2009) labels "open" questions. Walter Parker (2003) draws a distinction between the aims of classroom *discussion* and *deliberation*. "Discussion," he argues, "is a kind of shared inquiry, the desired outcomes of which rely on the expression and consideration of diverse views" (p. 129). The purpose of discussion is to create "shared understanding" through listening, questioning and working through ideas "in progress" (p. 129). Deliberation is a more specific type of discussion, one that aims "at deciding on a plan of action that will resolve a shared problem. . . . The opening question is usually some version of 'What should we do about this?'" (p. 131). To clarify this difference, students might *discuss* the meaning of the Second Amendment to the U.S. Constitution but *deliberate* the question "Should there be laws against the private ownership of assault weapons?" Both types of talk have democratic value, because, when done well, this sort of dialogue will give students practice giving reasons, listening, considering perspectives, evaluating views, and treating each other as political equals. But deliberation is particularly important for the formation of dispositions and values that support democracy because it requires students to consider the larger question, "How should we live together?" Deliberative theory assumes that participants "aim at finding fair terms of cooperation," "speak truthfully," and seek a solution that promotes the common good (Mansbridge et al., 2010, p. 66). When students engage in this type of talk, it encourages them to move from the self-interested thinking of "What is best for me?" to the deliberative question, "Which option seems best for society as a whole, given varied views and perspectives?"

Teaching students to deliberate political issues is an important element of democratic education. We note, however, that *how* to do this is a pedagogical challenge, in part because classrooms are unusual political spaces. On the one hand, schools are institutions that are able to provide young people with the opportunity to reason with others who may hold a variety of views; through this process, students learn that political disagreement and compromise are both valuable and normal parts of democratic decision-making. But students are also a "captive audience" of emerging citizens, and unlike adults in other public spaces, students are not able to easily exit situations that they find uncomfortable or offensive. Teachers often compel or cajole students to participate in discussions about topics they did not choose and in groups they have not selected. Finally, students also are being raised by other adult caregivers who may adhere to religious, cultural, or political values that are not well aligned with the aims of the school. Because classrooms are unusual political spaces, introducing political thinking to students in a way that is fair, age appropriate, and culturally sensitive, and that, in the end, prepares them for democratic life, requires teachers to make ethical choices. These include: Which issues will I address in my curriculum? How will I present them? What am I trying to accomplish? And how do my own opinions about this issue come into play?

Many teachers choose to avoid using political deliberations and discussions with students, often because they are unsure about how to negotiate the accompanying pedagogical challenges. Further deterring teachers is the increasingly polarized climate outside schools. Fear of parental and public backlash leads some teachers to retreat to lectures and the textbook. In Chapter 2, we will show how polarization is making it more difficult for teachers to create political classrooms; but rather than responding to what we see as a crisis in democracy by abandoning the values of deliberative democracy, we argue that engaging students in political deliberation is both possible and necessary.

Challenges to the Deliberative Ideal

It is important to keep in mind that deliberative theory presents an idea of what a better, more legitimate democratic society would look like; it is not a description of the world as it is. William Stanley (2010) argues that one important tension in social studies education exists between engaging students in activities that "transmit" the social order (preparing students for the world as it is) and those that "transform" it (preparing students for the society that ought to be). This tension also plays out in the political classroom. Teaching students to deliberate current political controversies prepares them to engage with the political world beyond school and, proponents hope, provides a foundation for thinking about controversies that will arise in the future. In this way, the political classroom is authentic to the world as it is. At the same time, the ideal deliberative space is one in which people enter as political equals and experience mutual respect. Further, participants engage in discussion with the intention to compromise, to listen, and to come to a fair (not purely self-interested) resolution. This is quite different from U.S. society as it is, in which some people do not experience mutual respect in the public sphere and where divisive partisan politics operate on the winner-take-all principle. As a result, teaching students to deliberate is transformative insofar as these are values that would make a stronger democracy but that are not widely practiced in contemporary American society.

Social inequality and political polarization are recurring themes in this book, because they complicate practices within the political classroom. We will discuss each of these in more detail in later chapters but provide a brief introduction here.

Social Inequality

Lynn Sanders (1997) argues that the liberal attachment to deliberation "between equals" as necessary for legitimate decision-making in democratic societies overlooks the reality that we do not live in a society of equals. Instead, we live in a political culture with citizens who are "already underrepresented in formal political institutions and who are systematically materially disadvantaged, namely women, racial minorities, especially Blacks, and poorer people" (p. 349). Consequently, "some citizens are better than others at articulating their arguments in rational, reasonable terms," making their views more respected and powerful (p. 349). Sanders argues that when we do not begin from a starting point of mutual respect and equality, attempts at deliberation are "often neither truly deliberative nor really democratic" (p. 349).

There are two ways in which the reality of social inequality creates challenges in the political classroom. First, when classrooms are heterogeneous along lines of social class or race, teachers need to be aware of how social divisions affect the classroom culture. If, for example, middle-class students are the majority and working-class students are the minority, there is a possibility that the well-off students will dominate discussions and exclude and silence others—behaviors that can then cause the minority to resist or disengage with the discussion. In our experience and research, this does not occur intentionally but is the result of some students being more practiced with the norms of deliberation and being unaware of how their familiarity with the type of classroom talk privileged by schools can deter others from participating.[4] It is important for teachers to be aware of and take steps to overcome dynamics like this within the classroom. Second, and more commonly, because schools in the United States have been rapidly resegregating since the mid-1980s, the deliberative space of the classroom is often a discussion among similarly positioned people in society (Frankenberg & Lee, 2002; Orfield,

Kucsera & Siegel-Hawley, 2012). When, for example, students deliberate an issue like immigration policy and there are not first- or second-generation students in the room, participants do not have to confront those most affected by the policy under discussion. Further, without this perspective, their discussion may end up reifying prejudiced views of undocumented workers and not live up to the ideal of deliberation, which is to expand understanding. In short, if the overarching question of the political classroom is, "How should we live together?," then teachers need to be very clear about who is and is not represented within their classrooms.

Polarization

Political polarization refers to moments when political discourse and action bifurcate toward ideological extremes. This causes a crowding-out of voices in the middle, leaving little room for political compromise. Polarization has occurred at various times in the United States (such as during the period leading up to the Civil War) and in other modern democracies, and it is a feature of democracy that will likely ebb and flow with the times (McCarty, Poole & Rosenthal, 2006). Scholars have established that the United States is currently polarizing once more, causing a reevaluation of fundamental principles, especially with respect to the role of the government in individuals' lives (Abramowitz, 2010; Bishop, 2008; Gutmann & Thompson, 2012; McCarty et al., 2006).

One of the reasons polarization is so troubling is that it reduces trust among citizens. Danielle Allen (2004) argues that trust is fundamental to democratic life because citizens must, to some extent, rely on strangers to make good judgments. Allen further explains that living in a democracy requires citizens to accept political losses; however, these losses can only be acceptable to the public if the losers trust that the winners will continue attending to the interests of the minority and resist operating from the position of "rivalrous self-interest." This accurately describes the political climate at the time of this writing: When there is little or no willingness to compromise, the message is that our political rivals cannot be trusted to govern with an eye to the nation's general interest, and politics becomes a game of winner-take-all. The research on why this is happening suggests that distrust and polarization fuel each other: Polarization causes distrust, and distrust causes polarization (McCarty et al., 2006).

We discuss this dynamic in greater detail in the next chapter, but it's worth noting how polarization affects classroom practice. Most importantly, as the example about President Obama's speech shows, political distrust outside schools caused some to be suspicious of what is happening inside schools. As a result, some teachers avoid topics that may be particularly heated in the community, while other educators decide to avoid political controversy altogether. Furthermore, political polarization can cause distrust within classrooms—between teachers and students and among fellow students. As we show in later chapters, creating a political classroom is particularly challenging in polarized times.

We want to be clear that we do not believe that merely teaching young people to deliberate will transform society; social inequality and political polarization are problems far too complicated to be corrected by schools. Nevertheless, deliberative principles can transform individuals, as these values can promote more productive classrooms, friendships, families, workplaces, and community organizations and can also shape how young people evaluate what is appropriate behavior in the public sphere. At the same time, school policies and practices can exacerbate social inequality and transmit the worst behaviors of polarization. Being able to think through these possible pitfalls is an important part of teaching within the political classroom.

About This Book

This book is unusual because it integrates social science research with philosophic thinking about ethical issues of teacher practice. The social science work is based on a mixed-method, longitudinal study of high school social studies courses that include deliberations of controversial political issues. We use this evidence to answer two overarching questions: (1) What did students experience and learn from these discussions? and (2) What effect do classrooms that engage young people in discussions of political controversy have on students' future political engagement and attitudes? Much of the book is based on "the study" we discuss below.

The Study

Diana Hess began collecting data with Louis Ganzler, a graduate student, in 2005. In 2006, Paula McAvoy joined the study team as a then-graduate student in philosophy of education—primarily because she, like Hess and Ganzler, had taught high school social studies for many years. Data collection was completed in the spring of 2009, and the sources included 1,001 students and 35 teachers from 21 high schools in Illinois, Indiana, and Wisconsin. We made a conscious effort to seek out what research has shown to be fairly unusual social studies courses: those taught by teachers who regularly involve students in discussions of political controversy (Kahne, Rodriguez, Smith & Thiede, 2000; Nystrand, Gamoran & Carbonaro, 2001; Nystrand, Wu, Gamoran, Zeiser & Long, 2003). We found such teachers in public schools, private schools, and charter schools. We also sought out teachers who do not use discussion because we wanted to compare their students to those who engage in discussion. We found teachers who do not employ discussion in all types of schools.

While students were in high school, we administered a teacher questionnaire and pre- and post-course questionnaires to students. The surveys asked about classroom climate, respondents' views on particular political issues, their level of engagement and interest in civic and political life, their political knowledge, and their views of classroom discussion. We also collected qualitative data that included classroom observations, interviews with teachers about their educational philosophies, and interviews with 225 students conducted during the last two weeks of the course. Students in this sub-sample were asked about the issues they remember discussing, what happened during the discussions, their attitudes toward discussion, whether they knew their teachers' views about the issues, and what other activities happened in class.

We asked participating students to consent to be contacted up to two times in the next few years. We contracted with the University of Wisconsin Survey Center to conduct two rounds of follow-up telephone interviews. In the first round of follow-up interviews, completed in 2007 after the mid-term elections of 2006, we collected responses from 401 former students. The second round, completed in 2009 following the 2008 presidential election, elicited 369 responses. These interviews took between 20 and 30 minutes and asked students closed questions about their current political views, levels of political and civic engagement, news consumption, experiences with voting and election coverage, and views of citizenship. We also asked a series of open-ended questions to determine what students remembered about their high school class, what they recalled about discussions, what effect they thought the class had on them, and whether they knew their teachers' views about the issues that were discussed. This study was unique in the field of social studies because of its size and because it included both quantitative and qualitative data from students and their teachers. In addition, it is one of the first longitudinal studies to include follow-up data from students after they have left high school (see the Appendix for more description of our research methods and data set).

As we collected and analyzed the data, we learned that even among teachers who are committed to including controversial political issues in their courses, there is a lot of variation in what they ask students to do. We also learned that both the content and quality of teachers' courses affected what students learned and how they reacted to the courses. One of the key differences we encountered is that teachers make very different decisions about what we term "controversial pedagogical issues." Some, for example, believe that teachers should never share their political views with the class, while others feel it is wrong not to. Some have students discuss and deliberate whether same-sex marriage should be legal; others see this as a human-rights issue for which there is one correct answer, and so they are more directive in teaching the issue. These decisions are challenging for teachers because they are examples of *ethical* questions or questions that require professional judgment. While data can help people test certain assumptions, ethical questions usually cannot be answered by data alone because they are questions for which people need to make value judgments. Most professions have a code of ethics that enumerates rules of right behavior, such as defining what constitutes sexual harassment, but there are many other issues for which professionals need to use their best judgment. We have used the data from the study to identify three questions for teachers' professional judgment that necessarily arise when they engage students in political thinking:

1. How should teachers decide what to present as a controversial political issue?
2. How should teachers balance the tension between engaging students in authentic political controversies and creating a classroom climate that is fair and welcoming to all students?
3. Should teachers withhold or disclose their views about the issues they introduce as controversial?

In this book, we present a framework for how teachers ought to think through these issues. We refer to this as "the framework" and explain more about it below.

The Framework

In his influential work on ethics and education, Richard Stanley Peters (1966) famously argued that the educated person can answer the question, "Why do this rather than that?" (p. 90). This person may be considered "educated" if she can rationally come to an answer based upon evidence acquired by using the standards of inquiry from multiple disciplines and consider how her actions affect other people. It is not, Peters explains, enough for someone to be a great scientist if that person is not able to think about a particular problem with consideration of how the problem fits within its historical moment or how various outcomes affect the lives of others. The process of education is an activity that intentionally brings about this "desirable state of mind in a morally unobjectionable manner" (p. 5). Peters further argues that teachers ought to be "educated," rather than "trained," in classroom practice. In other words, teachers should not be told the rules of good teaching but need to be educated about good judgment, which requires teachers to consider their options in light of evidence, aims, and their effect on others.

We argue that democratic education requires teachers to create a political classroom in which young people develop the skills, knowledge, and dispositions that allow them to collectively make decisions about how we ought to live together. Deciding to create a political classroom necessarily causes teachers to make judgments about their practice. The three questions we identified above are all ethical questions because they require teachers to ask themselves, "Why do this, rather than that?" The list is not exhaustive, and there are many more ethical decisions that teachers must make, such as, "Should I require all students to speak during class discussion?" or "Should I support tracking students based on ability level?" The three questions that we identified are ones that teachers in the study a) often disagreed about and/or b) struggled with during their careers. Many teachers we spoke with changed their minds about these questions over time. The study provides some evidence around the issues surrounding the questions.

Some teachers have very strong beliefs about what the "right" answer is to one or more of these questions. We, on the other hand, do not believe any of these questions has a single answer that ought to apply to all teachers in all cases. At the same time, we do not think that every decision a teacher makes about these issues carries equal ethical justification; there are better and worse responses. In short, we agree with Peters that the best approach to thinking about the three ethical questions we identified is not to create hard-and-fast rules that all teachers must follow but to educate teachers about how to make good judgments about their practice.

To that end, we work from the deceptively simple ethical framework that professional judgment requires teachers to consider the *context* in which they teach, the available *evidence,* and their educational *aims* (see Figure 1.1). This framework represents an approach to good judgment that is broadly in-line with John Dewey's (1916/2004) theories of education and what it means to reason about practice. Dewey promoted a social and ethical theory that recognized the relationship between empirical inquiry (evidence), the constraints and affordances available in particular environments (context), and values (aims).[5] As such, all three are relevant to decision-making.

By "context" we refer to the relevant characteristics of the classroom, school, and larger community. For example, teachers within the same school might teach students with very different abilities, languages, and socioeconomic and cultural backgrounds. The subject that one teaches, the size of the class, and the grade level of students also factor into the contextual equation at the classroom level that can alter the aims that a teacher has for a particular group of students. Further, the culture of the school matters. Within the study, we examined several schools with religious missions (two evangelical Christian schools and two Catholic schools), as well as an urban college-prep charter school that primarily enrolls students of color from poor and working-class neighborhoods. These schools had very different missions and cultures that, in turn, shaped how teachers made decisions. Context also applies to the political community and ethos beyond the school.

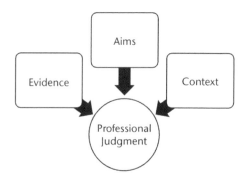

FIGURE 1.1 Framework for Professional Judgment

As the stories that opened this chapter show, the broader political climate always influences what happens within schools.

Good judgment also requires teachers to attend to relevant evidence. By this we mean current research about teaching and learning, what teachers know about their students, and standards of academic inquiry. In ethical decision-making, evidence helps teachers test their assumptions, identify constraints within various contexts, and make more-informed decisions. For example, surveying students about their initial beliefs on issues that might be discussed in class can help a teacher identify questions for which there is natural diversity in the classroom; this, in turn, gives students an opportunity to practice discussing issues across political differences. It is also important for teachers to understand the standards of inquiry in their subject areas and what counts as a well-reasoned claim that is worthy of students' consideration. There are clearly many issues about which people disagree, but in some cases the disagreement is based on bad evidence. Being able to evaluate public debates by evaluating the evidence used to support them will help teachers determine which issues have educational and democratic merit and are, therefore, worthy of inclusion in the curriculum.

Educational aims are an expression of a teacher's conception of what it means to be an educated person or a good citizen. Philosopher Joseph Schwab (1978) put it this way: "a curriculum is not complete which does not move the Eros, as well as the mind of the young, from where it is to where it might better be" (p. 109).[6] In his view, a good education is one that moves both hearts and minds toward where they might better be; the set of values and dispositions that one sees as "better" are one's educational aims. Within democratic education, teachers might educate toward aims such as political tolerance, development of a sense of justice, commitment toward one's community, patriotism, or appreciation for one's independence. Aims differ from educational "outcomes," which usually reflect measurable skills that students should master, such as writing an effective essay or learning to give a public speech. Ideally, outcomes are skills that contribute to the development of the larger aim. To clarify, if one characteristic of a "good" democratic citizen is valuing diversity (religious, cultural, or political), then developing the skills to listen and respectfully discuss an issue with people who hold different views is an important educational outcome that helps achieve this aim. Teachers, of course, have multiple aims when they work with students, and understanding how to make decisions about which aims matter in different moments is an essential part of making good judgments.

We use this ethical framework of "context, evidence, and aims" both as a tool for making good judgments and as a structure for the book, which consists of three parts:

Part I. In Chapter 2, we discuss the social and political context in which the study took place and why this is important both for interpreting the findings we present and for thinking about the professional judgment of teachers. Chapter 3 presents the major findings of the study and provides evidence for our view that, when done well, teaching young people to discuss political controversies is an important component of democratic education. However, the findings also suggest that social class differences predict which students are likely to become politically engaged adults—an inequality of outcomes that poses an important challenge for democratic societies, as well as for classroom practice. In Chapter 4, we examine the aims of the political classroom as they apply more generally to democratic education. At the same time, identifying appropriate aims is itself a controversial issue and a problem that requires professional judgment.

Part II. In Chapters 5 through 7, we use case studies developed from our study to introduce the reader to three examples of teacher practice. We describe what teachers *aimed* to accomplish in their courses, the *context* in which they are teaching, and *evidence* about what happened in these classrooms and what students say about their experiences. Throughout the book, we use pseudonyms when naming cities, schools, teachers, and students. Chapter 5 focuses on the government teachers at Adams High, a socially and politically diverse suburban public school where the 12th-grade government course is structured around an extensive legislative simulation. Ms. Heller, Ms. Matthews, and Mr. Hempstead run the simulation and teach toward the aim of "inclusive participation." The simulation involves the entire senior class and is carefully scaffolded to teach students both the legislative process and how to discuss policy issues with their peers in an open forum. Because the teachers believe that democratic processes must include all voices at the table, they are committed to keeping the government course non-tracked—a policy they must regularly defend to parents and administrators. In Chapter 6, we present Mr. Kushner at Academy High, an urban public school that is diverse along dimensions of race and social class. It is also one of three schools that we label a "Like-Minded School" because more than 80% of students surveyed hold political views that line up on one side of the political spectrum. Academy High is the most left-leaning school in the study, and we discuss how this context shapes Mr. Kushner's aim of developing what Allen (2004) refers to as "political friendship." In Chapter 7, the final case study, we introduce Mr. Walters at King High, a private evangelical Christian school. King High, also a Like-Minded School, has the most conservative students in the study. Here, we discuss Mr. Walters' aim of developing what we call "bounded autonomy" among his students. That is, he would like students to remain committed to their Christian faith while also developing political independence. Chapter 7 also presents overall findings about the effects that Like-Minded Schools have on future political engagement.

Part III. In the last section of the book, we return to the framework of professional judgment to discuss how teachers can apply it to three ethical questions that arise in the political classroom: Which issues should be included in the curriculum? How should teachers balance the competing values of authenticity and fairness? Should teachers share their political views on the issues they discuss in class? Chapter 8 addresses the first two of these questions. We explore a number of ethical controversies related to which controversial political issues should be included in the curriculum. We explain various criteria that could be used by teachers to determine whether an issue is a matter of legitimate political controversy (that is, one with multiple and competing views). Here we argue that it is helpful for teachers to deliberate with each other about this baseline question of how we should determine what to teach as controversial. Building on previous work, we then draw a distinction between empirical questions and political questions and argue that the political classroom should a) teach students to see the difference, and b) prepare students to deliberate controversial political issues. Further, understanding this distinction will help teachers to make choices about which questions are "open" and useful for discussion. Next, we explain what we learned from the teachers in our study about why some controversial political issues are especially sensitive, even when there is no question about whether they are "open" in the political world. For example, some teachers are leery of teaching about immigration issues if they know that some of their students are undocumented. We use the framework to show how teachers could approach the question of when it is ethical to include or exclude particular issues when they may be especially sensitive or personally challenging for some students. Chapter 9 addresses the teacher's decision to withhold or disclose his/her political views to the class. Elsewhere, we have presented findings from the study about what students think about political disclosure and withholding by their teachers, but here we build on this discussion to consider how context, aims, and evidence can help teachers make good judgments about this issue.[7]

We conclude in Chapter 10 with recommendations for how teachers ought to think about creating a political classroom—especially given the challenges posed by growing political polarization and social inequality. Despite the challenges, we hope that teachers do not shy away from political controversy and instead see their job as helping students to develop the skills and dispositions of deliberation so that young people are able to practice listening, reason-giving, and considering how their views affect others. Further, because classrooms are "unusual political spaces" in which young people develop their political identities, we believe that students deserve the opportunity to puzzle about the political issues they are inheriting in a way that models good thinking and reasoning. In our view, it is these experiences that best prepare future citizens to answer the question, "How should we live together?"

Notes

1   Parts of this chapter have been adapted from McAvoy, P., & Hess, D. (2013). Classroom deliberation in an era of political polarization. *Curriculum Inquiry, 43*(1): 14–47.
2   Congressman Gingrich was also supportive of President Obama's speech. See Barr, A. (2009, September). Newt Gingrich: "Every child" should read speech. *Politico.* Retrieved from http://www.politico.com/news/stories/0909/26865.html.
3   Mann did not actively support racially integrated schools. See Moss, H. J. (2009). *Schooling citizens: The struggle for African American education in antebellum America.* Chicago, IL: University of Chicago Press, for a detailed history of the fight for and resistance to

allowing African Americans access to public education in Boston, New Haven, and Baltimore. In addition, part of Mann's opposition to May was likely motivated by Massachusetts' election of 1840, during which the Democrats ran on a campaign to abolish the state Department of Education, which would have ousted Mann and halted the Common School Movement. See Katz, M. B. (2001). *The irony of early school reform: Educational innovation in mid-nineteenth century Massachusetts.* New York, NY: Teachers College Press.

4 Annette Lareau (2003) finds that middle-class children are raised to be comfortable talking with adults and with the kind of talk that is often rewarded in schools. Working-class children are often less familiar with these discussion norms. That said, we think it is also quite likely that a classroom with a majority of working-class students could also make a middle-class minority feel excluded or deter their participation. The point is that social class and racial dynamics within the school will play-out within the classroom and, therefore, put some students on unequal standing during a classroom discussion.

5 We recognize that Dewey would likely object to suggesting that aims, context, and evidence are distinct. We agree with Dewey that these are necessarily interrelated to judgment and use this framework to make more explicit what this reasoning might look like in practice. Thank you to Terri Wilson for pointing this out to us.

6 "Eros" here refers to love or passion—especially for knowledge or beauty. Schwab's point is that a liberal arts education should improve hearts and minds.

7 See Chapter 6, pp. 97–110, of Hess, D. (2009). *Controversy in the classroom: The democratic power of discussion.* New York, NY: Routledge.

PART I
Context, Evidence, and Aims

2

THE POLITICAL CLASSROOM
IN CONTEXT

In the witches' brew of fearmongering, unkeepable promises and poll-tested metaphors that both parties serve up to the electorate every four years, you can always find this predictable dash of inspiration: the image of Americans uniting and working together for the sake of the country. President Obama said in Charlotte, N.C. that America is "about what can be done by us, together." In Tampa, Paul Ryan said, "Whatever your political party, let's come together for the sake of our country." And Mitt Romney closed his convention speech with three invocations of "That America, that united America." But America is not united and it is getting less and less unitable with each passing decade.

(Haidt & Hetherington, 2012, para. 1–2)

This book, as noted in the previous chapter, grew out of a longitudinal study of high school classes in which students deliberate controversial political issues. The purpose of the study was two-fold: To examine what students experience and learn in classes that engage them in high-quality discussions of political issues and to identify the effect of those experiences on study participants' future political and civic engagement. Data collection occurred between 2005 and 2009.

Unbeknownst to us at the time, the study coincided with significant shifts in the political landscape. When we launched our research in January 2005, George W. Bush was beginning his second term as president, the United States was waging war in Iraq and Afghanistan, and Massachusetts recently had become the first state to legalize same-sex marriage at a time when 13 other states had recently defined marriage as applying only to unions between one man and one woman. A second round of data collection occurred during the 2005–2006 school year. That fall, the nation was trying to recover from Hurricane Katrina, which struck the Gulf Coast in August and caused more than $100 billion in damage, took the lives of more than 1,800 people, and set off a maelstrom of criticism about the federal government's slow and inadequate response to the crisis. By the time the study concluded in 2009, Iowa and Vermont had joined Massachusetts in granting marriage licenses to same-sex couples, while 27 states had passed "defense of marriage" amendments to their constitutions. Barack Obama, the nation's first African American president, had just been elected, the nation was facing its greatest recession since the Great Depression, and the Tea Party movement was emerging in opposition to federal responses to the economic crisis.

Throughout this period, the political climate was becoming increasingly divisive, polarized, and vitriolic. To cite just one example, congressional town hall meetings held in the summer of 2009 devolved into yelling matches over the proposed health care bill that came to be known as Obamacare. In one famous exchange illustrative of the prevailing political climate, a constituent asked Representative Barney Frank (D-Massachusetts) about the Affordable Health Care Act and accused him of "supporting a Nazi policy." Frank responded that her question was "vile, contemptible nonsense." He finished the exchange with the indictment, "Ma'am, trying to have a conversation with you would be like trying to argue with a dining room table. I have no interest in doing it." Frank's comment, circulated widely at the time, clearly reflects his frustration with the tenor of public discourse. Regardless of one's position about this exchange, it underscores the intertwined and troubling trends of political polarization and distrust in the public sphere.

In the next chapter, we present the major findings of our study, but it is important to keep in mind that the political classrooms that we studied existed within—and responded to—a particular political culture. Polarization, as we will show, is a serious problem for democracies, but it is also a problem for democratic education because young people coming of age within this climate are likely to view political dysfunction as the norm. Moreover, polarization threatens the very project of democratic education. When democracy is reduced to warring political camps, one reaction can be to keep politics out of schools; as a consequence, students are not taught how to deliberate about their differences. In this chapter, we discuss political context in more detail. In particular, we answer these questions: Why is polarization occurring in the public sphere? What effects does it have on democracies? What trends in school policy exacerbate and/or alleviate the problem? We also introduce the young people we studied and describe what we know about the political engagement of their generation.

How Did We Get Here?

Among political scientists, the discussion of polarization focuses largely on the behavior of the U.S. Congress and the relationship between the two major political parties. Polarization, in these studies, is a measure of the extent to which Democrats and Republicans vote along party lines and the extent to which the parties are internally consistent ideologically. Another way to think about this is to ask, How liberal are the Democrats and how conservative are the Republicans?

One need only look at titles of recent publications to deduce that polarization is on the rise. Examples include: *Going to Extremes: How Like Minds Unite and Divide* (Sunstein, 2009), *Polarized America: The Dance of Ideology and Unequal Riches* (McCarty et al., 2006), and *It's Even Worse Than It Looks: How the American Constitutional System Collided With the New Politics of Extremism* (Mann & Ornstein, 2012).

Nolan McCarty, Keith Poole, and Howard Rosenthal (2006) explain that polarization has not always been the norm:

> In the middle of the twentieth century, the Democrats and the Republicans danced almost cheek to cheek in their courtship of the political middle. Over the past thirty years, the parties have deserted the center of the floor in favor of the wings.
>
> (p. 1)

But the move toward ideological extremes is not just the story of congressional behavior; it has emerged alongside other troubling social trends, such as rising income inequality, anxieties caused by increases in immigration, and heightened ideological divisions among the public. It is important for teachers in the political classroom to understand these social trends because they greatly affect how political issues become controversial and how they are discussed.

Partisan Politics

In the last 35 years, the two major political parties in the United States have purified along ideological lines; as a result, philosophical differences between the two parties are clearer and more pronounced than they have been at any time in the recent past. Democrats are solidly the party of the Left; Republicans, the party of the Right, but for much of their histories, the major parties in the United States have been ideologically mixed (Green, Palmquist & Schickler, 2002; Mann & Ornstein, 2012; McCarty et al., 2006).[1] In the 1960s, the parties started sorting—that is, they were becoming ideologically homogeneous. A decisive turning point came when conservative Southern Democrats took a stand against civil rights legislation and shifted their allegiance to the Republican Party, ending longstanding coalitions within the Democratic Party. Partisan purification deepened with the second political trend to inform political polarization: the rise of evangelical Christians and their influence on the Republican Party. This movement, which began in the early 1970s, further marked the Republicans as social conservatives who saw themselves in opposition to what they perceived as a takeover of U.S. society by secular humanists (Green et al., 2002; Putnam & Campbell, 2010). The "culture wars" followed, especially around wedge issues such as abortion, school prayer, and gun control, which became defining causes for each party.

In addition to partisan purification, polarization has emerged as a result of changing political strategy by members of Congress. Representative Newt Gingrich

(R-Georgia) led the charge in the 1980s, when, as a junior member of the House of Representatives, he set out to take back control of Congress by organizing a unified Republican Party and by encouraging the use of oppositional, parliamentary-style politics. The strategy eventually worked, and in 1994, the Republicans became the majority party in both houses for the first time in 40 years (Abramowitz, 2010; Mann & Ornstein, 2012; Theriault, 2013). While the Democrats at that time were not above playing oppositional politics, the unwillingness to negotiate or compromise across party lines can in large measure be traced to the change in Republican strategy (Mann & Ornstein, 2012; McCarty et al., 2006; Theriault, 2013). These tactics traveled into the Senate through a group of lawmakers that Sean Theriault (2013) labels "the Gingrich Senators." These 40 senators were all Republican House members who moved to the Senate after 1978, the year Gingrich was elected to the House. Theriault's (2013) research identifies these senators as the group that brought the new Republican House strategy to the Senate floor, and in so doing, transformed the chamber from an "Individualized Senate" to the "Partisan Senate" that we see today (p. 9).

Abramowitz (2010) and Theriault (2013) both note that these changes are not altogether negative. Later, we discuss Abramowitz's findings that polarization has the positive effect of energizing the public and creating increased political engagement. Theriault reminds his readers that prior to this period, "political scientists lamented the lack of strong parties" that often failed to rally behind a unified strategy (p. 17). Today, the parties are more internally cohesive, but the result is often partisan gridlock. The unfortunate consequence is that Congress as a whole has become less willing to work through differences and more interested in maintaining political power (Mann & Ornstein, 2012; McCarty et al., 2006; Theriault, 2013). At the time of this writing, Congress's approval rating stands at 13% (Jones, 2014).

Economic Inequality and Immigration

Political scientists have engaged in a lively debate about why political polarization has increased so dramatically and relatively quickly. They agree that no single reason can explain the trend but that a host of factors probably coalesced. In their study of polarization, McCarty et al. (2006) described the emergence of polarization as a "dance" between economic factors and the behavior of politicians. They found that political polarization has occurred two times in the last 100 years, and they note that both periods have been highly correlated with the growth of income inequality. The first period of polarization took place in the years leading up to the 1929 Stock Market Crash. After World War II, economic disparity diminished, as did polarization (measured by congressional roll-call votes). Since 1977, however, this trend has reversed: Economic inequality has increased alongside political polarization. The researchers argue that as wealth moves into fewer—and more powerful—hands, political parties divide on the issue of the social safety net. They found that the congressional stalemate that occurs around redistributive issues, such as taxation policy and health care—whose handling *could* promote public trust and address growing inequality—ends up exacerbating the income gap, which in turn increases polarization.

Intertwined with the story of economic inequality is the impact of a rise in immigration. McCarty et al. (2006) found that the two most polarized periods in the last century also had higher percentages of noncitizens living in the United States. From 1880–1910, the percent of foreign-born residents remained around 14%, then dropped in the 1920s until it reached a low of 4.7% in 1972 (p. 9). It has since climbed to 12%. The rise of foreign-born residents is due primarily to an increase in legal immigration sparked by legislation passed in 1965 and 1990, though the researchers also note that during this time "the United States did little to contain illegal immigration" (p. 138). In their analysis of why a connection may exist between increased immigration rates and polarization, they postulated that even though those just arriving in the United States were on average poorer than middle-class Americans, their effect on economic inequality was small because the gap between rich and poor was already on the rise. "Immigration," the researchers concluded, "cannot have been a driving force in the onset of the increase in income inequality and political polarization" (p. 138). Instead, when they looked at voter trends by income, they found that as immigration rates increase, median-income voters become more resistant to redistributive social policy, such as raising the minimum wage, increasing taxes on the wealthiest, and expanding access to health care (p. 138).

It is this relationship *between* immigration and resistance to remedies for economic inequality—and not immigration itself—that exacerbates partisan divisions. Vanessa Williamson, Theda Skocpol, and John Coggin (2011) polled members of the Massachusetts Tea Party and found that 78% were concerned about immigration and border security—second to their highest concern, which centered on deficit spending (p. 33). This proportion is significantly higher than the 60% of Americans who in national surveys report that they are concerned about immigration (p. 34). The Tea Party attracts the more conservative members of the Republican Party, and the researchers found that although its members appear to be motivated by libertarian ideology, they are generally supportive of well-established government programs like Social Security and Medicare, to which they "feel legitimately entitled" (p. 26). In contrast, Tea Party members expressed strong opposition to new programs, such as the Affordable Care Act, which they regard as "'handouts' to 'undeserving' groups, the definition of which seems heavily influenced by racial and ethnic stereotypes" (p. 26). The views of Tea Party members illustrate the general finding by McCarty et al. (2006) that economic inequality and a rise in immigration reduce the willingness of the middle class to support redistributive policies. In part this resistance is motivated by a belief that those on the bottom are undeserving of assistance, and relatedly, if the government attends to the interests of the poor, it will fail to look out for the interests of middle-class workers (p. 33).

Rising economic inequality also greatly affects whose voice is heard in a democracy. Kay Lehman Schlozman, Sidney Verba, and Henry Brady (2012) draw upon multiple data sets and surveys to investigate the relationship between social class and political participation. One of their major findings is that compared to the poorest 20% of Americans, the richest 20% "is responsible for 1.8 times the number of votes, more than 2.6 times the number of hours [working for campaigns and political causes], [and] 76 times the number of dollars [spent on campaigns and political causes]" (p. 14). The more disposable income there is at the top of the economic distribution, the more opportunity wealthy voters have to spend it in support of their political interests. This, in turn, increases the amount of money it takes to win an election—a phenomenon whose legality was cemented by the Supreme Court decision in *Citizens United v. Federal Election Commission* (2010), which prohibited federal restrictions on campaign spending by corporations, associations, and unions. Amy Gutmann and Dennis Thompson (2012) argue that the ever-increasing amount of money necessary to run for political office lands politicians on an exhausting and expensive treadmill of continuous campaigning. Good campaigners, they note, appear firm in their convictions. Good legislators, however, need to be willing to compromise. This conflict of roles exacerbates the "do-nothing" culture of Washington, resulting in a more polarized and suspicious citizenry that grows increasingly skeptical of the political system's ability to address the most urgent problems facing the nation.

The Polarized Public

In *The Disappearing Center: Engaged Citizens, Polarization, and American Democracy,* Alan Abramowitz (2010) studied the relationship between political polarization and the "engaged public." Specifically, Abramowitz asks whether the American public is as polarized as political elites and examines what causes people to participate politically. Using data from the American National Election Studies, Abramowitz defines the "engaged public" as "citizens who care about government and politics, pay attention to what political leaders are saying and doing, and participate actively in the political process" (p. 4). They are, in other words, the type of citizens that social studies teachers typically hope to develop.

Abramowitz (2010) finds that the percentage of the U.S. public that counts as "engaged" has increased steadily during recent polarizing decades (pp. 19–20). Additionally, he finds that the two strongest predictors of those who are "highly engaged," when using a scale of six measures of engagement, are (1) identifying as a "strong partisan" (identifying with one of the two major parties); and (2) possessing a "strong" ideological orientation (liberal to conservative) (p. 24).[2] Lastly, Abramowitz shows that as the two parties polarize, the engaged public has responded by becoming more ideological and more partisan—what he calls "ideological-partisan polarization" (p. 37). This research shows that the more ideologically consistent citizens' views are across a range of issues, "the stronger their preferences will be with regard to political parties, candidates, and officeholders," and the more likely they are to be politically engaged (p. 7).[3]

In 2012, the Pew Research Center released a comprehensive report showing that Americans' values and basic beliefs are more polarized along partisan lines than at any point in the past 25 years. Unlike in 1987, when the series of surveys began, the divide between the views and beliefs of Republicans and Democrats is now greater than gaps based on gender, age, race, religion, or socioeconomic class:

> With regard to the broad spectrum of values, basic demographic divisions—along lines such as gender, race, ethnicity, religion and class—are no wider than they have ever been. Men and women, [W]hites, [B]lacks and Hispanics, the highly religious and the less religious, and those with more and less education differ in many respects. However, these differences have not grown in recent years, and for the most part pale in comparison to the overwhelming partisan divide we see today.
>
> (Pew Research Center, 2012, p. 1)

As this key finding confirms, demographic factors continue to explain some of the most important differences in Americans' political and social views. For example, African Americans and Hispanics are much more likely to support affirmative action than are Whites. When asked whether "we should make every possible effort to improve the position of Blacks and other minorities, even if it means giving them preferential treatment," 62% of Blacks and 50% of Hispanics agreed, as compared to 22% of Whites. This is a huge difference, to be sure—but, notably, that degree of difference has remained stable over the past 20 years, while the difference in how Democrats and Republicans answer the same question has grown far more pronounced over the same period. What was a 15% gap 20 years ago more than doubled to become a 39% gap in 2012. When comparing the views of Democrats, Independents, and Republicans across time, researchers found that the average partisan gap has nearly doubled.

Many Americans are not aligned with a political party, and for that reason, one might think that these citizens would not be part of this trend toward polarization. However, the Pew Research Center Report (2012) showed that even Independents are more polarized now than they were in the past:

> The growing partisan divide over political values is not simply the result of the declining number who identify with the party labels. While many Americans have given up their party identification over the past 25 years and now call themselves independents, the polarization extends also to independents, most of whom lean toward a political party. Even when the definition of the party bases is extended to include these leaning independents, the values gap has about doubled between 1987 and 2012.
>
> (p. 1)

These political trends are further intensified by social changes "on the ground." In *The Big Sort: Why the Clustering of Like-Minded America Is Tearing Us Apart*, Bill Bishop (2008) draws upon social science research to show that since the 1980s, the public has been "sorting" itself into more politically homogeneous communities.[4] When we live and work among people who generally think as we do, our views tend to become more extreme and less tolerant (Mutz, 2006; Sunstein, 2001, 2009). As a result, people in like-minded social networks are more likely to vote, but they are largely motivated by the fear that, in their view, the irrational other side cannot be trusted to govern from a position of goodwill. Conversely, Diana Mutz (2006) has shown that people who socialize in ideologically mixed groups are more politically tolerant but also less likely to vote. This means that, in general, people who show up to the polls are likely to hold more extreme views (Mutz, 2006; Putnam, 2000). The move to create ideologically homogenous communities, which makes it less likely that people will engage with or take seriously views different from their own, ferments extremism and causes the demonization of legitimate political difference.

Journalism

Contributing to citizens' distrust of political opposition is a sea change in journalism and the ways that people access information. While the 1980s marked the beginning of 24-hour news channels that often fill time with partisan commentary, the 1990s saw a shift away from printed newspapers to the Internet. The Internet has certainly produced an explosion of alternative news sources—in many ways democratizing information—but it also allows people with more extreme views to find each other and strengthen virtual communities of like-mindedness (Sunstein, 2001). The Internet, moreover, has changed the rules of journalism. *Atlantic Monthly* contributor Mark Bowden (2009) describes how partisan bloggers operate with what he refers to as a "winner-take-all" view of democracy:

> I would describe their approach as post-journalistic. It sees democracy, by definition, as perpetual political battle. The blogger's role is to help his side. Distortions and inaccuracies, lapses of judgment, the absence of context, all of these things matter only a little, because they are committed by both sides, and tend to come out a wash. Nobody is actually right about anything; no matter how certain they pretend to be. The truth is something that emerges from the cauldron of debate. No, not the truth: *victory*, because winning is way more important than being right.
>
> (p. 3)

When the media adopts a "winner-take-all" strategy, it becomes difficult for the public to sort through the noise of constantly disputed facts to form opinions based on reliable information. The result is a political sphere in which deliberation comes to a standstill. If, for example, the public cannot agree about the existence of climate change, we cannot discuss how to effectively address the problem. Further, the public will form polarized groups of "believers" and "nonbelievers." Indeed, Gordon Gauchat (2012) showed that trust in scientific sources has become a partisan issue. He found that since the 1970s, liberals and moderates have had a consistent trust in the scientific community, but conservative trust has steadily declined since the 1980s, with the most significant drop among educated conservatives. Gauchat posits that the solution to this partisan divide is not likely to be more or better information, because the divide appears to be grounded in ideology rather than in a lack of information (p. 182). Of course, these changes in media and journalism are not operating in a vacuum, and indeed they complement the dynamic behavior of a political order that is playing by the same rules.

It is clearly not possible to point to a single cause of political polarization, and thus there does not appear to be any easy solution to what we see as a crisis in democracy. What is clearer is that the most destructive aspect of this political reality is the loss of public trust. McCarty et al. (2006) agree:

> It is not hard to speculate how declining trust can lead to policy stalemate. If the two parties cannot agree how to solve a problem, it is hard to mobilize the public around any policy response. It is even worse when one side says the proposed policy ameliorates the problem when the other says it exacerbates it.
>
> (p. 180)

Benjamin Barber (1984) famously argued that democracies exist along a continuum from "strong" to "thin," with "strong" describing systems that include more voices and greater participation from the public as a whole and "thin" describing those that demand less from citizens and give more decision-making power to elected representatives. The current era of polarization is not just a thin version of democracy; it undermines democracy. A thin democracy may demand less from citizens but nevertheless could be effective at addressing social problems if elected officials are able to work together. A thin *and* polarized democracy becomes trapped in a partisan feud that exacerbates social problems. Because the causes of polarization—partisanship, economic inequality, residential sorting, and a polarized media—are so entangled, it is difficult to identify a way out of the situation.

We are not so idealistic as to believe that schools are the solution, but schools and democratic educators do have a role to play. First, schools should be aware of policies that make them complicit in the development of polarization and social distrust. Second, democratic educators need to be aware of these social and political trends, teach students that they are inheriting a democracy in distress, help them recognize and imagine what a stronger democracy might look like, and develop in students the skills and dispositions to respond productively to questions that ask, "How should we live together?"

Policies That Work Against the Political Classroom

One challenge to creating a political classroom that does not reify the behaviors and values of polarization is structuring courses so that students encounter people who are different from themselves in ways that make democratic deliberation truly democratic. We identify two related trends in education policy—racial segregation and tracking—that make it particularly difficult for students to experience deliberations across difference.

During the first decade of the 21st century, when this study was taking place, the national debate about whether schools and classes should be purposely created to educate students of different races, ethnicities, and social classes together was taking a backseat to other discourses on education (Apple, 2001). While remarkable progress was made in desegregating schools between 1970 and 1990, the tide began to turn as the '90s wore on, propelled in part by three Supreme Court decisions that undercut state and school-district desegregation policies.[5] By 2012, as Gary Orfield, John Kucsera, and Genevieve Siegel-Hawley (2012) documented in a report with a particularly evocative title—*E Pluribus . . . Separation: Deepening Double Segregation for More Students*—it was clear not only that the desegregation project had stalled, but also that it was being reversed. In its place, discussions of how to remedy achievement gaps ruled the day. While previously many had defined education-related "civil rights" as a goal that would be achieved by educating students of different races together, today many are arguing that the "new civil right" of educational opportunity should be framed as access to good schooling—irrespective of whether such schools enhance racial isolation or promote broader democratic values of social inclusion. Similarly, while there had been a robust debate in the 1980s and 1990s about whether schools should use various forms of academic tracking or, conversely, dismantle them as vestiges of inequality, in the early years of the new century it became clear that tracking had won in most school districts and schools, especially in the suburbs (Oakes, 1985).

In 2005, at the beginning of our study, one of the first places in which we collected data was Washington High School, a wealthy school in a suburb outside a major Midwestern city. Students at this school were tracked in virtually all their academic courses and in all four grades. By senior year, when students took the required American Government course, they were placed in five different "tracks" to learn about the nature and structure of U.S. democracy: transitional, regular, accelerated, honors, or Advanced Placement (AP). Our research team remembers being somewhat astonished by the number of tracks. Was it really possible, we wondered, that a school with a total student population of fewer than 2,000 could create this many tracks for a single course that actually reflected meaningful differences among students? Given that Washington High School was marked by the highest degree of racial homogeneity of any in the study (90% of its students were White), we investigated whether social-class differences aligned with how students were tracked. Students in the honors and AP sections of the American

TABLE 2.1 Washington High School: Distribution of Students in Top Two Tracks by SES

	Socioeconomic Status			
	Lowest Quartile (%)	Second Lowest (%)	Third Lowest (%)	Top (%)
AP Track	5.4	16.2	21.6	56.8
Honors Track	14.7	14.7	50.0	20.6

Government courses participated in the study.[6] As Table 2.1 shows, students in the top two tracks were quite wealthy compared to our sample as a whole. We learned that students in the AP sections had a statistically significant higher socioeconomic status (SES) than students in the honors sections: In the top track, more than 80% of students were in the top half of the SES distribution in our sample; in the next highest track, more than 70% were in the top half. It is remarkable that a significant difference exists between the SES of students in these two tracks, providing evidence of the way in which tracking, even in a school noted for the overall wealth of its students, is a powerful sorting mechanism.

We later learned that tracking was being changed for American Government students at Washington High in the 2006–07 school year. No longer would students be placed in honors or AP classes; instead, these two tracks were being merged so that more students would have access to the AP course. The "democratization" of the top track at Washington High was part of an explosion in the number of students taking AP courses in high schools across the nation. Even though it minimally diminished some of the most fine-grained tracking at this school, the creation of AP courses works in the opposite direction at many other schools: It enhances the racial and social-class segregation and isolation within schools (Oakes & Wells, 2004). This example of Washington High aligns with other research that finds that in practice tracking sorts students not by ability but by social class (Oakes, 1985; Oakes & Wells, 2004). For the purposes of the political classroom, which aims to have students discuss public policy with others who are differently affected by policies and who view the world from different social positions, tracking in social studies courses and the resegregation of schools undermine the democratic potential of the classroom.

The explosion of AP courses in the last 40 years is similarly problematic. The AP program started in the early 1950s, when a few advanced courses were offered to students at elite private high schools. Now, there are close to 40 AP courses, ranging across a broad swath of subjects. In many cases, these courses are offered as the top academic track in public and private schools. Students are enrolling in these courses in record numbers, driven in part by intense and effective marketing by the College Board (the non-profit organization that runs the AP program), federal and state legislation that rewards states and school districts that increase the number of students enrolled in AP courses, and high school rating systems that equate access to AP classes and the percentage of students who take and score well on AP tests to the overall quality of the school. Consider this stunning change: From 1952 to 1954, just 959 AP exams were taken in a total of 10 subjects (College Board, 2011a). During the 2011 school year, 3,365,617 AP exams were taken by 1,926,204 students, 88% of whom were from public high schools (College Board, 2011b). This number underrepresents the number of students enrolled in AP courses, because as much as 40% of students in these courses do not take the exam (which is not required in many school districts). It also is frequently the case that a single student takes multiple AP courses, effectively creating a "school within a school" for the top track. As a result, even if students attend one of the increasingly unusual schools in the United States that has a student population with a high degree of racial, ethnic, or economic diversity, many students on the AP track take classes with peers who are likely more similar to them than not.

The increase in the number of AP courses in high schools and in the number of students enrolled in these courses has been especially dramatic in social science and history courses. Of the 40 AP courses offered by the College Board, American Government is the fourth most popular course (and test). In 2005, when our study started, 129,323 students took the AP American Government test (College Board, 2005). By 2011, the number had risen to 225,837 students (College Board, 2011b). In some schools, especially in urban areas, the increase has provided more African American and Latino students access to a curriculum that one prominent social studies scholar has labeled the "gold standard" because it is developed by experts; most high school courses, in contrast, are typically developed by an autonomous teacher operating without the benefit of deliberation and without the accountability created by a national, standardized exam (Parker et al., 2011, p. 534).[7] However, the creation and widespread adoption of AP courses has reified existing racial and social-class segregation within some schools and, in some cases, the boundaries and structures of the AP curriculum and exam have made it difficult for teachers to put in place elements of the political classroom that we and other civic educators recommend.[8]

The prevalence of resegregation and tracking in U.S. high schools is ubiquitous but not universal. Some schools are more racially and economically diverse than they were in the past; at others, tracking has not taken hold. It is rare, though, to find a school that is diverse, not entirely tracked, and that refuses to offer the popular AP course in American Government. For this reason, we were intrigued when we learned about such a school and pleased when its teachers enthusiastically agreed to participate in the study (see Chapter 7 for a discussion of this school).

The Millennial Generation

The central questions of our study probe the short- and long-term impact that pedagogy within the political classroom (deliberation) has on the civic and political development of young people. Schools are just one of many institutions that affect the political socialization of participants in a democracy. Families, extracurricular activities, and religious organizations also have been shown to positively affect political engagement (Campbell, 2004; Flanagan, 2013; Schlozman et al., 2012). Before turning to the young people and teachers we studied, we discuss the political engagement of their generation and the influence of social and political factors on their development.

While there have always been differences between the political and social views of young people compared to those of older Americans, another significant change involves the growing contrast between the opinions of younger people and their elders. One major difference is political affiliation (or lack thereof), as Table 2.2 illustrates. Note two especially important ways in which the youngest cohort, the Millennials, differs from the others: It is more racially diverse and much more likely to claim "Independent" as its political affiliation.

In addition to differences in political affiliation and cohort demographics, there are other important ways in which the views of young Americans are strikingly different from those in older age cohorts. Table 2.3 identifies some issues for which there are major differences based on age (these include same-sex marriage, the role of government, legal status for undocumented workers, and legalization of marijuana) and other issues for which the generational cohorts hold similar views (these include abortion, gun ownership, and the Affordable Care Act).

It is important to note that with some of these issues, age and the time in which a cohort came of age are clearly the driving factors. For example, irrespective of race, ethnicity, and gender, the youngest adults are more likely to support gay rights than are older Americans. Polls show that gay rights are supported by an overwhelming majority of young Americans—even those who affiliate with

TABLE 2.2 Demographic Differences by Generation

| | Generations | | | |
	Millennial	Generation X	Baby Boom	Silent
Demographics				
Age	18–33	34–49	50–68	69–86
Percent Share of Adult Population	27	27	32	12
Percent Non-Hispanic White	57	61	72	79
Percent Non-White	43	39	28	21
Political Affiliation				
Percent Democrat	27	32	32	34
Percent Independent	50	39	37	32
Percent Republican	17	21	25	29

Note: This table was created using data from the Pew Research Center, 2014, *Millennials in Adulthood*.

TABLE 2.3 Ideological Differences by Generation

	Generations			
	Millennial (%)	Generation X (%)	Baby Boom (%)	Silent (%)
Support Same-Sex Marriage	68	55	48	38
Support for Legal Status for Undocumented Immigrants	55	46	39	41
Support for Bigger Government & More Services	53	43	32	22
Support Legalization of Marijuana	69	53	52	30
Believe abortion should be legal	56	59	52	42
Believe controlling gun ownership is more important than controlling gun rights	49	48	44	51
Approve Health Care Law	42	43	41	39

Note: This table was created using data from the Pew Research Center, 2014, *Millennials in Adulthood*.

the Republican Party (Pew Research Center, 2013a). However, only 33% of the Boomer generation and 32% of the Silent generation feel the same way (Pew Research Center, 2014). What accounts for this difference? Patrick Egan argues that younger Americans grew up when gay people were portrayed more positively in the culture than has been the case in the past (Bollier, 2014). This view was supported by Vice President Joe Biden, who argued on *Meet the Press* that a popular television show that ran from 1998 to 2006 and featured an openly gay corporate lawyer made the difference: "I think *Will & Grace* did more to educate the American public than almost anything anybody has ever done so far" (Barbaro, 2012, p. 2).

The fact that the youngest cohort of adult Americans is more racially diverse than the other cohorts further helps explain their greater liberalism compared to the less-diverse older cohorts. However, other issues illuminate significant differences *within* the cohort of young Americans. Table 2.4 illustrates the degree of ideological variance within the Millennials and shows that views among this segment of the population are strongly correlated with race. For example, while 53% of all Millennials favor a bigger government with more services (see Table 2.3), just 39% of White Millennials do (Table 2.4). Notice also that only 9% of non-White Millennials identify as members of the Republican Party, and members of this group are far more supportive of President Obama. The important point here is that even though Millennials are more liberal overall than their elders, there is still significant variance within the cohort. This variance is partially attributable to the racial diversity within the group.

TABLE 2.4 Ideological Variance Among Millennials

	Pew Racial Classification	
	White (%)	Non-White (%)
Democrat	19	37
Independent	51	47
Republican	24	9
Approve the job President Obama is doing	34	67
Favor same-sex marriage	70	67
Favor legalization of marijuana	73	63
Believe in bigger government or more services	39	71
Approve of health care law	44	68

Note: This table was created using data from the Pew Research Center, 2014, *Millennials in Adulthood*.

That being said, even a cursory analysis of recent election results shows that younger voters are much more likely to support more progressive candidates than are older voters, and this difference is increasing dramatically. In an analysis of this generation gap, the Pew Research Center (2011) reported:

> The age gap in voting, which began to open in the 2004 election and became a major factor in Barack Obama's 2008 victory over John McCain, is not the political norm. In fact, for most of the past four decades, there was little difference in the voting preferences of younger and older Americans. As recently as the 2000 election, younger and older voters—as well as those in-between—were virtually indistinguishable.
>
> (p. 25)

As a case in point, consider the magnitude of this difference: in 2008, 66% of Millennials who voted cast their ballots for Barack Obama, while only 45% of older Americans did so (Pew Research Center, 2011). This difference narrowed slightly in 2012 from 60% compared to 48% (CIRCLE, 2012a).

A persistent gap also exists in electoral participation of young adults (ages 18–29) versus older voters: 49% of young adults voted in 2004, compared to 68% of those over 30, and this gap has remained fairly consistent since 1972 (CIRCLE, 2008; 2012b). Moreover, the economic and educational gap between young people who vote and those who do not is typically large. Young people who have had some post-secondary education are more likely to vote than those who drop out of high school or who graduate but do not continue their education (CIRCLE, n.d.). Poor young people have been much less likely to vote than those with more wealth, and African American and White young people historically have been much more likely to vote than Hispanics and Asian Americans (CIRCLE, n.d.). While such gaps also exist among older people, they are more pronounced among young people. In other words, voting rates among young people are even lower and more unequal than among older people.

The Study

Against the backdrop of political polarization and its associated trends—including a public school system that is sorting students by race and social class and a generation of young people who are breaking to the left of older generations—we went into classrooms to study teachers and students engaged in discussions of controversial political issues. The research began in 2005 with nine schools in Illinois and Indiana in which at least one social studies teacher was participating in a deliberation project—either the Choices for the 21st Century Education Program, which sponsors the Capitol Forum, or the Constitutional Rights Foundation Chicago (CRFC) Illinois Youth Summit program.[9] Teachers who participated in these programs received written curricula and professional development from the sponsoring organizations, and their students were invited to deliberate with peers from other schools at large-scale events.

During the spring semester of the 2004–05 school year, Hess and a team of graduate students at the University of Wisconsin–Madison observed classes in these nine schools and interviewed 15 teachers along with a large sub-sample of 57 students. We also observed the multi-school deliberation events and accompanying professional-development activities for teachers. Toward the end of the semester, we administered a "baseline" survey to 250 students in these courses. In this first round of data collection, we were primarily interested in learning about what was happening in the classes and at the deliberation events. Much of what we sought to understand was purely descriptive: What issues were teachers including in the curriculum and why? What kinds of discussion and deliberation methods were teachers using and why? What caused teachers to become part of the deliberation programs in the first place and what happened at these programs? We were interested in identifying similarities and differences among students in the classes being observed.

During the 2005–06 school year, we retained some of the teachers from the first year but also broadened our sample to include a third state, Wisconsin. We recruited teachers who reported engaging their students in issues discussions but who were not involved with either of the deliberation programs. Broadening the sample ensured that we had teachers who integrate issues discussions into their classrooms but who use other materials and approaches. We administered a pre-survey in the first two weeks of the course and a post-survey during the last two weeks of the course. During the 2007–08 school year, we returned to one of the schools (Academy High) for further data collection because it had become clear that this was a particularly interesting example of how students learn in an ideologically homogeneous community. We also added another evangelical Christian school to increase our private school sample. Table 2.5 provides information about the number of participating students, teachers, and schools from the three states.

The longitudinal data were collected in the spring of 2007 and the spring of 2009. We contracted with The University of Wisconsin-Madison Survey Center to complete phone interviews with students who had been study participants while they were in high school. The Survey Center successfully contacted 401 students in 2007 and 369 in 2009. In the Appendix, we explain the data collection and sample attrition in detail, but it is important to note that we were able to obtain parent and student consent for the follow-up interviews from just 600 of the 1,001 students. As a result, our overall response rate for the follow-up interviews (after high school) was roughly 40% of the possible follow-up sample. However, that is more than 70% the portion of the sample that we could draw from given the consent situation. Table 2.6 provides information about the number of

TABLE 2.5 Study Sample by State

	Illinois	Indiana	Wisconsin	Total
Students	490	174	337	1,001
Teachers	18	7	10	35
Schools	10	5	6	21

TABLE 2.6 Participants and Study Stages

	2005	2005–2006	2007–2008	Total
Students	250	675	76	1,001
Interviewed	57	146	22	225
Pre-survey	250	673	76	999
Post-survey	N/A[a]	464	61	525
Follow up (07)				401
Follow-up (09)				369
Schools	9	16	2	21[b]
Teachers	15	24	2	35[b]

Notes:

[a] In 2005, participants took a one point-in-time survey, so there were no post-questionnaires for this group.

[b] Some teachers participated with more than one cohorts of students and duplicates are not counted toward this total.

students in each wave of the study, which surveys they took, and whether they were interviewed.

The Sample

We are often asked whether the sample of students, teachers, and schools in the study is representative and, if so, of what. Clearly, this is an important question because it influences the kinds of claims we can make and thus what can be learned from the study. The samples are *not* representative of the broader population of high school students and teachers in the three states. Given that we were seeking teachers who engage their students in classroom discussions and that this approach is quite rare, we were not able to construct a sample that included enough teachers who used discussion *and* that was demographically representative of the schools, teachers, and students in the three states.

The pool of participants might best be described as a purposeful sample that represents a number of different dimensions: classroom pedagogy, ideological diversity of the school community, student demographics, and school type. Of the 21 schools in the study, there were 16 traditional public schools, one charter school, and four private religious schools. It would be dishonest not to acknowledge that funding constraints affected our sampling, as well. Had we had unlimited funding, we would not have limited ourselves to Midwestern states. Even though our student sample was not technically representative of the student populations in the three states, Table 2.7 illustrates that it was roughly similar with respect to some of the key demographic characteristics. (See the Appendix for more details about the sample.)

TABLE 2.7 Study Sample and Public High School Demographics in Three States

	Illinois		Indiana		Wisconsin	
	State Public High Schools (%)	Study Sample (%)	State Public High Schools (%)	Study Sample (%)	State Public High Schools (%)	Study Sample (%)
African American	20.1	6.0	12.0	2.9	9.7	3.0
Asian	3.9	5.8	1.3	1.7	3.6	2.4
Latino	16.6	17.0	5.2	2.3	5.7	2.4
White	59.2	64.9	81.3	86.2	79.5	88.2
Other	0.3	5.4	0.3	4.6	1.5	2.7

Note: State public high school enrollment data for Illinois, Indiana, and Wisconsin was retrieved from the National Center for Education Statistics, 2007–2008 Common Core of Data in ELSi, http://nces. ed.gov/ccd/. Study sample refers to the students in the study.

The Students

The total study population included 1,001 students, but the sample size and composition varied from wave to wave. Generally speaking, the study sample showed similar demographic characteristics to the youth population in the states where the data collection occurred. Like the population in those states, the sample was predominantly White (76.4%), followed by a modest Hispanic/Latino population (9.5%), and less than 5% each for African Americans, Asian Americans, and students with multiple racial/ethnic origins. While we do not know how many of the students were in sheltered or ESL classes, 13.5% reported that a language other than English was primary in their homes, and 7.9% were born outside the United States. As the study progressed, the sample became less diverse, and by the second follow-up, 87.1% of the sample was White. We found that students we were able to contact in the follow-up phone surveys were significantly higher in SES than in the post-survey sample.[10] What this likely means is that students who had higher SES levels were more likely to stay in the study than were those with lower SES levels. The sample started out as a slightly female-dominant group (55.3%), and the gender ratio remained relatively stable throughout the study. The majority of students identified as Christian, but many claimed no religious affiliation or said that they identified with a religion that was not Christian, Jewish, Muslim, or Hindu.

When students were in high school, the surveys administered at the beginning and end of their classes asked which candidate they would have voted for in the 2004 presidential election in which President George Bush, Senator John Kerry, and Ralph Nader were the leading candidates. We also asked students about their opinions on eight policy questions, such as whether they were in favor of the death penalty and whether they thought civil unions should be recognized between same-sex partners. Using this information, we were able to identify a student's political leanings and create measures of each student's ideology (liberal to conservative) and coherency (to what extent views align with one side of the political spectrum). When we examine the sample composition by political ideology and age, we note that those categories remained relatively stable over time. That is, the mean and standard deviation of those indicators remained similar for all four waves. The fact that the ratio of women to men, religious preferences and religious attendance, and political ideology did not shift appreciably over the course of the study suggests that there was no selective attrition by specific groups based on those factors. In other words, even while the sample size shrank, the representation by politically conservative youth remained proportionally similar across waves.

Politically, students in our sample were fairly similar to young people in their respective states; and fortuitously, there were important differences in the partisan makeup of the three states' populations. Illinois leaned Democratic, Indiana had been solidly Republican but voted for Barack Obama in 2008, and Wisconsin was politically diverse. Given that the political environments in which young people come of age are an important factor in their political lives, it was useful to have different political climates in the states and across the many communities in which the schools are located—rural, urban, and suburban.

The Teachers

Most of the 35 teachers who participated were recruited specifically because we knew they were using deliberation-based curricula that focused on controversial political issues. In many of the schools, we also included teachers who were teaching similar classes but who reported not focusing as much on classroom discussion or controversial political issues; these were teachers who primarily lectured. We did so to compare what effects teaching and learning with different pedagogical approaches might have on outcomes related to political and civic engagement.

There were important similarities and differences among the teachers. As a group, they were quite experienced: the average number of years teaching was 13, with about 33% teaching nine or fewer years, 43% between 10 and 15 years, and 24% more than 15 years. With respect to teachers' academic majors as undergraduates and graduate students, the majority had BA or BS degrees in history or political science, and the majority of teachers we interviewed also had master's degrees. All were certified to teach in their respective states (even if they taught in private or charter schools). We also surveyed teachers on their political views and found that they held opinions that cross the political spectrum. Nine of the 26 teachers who completed the survey had consistently conservative views on most political issues, nine clearly leaned to the left, and the other eight held moderate political views. This ideological range within the teaching sample aligns with recent research that shows that the political views of high school social studies teachers reflects the political diversity of the non-teaching public (Commission on Youth Voting and Civic Knowledge, 2013).

Political Engagement and the Study Sample

The period in which the study took place (2005–09) and the subsequent years are notable for the nature and degree of major changes in the political, economic, and social landscape that could not help but influence what was happening within schools. We now turn to the ways in which teachers and students in the study were influenced by these trends.

Study Participants' Political Views

In *Controversy in the Classroom* (Hess, 2009), an entire chapter is devoted to the nature and range of ideological diversity in the classes that we studied. In Chapter 7 of this book, we build on that foundation to discuss in more detail how the

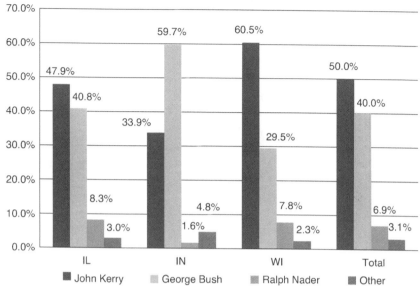

FIGURE 2.1 Students' 2004 Presidential Preferences by State

Note: The total number of students who answered this question in all states is 948.

level of political homogeneity within communities—and classrooms—influences students' learning and political engagement after they leave high school. Here, we situate our sample within the broader political trends described earlier in the chapter. As Figure 2.1 illustrates, in answer to the question about which presidential candidate they would have voted for in 2004 had they been old enough, a majority of students in Indiana favored President Bush, while the students in Illinois and Wisconsin favored Senator Kerry.

At the classroom level, most students were in environments in which there was a diversity of views about presidential preference: 53% of students were in classes in which fewer than 70% of their classmates selected the same presidential candidate. We labeled four schools Like-Minded Schools because, in addition to other factors, more than 80% of the students would have voted for the same candidate. We discuss Like-Minded Schools in Chapters 6 and 7.

We were interested to see whether students' electoral choices in the historic 2008 presidential election would continue to be reflective of the states (and communities) in which they went to high school or whether their voting preferences would change. Figure 2.2 shows the percentage of young people in our sample who reported voting in the 2008 federal election and which candidate they reported voted for: Barack Obama, John McCain, or other. Compared to whom they said they would have voted for in 2004, the students in the

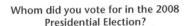

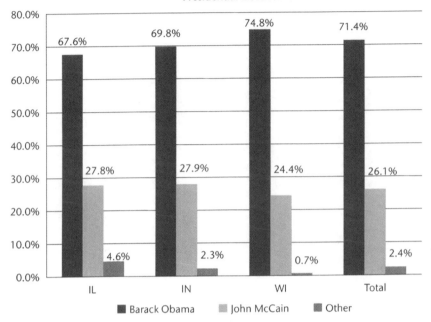

FIGURE 2.2 Students' 2008 Presidential Preferences by State

Note: The total number of students who answered this question in all states is 265.

sample moved to the left in the 2008 election as a group and were roughly in line with how their age-cohort voted. In the 2008 presidential general election, Illinois young people (18–29) voted 71% Democrat, 27% Republican; Indiana's young people (18–29) voted 63% Democrat, 35% Republican, 2% other; and Wisconsin's young people (18–29) voted 64% Democrat, 35% Republican, 1% other (CNN, 2008).

Digital Citizens

The students in our study are part of a generation of "digital natives," defined by Marc Prensky (2001) as those born at a time when working with new technologies was the norm; in contrast, their elders—described by Prensky as "digital immigrants"—faced a much steeper learning curve to become conversant with these new technologies. Consequently, we were interested in examining the role that new technologies played in enabling young people to learn about politics, as well as the ways in which study participants engaged and communicated politically. Specifically, we focused on two questions: Where do young people go for information about political news, current events, and political issues? And in what ways, to what extent, and in what venues do young people exchange their political views and engage in other forms of political activity online?

Young People as News Consumers

There is a strong relationship between following the news—regardless of the source—and civic engagement (Lopez et al., 2006). Those who regularly follow the news in any medium are more involved in public life than those who do not (Lopez et al., 2006). Young people are more likely now than in the past to learn about the news from online sources than from print newspapers, radio, TV, or news magazines. For example, in the 2008 campaign, 34% of young adults used the Internet as a major source of election news, compared to 20% who relied on a print newspaper (Smith, 2009). Among the young people in our study, a comparison of the post-surveys to the follow-up interviews revealed a marked decrease in print newspaper, TV, and radio as sources of information about the news, and a huge increase in the use of online resources (including organization websites, blogs, online versions of newspapers, and social networking sites). While reliance on online sources increased among all age groups, the increase for young people was particularly dramatic.

Moreover, there is a positive correlation between the use of online sources and youth civic and political engagement. This is true even when controlling for the effects of education (Lopez et al., 2006). This positive relationship reflects a more generalized trend of online political consumption and some forms of online political production (such as posting material about a political or social issue) as *less* marked by SES disparities (Smith et al., 2009). Further, there is evidence that

TABLE 2.8 Media Consumption by Students in the Study in 2005, 2007, and 2009

	2005 (%)	2007 (%)	2009 (%)
TV			
Never	6.8	21.1	24.9
Daily	29.1	13.8	10.3
Internet			
Never	21.0	22.8	11.1
Daily	16.0	24.3	36.3
Newspaper			
Never	17.0	27.6	29.0
Daily	15.4	12.0	7.3
Radio			
Never	25.1	41.4	55.8
Daily	19.7	11.3	9.2

video games can be good sites for civic learning—and that civic gaming is not beset by the kinds of class distinctions that we often see in school-based democratic education (Kahne, Lee & Feezell, 2012; Lenhart et al., 2008). Yet, the online world also can be a site of political polarization. Politically active Internet users are increasingly seeking news from sites that match their political views—and this trend is even more pronounced among young people (Smith, 2009). This partisan information-seeking is part of a larger demographic trend in the United States to associate with those who hold the same political views—thereby increasing ideological amplification (Schkade et al., 2007). The "Big Sort"—as Bishop (2008) has described—has moved online. This new venue for youth engagement proved to be a great resource for Barack Obama's 2008 campaign. In the study's final phone survey in 2009, we found that almost 40% of those who played online games recalled seeing a campaign ad for Barack Obama.

Young People as Political Producers

Social networking sites (such as Facebook and Twitter) are locations for youth news consumption, production, and interaction. These are the spaces in which young people are the most likely to communicate with one another about politics. For example, in our final phone survey, 65% of social networking site users (a group that comprised almost 60% of our respondents) reported that they had been invited to a political event by a friend who made contact via the social networking site and more than 60% sometimes or regularly used these sites in order to *disagree* with a friend's message or posting about a political view.

Young people use social networking sites to communicate their ideological views and political preferences and to assess the ideological diversity of their online friendship group. There are two major categories of online political activities: those for which there is a clear offline counterpart (for example, e-mailing a letter to a government official versus sending a printed letter via post) and those for which there is no clear analogous offline activity (for example, the use of blogs and social networking sites). The evidence is fairly clear that young people are *less likely* than older adults to engage in online activities for which there is an offline counterpart (Lenhart et al., 2008).

With respect to online political activities for which there are no clear offline counterparts, young people are much *more likely* to participate than older adults, and, significantly, it appears that these activities are not strongly associated with socioeconomic status (Cohen & Kahne, 2012; Smith et al., 2009). That is, the Internet may be a space for new forms of civic engagement that can help diminish what has been called the democracy divide, which is clear and persistent in the rate political participation between young people with more or less education (Hess, 2009, pp. 169–170). Moreover, young people who engage in online political activities (as compared, say, to those who use social networking for purely social reasons) are much more likely to engage actively in their own communities in more conventional offline political and civic activities, such as volunteering or attending a public meeting to discuss community issues (National Conference on Citizenship, 2009). Young people who are highly engaged online come from diverse economic and educational backgrounds and also are highly engaged offline. It is not clear whether this is a causative relationship. Further research is needed to understand in a deep way whether online political activity *transfers* to offline activity—which, arguably, remains the coin of the political realm.

Conclusion

In this chapter we discussed the political climate in which this study was conducted, and highlighted how political polarization (1) puts democracies at risk; and (2) is fueled by troubling social trends such as economic inequality and ideological sorting.[11] We also discussed how educational policies, such as tracking and resegregation, may be weakening an already weak base for teaching young people to be politically engaged. Finally, we introduced the study sample and discussed how the Millennial generation is being politically socialized.

We conclude with the observation that while politicians, pundits, and bloggers were simultaneously denouncing and participating in highly divisive political discourse during the years data were being collected for this study, the most skilled teachers in the classrooms we observed were teaching students to engage in "civil discourse" by deliberating controversial political issues. When we asked teachers why they had adopted this approach, they said it was to prepare students for democratic life—not only to help them become more informed citizens but also to teach them how to talk about politics, which teachers viewed as an important democratic skill. They also saw this approach to discussion as purposely designed to counteract divisive contemporary political discourse. Mr. Voight, one of the teachers in the study, explained:

> I believe we need a better discourse in the country. These kids have grown up in an atmosphere where they're impressionable, [with people] yelling at each other . . . a talking-heads revolution . . . I don't know if they know that people can talk and disagree without yelling at each other. My goal in [class] is to get them to be able to disagree . . . and be able to talk about it, and be able to walk away and not go out and poke each other. I think we've lost that in our country.

Even though Mr. Voight and other teachers were interested in encouraging their students to improve on rather than replicate what was going on in the political world outside school, they were experienced and savvy enough to understand that political education within schools would be shaped—for good and ill—by political, economic, social, and technological developments beyond the classroom.

Notes

1 We note that what is labeled a "leftist" perspective in the United States would be considered center or even center-right in many other nations.

2 These two predictors are followed closely by age and education.

3 Other research also supports this finding: See, as examples, Budge, Crewe & Farlie (1976/2010); Mutz (2006); and Rosenblum (2008). Lupu (2014) shows that this relationship is likely causal. As citizens perceive polarization increasing, they become more partisan.

4 Abrams and Fiorina (2012) argue that Bishop's work may overemphasize the extent to which people have geographically sorted themselves, but they do not dispute the fact that some sorting has occurred and that political amplification is happening.

5 *Freeman v. Pitts*, 503 U.S. 467 (1992); *Missouri v. Jenkins*, 515 U.S. 70 (1995); *Parents Involved in Community Schools v. Seattle Public Schools*, 551 U.S. 701(2007).

6 As explained in the Appendix, the design of the study was not to include all government courses in a school in the sample, but to select a class in which the teacher was including political issues discussions and to compare it with a demographically similar class in which the teacher was not including such discussions.

7 Parker and his colleagues at the University of Washington are engaged in a multi-year, multi-course design project to change the nature of teaching and learning in AP courses and to make them more accessible to students who are traditionally placed in lower tracks. The initial focus of the team was on the AP American Government course. For information about this work, see Parker, W., Mosborg, S., Bransford, J., Vye, N., Wilkerson, J. & Abbott, R. (2011). Rethinking advanced high school coursework: Tackling the depth/breadth tension in the AP U.S. Government and Politics course. *Journal of Curriculum Studies, 43*(4), 533–559.

8 For school-based recommendations conducive to a political classroom, see Kahne, J. E. & Sporte, S. E. (2008). Developing citizens: The impact of civic learning opportunities on students' commitment to civic participation. *American Educational Research Journal, 45*(3), 738–766.

9 For the Illinois Youth Summit, see http://www.crfc.org/student-programs/illinois-youth-summit (Constitutional Rights Foundation, n.d.), and for the Choices Program, see http://www.choices.edu (Brown University, n.d.).

10 The SES score was standardized in this study and, therefore, had a mean (average) of zero at pre-test. Mean SES was still zero at post-test, suggesting that the social class of the sample students remained about the same as a group. However, at both of the follow-up surveys, SES went up by 0.2 standardized units, suggesting that lower SES students were less likely to remain in the study than high SES students.

11 Parts of this chapter have been adapted from McAvoy, P. & Hess, D. (2013). Classroom deliberation in an era of political polarization. *Curriculum Inquiry, 43*(1): 14–47.

3

EVIDENCE FROM THE POLITICAL CLASSROOM

Democratic dispositions—to be open-minded, to trust others, to be committed to finding common ground that transcends differences—do not happen by default. People are not born with democratic dispositions. Rather, formative institutions and experiences are critical. Consistent with a civic republican or strong democracy vision, citizens obtain their freedom by being members of and participation in political communities and deliberation with fellow citizens to determine how, collectively, they want to live.

(Flanagan, 2013, p. 163)

In 2005, Diana Hess launched a multi-year study to better understand discussion of controversial political issues as a component of school-based democratic education. The primary aim of this research was to examine students' experiences and learning in courses that engage them in deliberation of political issues. In the years leading up to the study, Hess analyzed the existing literature and spoke to teachers, teacher educators, and staff of nonprofit civic education organizations about their concerns regarding classroom discussion of controversial political issues.

From this investigation, three overarching questions emerged: First, what are the differences in this approach when it is implemented well, not implemented well, or not implemented at all? For example, how does a teacher's ability to teach discussion skills, prepare students for discussion, and facilitate the classroom discussion influence students' experiences and learning? This question focuses on the effects of such discussions in both the short and the long terms. Presuming there would be some important differences, the educators posed a second question: Other than the quality of instruction, what accounts for differences in the effectiveness of discussions on controversial political issues? For example, what role does the mix of students in the class play? Does it make a difference whether there is a wide range of opinion among students' views on the issues being discussed? What contrasts emerge when the community in which the school is located is more or less politically diverse? Even though some literature describing teachers' practices in this arena already existed, the educators were interested in a third question: What could teachers do to *improve* the quality of political discussions? With this advice in mind, Hess developed the study with guidance from an expert group of civic education researchers.[1]

This chapter concentrates on what was happening in the classrooms we studied by addressing the three questions listed above. We will demonstrate that both the quality and quantity of discussions of controversial political issues matter in important ways that are directly connected to the aims of democratic education. We will further show that students in classes with rich and frequent discussions of controversial political issues describe these courses as engaging, become more confident about their ability to participate competently in discussions, demonstrate increased political knowledge, and display more interest in politics. They follow the news more regularly, are more likely to engage in political discussions with people with whom they disagree ideologically, and are more interested in listening to opinions different from their own. Finally, students in these classes are more likely to intend on voting in the future.

Students' classroom experiences are certainly not the only factor that accounts for their learning. These experiences interact in powerful ways with the kinds of civic and political knowledge, attitudes, and experiences that students bring into the classroom. Moreover, given what was explained in Chapter 2 about the ways in which social class and other demographic factors affect political views and political participation in contemporary America, it should come as no surprise that these factors influence student experience and learning in the classroom, as well as civic and political engagement later in life.

The interplay between what students bring into the classroom and what they experience in school is complex and does not lend itself to easy or definitive answers. This is especially the case as we examine the relationship between the kinds of experiences and contexts in the classes we studied and what we learned from the follow-up interviews conducted after the young people graduated high school.[2] While we have clear evidence that students develop into very different sorts of citizens, it is much less clear what the relationship is between what they experienced in the classrooms we studied and what they reported believing, caring about, and doing as political beings as they got older.

This chapter is divided into three parts. We begin by explaining that the various teachers' classes we studied differed by the quality and quantity of discussion, creating three categories: Best Practice Discussion, Discussion, and Lecture. We then explain the differences in how students experience and learn in these three types of classes, focusing on what we learned from observations and interviews together with pre- and post-course surveys and phone interviews conducted in 2007 and 2009. Next, we explain two other factors that influenced the outcomes we measured: the knowledge, civic and political experiences, and civic dispositions students started with at the beginning of the class (which we call their "prior civic exposure") and their SES. While the type of classroom students were in clearly influenced how they experienced and learned from the course, both their prior civic exposure and SES turned out to be quite important in predicting outcomes at the end of the course. Finally, we examine how these factors—the kind of classroom students were in, their prior civic exposure, and their social class—influenced outcomes after high school as assessed on the two follow-up phone surveys (the first in 2007 and the second in 2009). In this chapter, we concentrate on what we learned, then on the methods used, which are explained in detail in the Appendix.

Creating a Typology

We began by analyzing the qualitative data from the first two years of the study—field notes from classroom observations and interviews with students and their teachers—in order to sort each class into one of two categories: "Discussion" or "Lecture." This initial categorization was not an evaluation of the quality of the discussions, but rather a judgment about whether students reported engaging in discussion at least 20% of the time.[3] We set 20% as the demarcation line based on previous observational research that showed that classes in which there is little or no discussion are more likely to be the rule than the exception. For example, one study on the frequency and quality of discussion in 48 social studies classes revealed that in 90% of the classes there was no discussion and that the discussions occurring in the remaining 10% of the classes were very short: 31 seconds on average (Nystrand, Gamoran & Carbonaro, 2001). As Walter Parker (2006) notes, "most indicators point to a very weak culture of discussion in U.S. schools" (p. 12). Thus, even though our threshold may seem low to some readers, we think a class in which students are talking seriously with one another about content at least 20% of the time probably far exceeds the norm.

The next step was to create a second set of categories to distinguish between the *qualities* of the discussion activities. Using a coding rubric that drew on classroom observation notes and the student and teacher interviews, we divided the classes in which discussion was happening at least 20% of the time into "Best Practice Discussion" and simply "Discussion" and ended up with three unique categories:

1. Best Practice Discussion: Students in these classes engaged in discussion of controversial political issues more than 20% of the time. These discussions also involved: students preparing in advance, significant student-to-student talk, and high levels of student participation.
2. Discussion: These classes also engaged in discussion 20% or more of the time, but fell short of Best Practice Discussion because most of the talk was student-to-teacher and not student-to-student, students were often not expected to prepare for discussions, and participation was not as widespread.

3. Lecture: These classes did not meet the threshold of using some form of discussion at least 20% of the time. The dominant pedagogical strategy was teacher lecture, some of which we assessed as very high quality.

Next, we evaluated on a class-by-class basis whether students were "engaged and learning," regardless of whether the course had previously been categorized as Best Practice Discussion, Discussion, or Lecture. Here, we sought to learn if students reported high levels of engagement in class activities, were excited about what they were learning, and found the course contributing significantly to their education. For this step, we relied on classroom observations and student interview responses about how the class compared to other social studies courses they had taken, the rigor of the course, their evaluation of the content and skills they were taught in the course, the classroom climate, and the extent to which they were engaged in the course. Table 3.1 shows the results of this sorting process.

We "tested" our qualitative assessment of the class categorization by using quantitative data to examine the extent to which students experienced their classrooms as places to investigate issues and explore their opinions and those of their peers, a construct known in the field of civic education as "open classroom climate" (Hahn, 1998; Torney-Purta et al., 2001). On the post-course survey, students were asked the following questions to measure the climate: Did the teacher encourage students to discuss political or social issues about which people have different opinions? Did the teacher present several sides of an issue when explaining it in class? Did students in the class feel free to disagree openly with their teacher about political and social issues? Did the teacher respect students' opinions and encourage participation? Did students feel encouraged to make up their own mind about the issues? Were students required to memorize dates and definitions?

After controlling for a number of demographic factors that prior research has found to predict a student's assessment of an open climate, we learned that students with Best Practice Discussion teachers rated their classes significantly higher in open classroom climate than those in the non-Best Practice Discussion classes,

TABLE 3.1 Number of Teachers, Students, and Schools by Classroom Type

Discussion Category	Teachers	Students	Schools	Teachers classified as "Engaged and Learning"
Best Practice	11	443	9	11
Discussion	7	234	6	4
Lecture	7	178	7	4
Not Rated	10	146	9	Not rated[a]

Note:

[a] There were ten teachers for whom we did not have enough qualitative data to make a classification.

and students in both types of discussion classes rated the climate as more open than did students in the Lecture classes. It is important to point out that most students in the study, regardless of the type of class they were in, reported a fairly open classroom climate, and this is generally true for students in the United States (Hahn, 1998; Torney-Purta et al., 2001). But because students in the Best Practice Discussion classes did have significantly higher scores on this scale, and those in Discussion classes had higher open-classroom climate scores than those in Lecture classes, we are confident that our categorical scheme represented meaningful distinctions.

What Students Experience and Learn in Classroom Types

Once classes had been sorted into the three types, we analyzed the student and teacher interviews to answer three questions: (1) How is engagement and learning different across classroom types? (2) Are students hearing multiple perspectives in their classrooms, and what do they learn from this? (3) What do students report learning in Best Practice Discussions?

Engaged and Learning

In addition to the quality and quantity of classroom discussion of controversial political issues, we were also interested in whether students were engaged in class activities and whether they were learning from these classes. All Best Practice Discussion teachers were rated as teaching courses with high levels of learning and engagement (see Table 3.1). Further, discussion stood out as the activity that contributed the most to student learning and enjoyment in the class. When students were asked to compare this class to other social studies classes they had taken, they often described the class as more active and less "boring." As a student in Ms. Green's class explained:

> I would say it is one of my top choices. I don't really like my other classes because they are more like cut and dried: "Here is the homework." There is no discussion, you know? "Here is the book. Learn from the book." But in Ms. Green's class, you participate, and we voice our opinions and stuff like that.

Similarly, one of Ms. Heller's students said, "Compared to my other classes, I really like this class because it is non-stop talking. . . . Everything is basically one large debate."

Students also spoke a lot about what *they* were doing in the course, as opposed to what the teacher was doing. For example, a student in Ms. Ingles's class noted:

> [W]e got together in groups, [based on] whether you are for or against the death penalty. And she gave us different books and stuff, different papers

that people have written. And then we kind of discussed them, looked for important points that could back up our side of the story and how we felt about it. And then we had the formal debate and then we just discussed it afterwards.

It is clear from this short quote that students in Ms. Ingles's class were researching and preparing for discussion and doing much of the intellectual work in the classroom, instead of spending the preponderance of class time listening to a teacher's lecture. This dynamic influenced how students viewed their role within the classroom.

The contrast with the other class types illustrates the finding that students in Best Practice Discussion classes felt more responsibility in the classroom. We found that there were Discussion and Lecture courses in which students reported learning a lot and found that the class was engaging. In the Discussion category, four teachers' primary pedagogical technique was a combination of discussion, recitation, and lecture that was highly interactive. Students were asked to report how much of the class time was spent in lecture and how much time was devoted to discussion. In these cases, students often reported large amounts of lecture and were stumped when asked about discussion, because as one student put it, "the lectures sort of are like the large-group discussion, but he is sort of leading it." In these classes most of the talk is teacher-to-student-to-teacher, but it is not merely recitation. Instead, these teachers presented information and then posed problems and controversies for students to consider, akin to a Socratic dialogue. A student in Mr. Xander's senior government class provided more detail:

It is not just taking notes and stuff. Like he really talks with you about everything and discusses everything by asking you questions and stuff. And, I don't know, it is more like you are just talking. And he says the most random things. And he has all these stories that are incorporated and help you think of things and stuff. So, yeah, it is really fun.

When done well, these courses engage students, primarily because the teacher is seen as a knowledgeable expert and often a charismatic presence in the classroom. Similarly, in the Lecture classrooms, four teachers were engaging storytellers who often presented content-rich lectures—so much so that students often labeled these teachers "legends." Humor was a common component in these classes. As one student in Mr. Kuehl's class described, "I would say you walk in and you sit down. You shut up. You take notes. And you laugh a lot."

We note these classrooms in order to acknowledge that we do not believe Best Practice Discussion is the only way in which students find their classes to be valuable, nor do we argue that there is a single way to be a an effective and engaging teacher. However, students in Best Practice Discussion classes describe learning in very different ways. The engaging lecturers are knowledgeable and entertaining, but they regard learning as primarily about content knowledge. The Discussion teachers appreciated the value of student talk, to be sure, but also held more control in the classroom; this often resulted in diminished emphasis on student-to-student exchanges. While students who were not in the Best Practice Discussion courses spoke about the personality of their teacher and of his or her deep content knowledge, students in Best Practice Discussion courses felt that they were learning more than just the content and that they were learning from their peers as well as from their teachers.

These differences were evident in the longitudinal follow-up surveys, as well. One particularly clear example is seen at Academy High, a school that is the focus of Chapter 6. Mr. Kushner and Mr. Kuehl both teach senior elective courses that could have provided very similar opportunities for engaging students in discussion of controversial issues. On the basis of qualitative data, we classified Mr. Kushner's classes as Best Practice Discussion and Mr. Kuehl's classes as Lecture. We also found that students in Mr. Kushner's classroom reported, on average, a significantly higher perception of open classroom climate than did students in Mr. Kuehl's classroom. The classroom average for Kushner was 4.12 on a scale of 1 (not an open classroom climate) to 5 (a very open classroom climate) and for Kuehl it was 3.77. In both of the follow-up interviews after students had left high school (conducted in 2007 and again in 2009), we asked the same open-ended question: "What do you remember about the course?" In the interviews with 37 of Mr. Kuehl's former students, they reported remembering that the content was "interesting" and that Mr. Kuehl was a great storyteller. A typical response went like this: "He was a really kooky and really neat guy. He knew a lot of stuff—just tons of information. The class material was very stimulating and interesting, and I still think about some of the stuff." Students were nearly unanimous in praising Mr. Kuehl as a "great teacher," but the comments are also almost all about his personality, which many called "hilarious." In 62 follow-up interviews with Mr. Kushner's former students, we were struck by how often the word "we" was used to describe the class: "We talked about . . . ," "We had a lot of discussions . . . ," and "We tried to look at both sides. . . ." In both years of follow-up surveys, only three students in Mr. Kuehl's class used the word "we" when answering this question, while 28 of Mr. Kushner's students did. As with Mr. Kuehl, students talked about Mr. Kushner being "a really good teacher" and the class being "one of my favorites." But it was notable that most of the comments did not focus on Mr. Kushner but rather on what students did in the class. Students spoke about discussions, debates, and group work and named specific issues that they talked about, such as gay marriage and abortion. They also remember learning from their peers and about multiple perspectives on issues even though many students in their classes were ideologically similar.

To sum up, while we find that students see value in the three types of classes (Best Practice Discussion, Discussion, and Lecture), young people experience engagement differently across the classroom types. Students in Lecture classes are often engaged, to be sure, but their comments often sounded as if they appreciated being entertained. Students in Discussion classes can choose to engage with the teacher in a dialogue, but they are not routinely required to engage with one another. Best Practice Discussion students are engaged with one another and as a result feel more responsibility for contributing to the learning that occurs in their classroom.

The Value of Multiple Perspectives

In addition to examining levels of engagement within classrooms, we were quite interested in the extent to which the different types of classes influenced the value students placed on learning multiple perspectives on issues. As explained in Chapter 2, one of the effects of political polarization and the increasing ideological make-up of so many communities in the United States is that citizens are not routinely exposed to political views on important political issues that differ from their own. Students in Best Practice Discussion classes appreciate hearing the views of their peers and report that this interaction contributes to their learning. In comparison to students in Discussion and Lecture classes, students in Best Practice Discussion classrooms were much more likely to report that it is important to consider other points of view before making a decision and that political issues are more complicated than they previously thought.

The qualitative data show that students enjoy hearing what their peers think about different issues and that engaging with multiple perspectives teaches young people to appreciate political diversity. This finding was particularly pronounced at Adams High, where all members of the senior class participate in a non-tracked, semester-long legislative simulation that is the focus of Chapter 5. We collected data from three of the teachers running this program (Ms. Heller, Ms. Matthews, and Mr. Hempstead). During the semester, students spend time in class and in an online forum debating bills written by their peers, and twice each semester they meet in the school theater for a legislative session run by elected student leaders. One student in Mr. Hempstead's class explained how the diversity of views affected her:

> I was influenced by other people. I got to hear personal experiences. I learned more about different issues rather than, you know, abortion, [and] the death penalty—the ones you hear about all the time. And I just, I don't know, I think this class really helped me just mature and see different sides of, you know, life other than mine.

Many students also spoke of becoming more open to considering differing perspectives as a result of class discussions; this is hardly an easy thing to learn. As one of Mr. Voight's students explained:

> [Discussing issues] challenges the way you think about everything. It is difficult looking at your own perspectives, and I don't know, seeing what other people think. Being open minded is difficult, I guess.

The challenge of confronting different perspectives also helped students clarify their own views. A student in Ms. O'Brien's class reflected: "Taking this class and getting the different sides of it, debating with it in class . . . I definitely have a viewpoint now." This finding was also apparent in post-course surveys. Students in the Best Practice Discussion classes were significantly more likely to believe in the importance of listening to many sides of a political issue before taking a definite stance.

Best Practice Discussion students also reported an appreciation of the complexity of political issues, a view that was almost never mentioned in the other two types of classes. This finding was seen across the Best Practice Discussion classes but was particularly strong in classrooms where students had to come to a decision about the issues. For example, Mr. Murphy used materials from Choices for the 21st Century Education Program (developed at Brown University) in his International Relations course; these activities often ask groups of students to read about multiple viewpoints and then attempt to reach a consensus about a policy issue. During the discussions, students have to weigh trade-offs among policy options. As a result, students realized how difficult it is to make decisions when outcomes are uncertain. One student described what he learned:

> Things are never as simple as you would like them to be. And, for me, actually, it is increasingly harder to determine what is the right policy to pursue because as you get into these gray areas and there are so many unknowns it is like, "How do I really know how this is going to play out?" And it is kind of like a guessing game whereas . . . you would think it would be a lot more concrete. Like, "This is right and this is wrong." And, really, that is not the case in my eyes.

Students who experience the Adams High legislative simulation also develop an appreciation for the difficulty involved in making policy decisions. One of Ms. Heller's students explained that she developed more sympathy for legislators:

> Seeing it up close, you have more respect for the people that run our country just all of the long, drawn-out processes that have to go on. And sometimes we bash the people that run our country when, actually, it is not an easy job, and there is so much behind-the-scenes work that goes on that nobody really knows about until you kind of experience something like this.

We believe that these outcomes—the recognition of complexity and the need for intellectual humility—are essential if schools are aiming toward the creation of democratic citizens. Many of the Best Practice Discussion teachers are, in fact, concerned that the political climate has become "too divisive" and see classroom discussion as a means of challenging the pitfalls associated with simplistic thinking. Our findings show that these educators are successful in teaching a habit of open-mindedness, as evidenced by their students' willingness to consider diverse points of view.

Recognizing Diversity in the Classroom

Of course, students can only learn how to consider diverse points of view if they are in classes in which multiple perspectives are present and if students' awareness of these perspectives is activated by the pedagogical choices of the teachers (Hess, 2009). By way of explanation, consider the different experiences that high school seniors at Washington High School had in a Best Practice Discussion class compared to a Lecture class. Washington High School required seniors to take a course in American Government, but students were tracked based on teachers' recommendations. As noted in the previous chapter, students in the AP course had, on average, a higher SES than those in the next highest track (which was an honors class), even though these were the top two tracks out of five. Moreover, the curriculum and pedagogy varied tremendously between the teachers who taught the two tracks. The first teacher, Ms. Brown, taught three sections of the second track, while the second teacher, Mr. Lincoln, taught two sections of the top track (the AP Government course). The contrast between the two cases illustrates that Best Practice Discussion classes socialize students into seeing disagreement as a normal part of democratic life, while students in Lecture classes are left to assume that most people agree about political issues.

Best Practice Discussion Class. Ms. Brown wants her students to engage actively in politics and directs her curriculum toward that goal. Her students meet politicians, work as election judges, learn how to vote, participate in legislative simulations and moot courts, and frequently discuss highly controversial political issues that affect the world outside their school. Ms. Brown's class was a microcosm of the political diversity that exists in the nation: half the members of the class reported that they would have voted for Bush in the 2004 presidential election, while the other half said they would have voted for Kerry. Because their views on many political issues were divided, genuine conflict surfaced in the discussions of controversial issues in Ms. Brown's class; some of these discussions were based on curriculum materials from Choices for the 21st Century Education Program. Ms. Brown valued those curricular materials because she believed they provide essential background on complex issues without compromising either clarity or complexity. This background, in her view, helped to prepare students for meaningful discussions on controversial topics such as immigration, terrorism, and global trade. The students we interviewed in her classes reported that they addressed controversial issues two to three times a week in discussions varying from 20 to 50 minutes.

During a lesson we observed, students engaged in a culminating discussion about what they learned and how their views changed as a result of a unit of study on current issues in international policy. Ms. Brown took on a facilitating role, allowing students to speak and respond to one another. Frequently, she would ask questions designed to provoke students to consider an alternative point of view. Ms. Brown's questions did not appear ideologically motivated; she seemed more interested in highlighting the controversy of the issue under discussion. Even though Ms. Brown did not explicitly voice her own views in this discussion, we have conflicting data from students about whether she remained mute about her opinions (we return to data about students' perception of Ms. Brown's political views in Chapter 9). In the discussion we observed, one student claimed that all scientists agree that global warming is harmful and another student disagreed. Ms. Brown then asked students what should be done about global warming when not all scientists can agree on its effects. Toward the end of the period, a student suggested to the class that the United States should not spend any of its money on aiding people who were affected by the tsunami that devastated many countries in Southeast Asia in December 2004. Several members of the class strongly disagreed, producing palpable tension in the room. Ms. Brown neither took sides in the controversy nor appeared to act as if the conflict among students was unusual. Every student who was interviewed described this class as having frequent discussions of controversial issues that were characterized by widespread participation, multiple and opposing perspectives, and the freedom to express one's views. Moreover, the students recognized that there were many different opinions in the room, a phenomenon they found both interesting and natural.

According to the students we interviewed, conflict was a normal element of the discussion of controversial issues in Ms. Brown's classes. While acknowledging that discussions "sometimes did get a little tense," the students viewed conflict as a regular and not undesirable component of the course. Indeed, the presence of conflict often spurred students into joining a discussion they might otherwise have avoided. One student said she did not often participate in class discussions but "when something really rubbed me the wrong way, I would definitely participate." Students were not reluctant to disagree with each other.

Students report talking more about politics as a direct result of taking classes that incorporate discussion of controversial issues. One student found that he "was able to engage in conversations with adults more than before." Some students were inspired to become more active in politics. "This class actually made me want to get into politics a little more than before," said one student. "It made me feel like you have to almost be in politics to be able to change things." Students also became aware of the complexity of political issues. One student, who described her family members as "stubborn" because they "didn't listen to what anyone else has to say," believed that the frequent discussions in Ms. Brown's class helped her appreciate the many political perspectives of her classmates and often led to further contemplation: "To finally be in a classroom where if you have an opinion, but then you get to hear what someone else has to say about the other side of it—you are just like—'Now I think we should think about it a little more.'" Another student reported that the frequent discussions "make me think deeper on every issue, not just government issues."

Lecture Class. Mr. Lincoln has more than a decade of classroom experience and teaches in the same school as Ms. Brown. On our observation day he lectured for most of the class period. We note that Mr. Lincoln was a very skillful lecturer, had a robust knowledge base to draw on, was an engaging speaker, and had structured the content clearly by including many examples. Moreover, there were a few times during the lesson that Mr. Lincoln asked students open-ended questions and received quick responses. Mr. Lincoln characterized the lesson we observed as "a fairly typical day" and described his own teaching as "instructor-centered." Mr. Lincoln recognized that his teaching relies heavily on lectures but, with the "condensed time" of the semester course coupled with his obligation to prepare students for AP exams, "you can't do as many interactive activities with the students" as he did in non-AP classes.

Discussion of controversial issues was not a frequent part of Mr. Lincoln's curriculum, and his class, therefore, served as a contrast to Ms. Brown's. However, his students indicated that they had brief discussions of controversial topics, such as abortion, the death penalty, and gay marriage. Throughout the year, Mr. Lincoln brought in newspaper articles on relevant current events. Students were required to give a talk on current topics, some of which were controversial. One student characterized the controversial-issues discussions as infrequent and unplanned: "If it happened to come up and someone had a question about it, then we talked about it. But it wasn't like, 'Today we are going to talk about the death penalty.'"

Because controversial-issues discussions were infrequent in Mr. Lincoln's AP classes, conflict was rare in his classroom. It was not entirely absent, however. One student described an activity in which students ranked the best U.S. presidents. The student described "a division" between those who ranked Democrats and those who ranked Republicans highest. According to the students we interviewed, class members felt free to express their opinions in Mr. Lincoln's classroom; no one felt that Mr. Lincoln tried to convince them to take a particular political position. All the students we interviewed agreed that Mr. Lincoln did not reveal his political views, and none of the students knew his position on any issue. "We really can't put our finger on where he is," said one student, echoing the sentiments of the others we interviewed.

When asked about how the course would affect them in the future, the students in Mr. Lincoln's class believed that they had a better understanding of how government functions. This increased knowledge appeared to affect them in at least two ways. First, students paid more attention to current events and politics. One student noted that she was "more aware of how things happen and why they happen." Second, at least one student felt the course affected him as a citizen.

Mr. Lincoln's class, he told us, "is going to influence my participation in things like voting or jury duty or responsibilities as a citizen of the nation. And maybe it also fosters my awareness of political news or current events."

The students we interviewed in Mr. Lincoln's classes were unanimous in their perception that there was not a wide range of political ideology among class members and characterized their peers as being politically "in the middle." Our quantitative data reveals a more complex and varied ideological spectrum among the students. Many students in Mr. Lincoln's class were, in fact, not in the middle: indeed, of the 37 students in the study, 12 were politically liberal and 12 were conservative, with the remaining 13 falling somewhere in between. In fact, there was a greater range of political ideology in Mr. Lincoln's classes than in any of Ms. Brown's classes.

We believe that a probable explanation for students' belief that their classmates possessed less political diversity than actually existed can be found in the work of John Hibbing and Elizabeth Theiss-Morse (2002), who find that Americans consistently underestimate the level of disagreement that exists among the electorate. Most voters believe that they are moderate and that the majority of other voters are, too. The condition that allows this misperception to flourish is a lack of exposure to disagreement. Discussion of controversial issues would bring these differences to the surface. Since most Americans eschew political conflict, they are unaware of how many different political opinions reasonable people may hold. Mr. Lincoln's class, in this sense, can be viewed as a microcosm of American political life. Since controversial issues were not discussed in the class, awareness of the political diversity among class members remained dormant. Students were rarely exposed to the opinions of their classmates; as a result they were left with the sense that most students shared their beliefs.

Increased Interest in Political Discussion

The qualitative and quantitative data showed that students in Best Practice Discussion classrooms were more likely to report that they are more interested in politics as a result of taking the course, more likely to enjoy political talk, and more comfortable with disagreement.[4]

During the in-class interviews conducted during the last two weeks of the class, students were asked what impact they thought the course would have on their futures. Students across all pedagogical categories tended to report that they were more prepared and more likely to vote; this was borne out in the 2008 election when the rate of voting of the students in the three kinds of classes was uniformly high. Many also reported feeling that the class prepared them academically by providing the foundational content needed to progress through the educational system. Students also mentioned learning to do research, write, think, and speak publicly as skills that would be useful for their future. However, the survey data show that the Best Practice Discussion students were more likely to report an increased interest in politics because of the course than were other students. When compared to all other predictors in the model, the Best Practice Discussion classroom was by far the strongest predictor. Further, these students were more likely to report enjoying political discourse.

These findings were particularly salient at Adams High School, where students participate in the legislative simulation described above. The all-encompassing nature of this activity greatly affects the culture of the school, and particularly the senior class, as one student noted:

> Senior year is big. Everyone is talking about politics. On the volleyball game bus last week we were talking about the immigration bill. It was the hot topic in class. It is just fun because the sophomores and freshmen are looking at us seniors like, "What are you guys talking about?" We are back there and having a debate on the bus.

In the qualitative analysis of what students told us about the importance of political talk, it was clear that they appreciated being inducted into the world of adult discourse. A student in Ms. Brown's Best Practice Discussion course articulates this view:

> So I guess one of the big things is just being aware of political aspects and being able to engage in conversations with adults more than before, like mainly politically or with any kind of social issue or public issue that is relevant in any shape or form. That is really the big part of it.

It is noteworthy that among students in Lecture classes, responses about the impact of the course were individualistic; most concerned voting and their students' own academic achievement. Members of Best Practice Discussion and Discussion classes not only became more interested in politics, but also came to view politics as a social activity—one shared with friends, family, and co-workers. Further, they learned that disagreement is a normal part of political life. We believe this shift can be attributed to the fact that Best Practice Discussion teachers model and teach the norms of what some students call "civilized talk" and what the teachers call "civil discourse." Within their classrooms, most Best Practice Discussion teachers explicitly taught the norms of political talk and structured activities so that students had multiple opportunities for practice. Further, they monitored student talk so that ideas were not called "stupid" and discussions rarely got "heated." Similarly, in the Discussion classes, the teachers held more control over the discussion and provided models of how to challenge another's views respectfully.

It is clear from what we have described that many of the classes we studied were important sites of political learning, and that this was especially the case for students in Best Practice Discussion classes. While thus far we have drawn on both the quantitative and qualitative data to compare and contrast students' experiences in various classroom environments, in Table 3.2 we display the data gleaned from the post-course survey as divided into four distinct categories: classroom discussion, political participation, knowledge and interest, and news and political talk.

TABLE 3.2 Classroom Practice Effects Observed at Post Survey

	SES	Prior Civic Exposure	Discussion	Best Practice
Classroom Discussion				
Deliberative values	+	+	0	0
Discussion efficacy	0	+	0	+
Share ideas in class	0	+	0	0
Political Participation				
Willing to volunteer	+	+	0	0
Political efficacy	0	+	+	0
Expect to vote	0	+	0	0
Vote every election	0	+	0	+
Knowledge & Interest				
General knowledge score	+	+	0	+
Democracy knowledge score	+	+	+	0
Interesting issues	0	+	−	0
More interest in politics because of class	0	+	0	+
News & Political Talk				
Frequency of news discussion	+	+	0	0
Frequency follow news	+	+	0	+
Total news consumption-breadth and frequency	+	+	0	0
Political talk with friends	+	+	0	0
Political talk with parents	+	+	0	0
Political disagreement in conversation	+	+	+	+
Willing to listen to those who disagree	0	+	0	+

Note: Multiple Linear Regression analyses were used to examine the impact of Discussion and Best Practice Discussion on four domains of outcomes (underlined and in italics). For each analysis, Discussion and Best Practice Discussion were entered as dummy variables (0=not used, 1=used) with Lecture as the reference group. Demographics, ideology, prior civic exposure, and age were also entered as controls. Significant positive values for Discussion, for example, can be interpreted as meaning that students in classrooms rated as Discussion are more likely to report the outcome than students in classrooms rated Lecture. Similarly, significant positive values for Best Practice Discussion can be interpreted as meaning that students in these classrooms are more likely to report the outcome than students in Lecture classes. See the Appendix for the effect sizes. (+) = statistically significant positive effects; (0) = no effect; (−) = statistically significant negative effect.

dents in the Best Practice Discussion classes scored higher on the
ey on seven of the composite scales and items, students in Discus-
ed higher on four items (and lower on one). In a separate analysis,
her students in Lecture classes showed significant growth in any
s between pre-survey and post-survey. We found no significant
change. more dramatic, however, is the way in which students' SES and
their prior civic exposure influenced outcomes as measured at the conclusion of
the course. For ten of the items, the changes were influenced by students' SES, and
for *all* of them the changes as measured on the post-course survey were predicted
by students' prior civic engagement as measured at the beginning of class.

The Impact of Social Class

As economic inequality increases in the United States, one of its most troubling
effects is the growing cleavage between the political and civic participation of
young people based upon their social class backgrounds. Other research consistently has shown that on virtually every possible measure of engagement, young
people from higher SES backgrounds are more likely to participate in the civic
and political realms than those from lower SES backgrounds (Commission on
Youth Voting and Civic Knowledge, 2013; Kahne & Middaugh, 2008). Moreover, in *Teenage Citizens: The Political Theories of the Young*, Constance Flanagan
(2013) explains that the social class backgrounds of adolescents matter tremendously in their views of the world, in part because the education level of their parents
influences their exposure to information and political discussion at home. While
Kahne, Rodriguez, Smith, and Thiede (2000) showed that high-SES students received
higher-quality school-based civic education, in our study students in the Best Practice
Discussion classes were more likely to be lower SES, which offers an opportunity to
assess whether exposure to this form of civic education can mitigate or perhaps even
trump the typically negative effects of low SES on civic and political participation.[6]

As Table 3.2 illustrates, the SES of the students is still a powerful influence on
the outcomes we measured, but note that student development in Best Practice
Discussion and Discussion classes, controlling for SES and their prior civic exposure, is important for some of the dependent variables and not for others. This
finding illustrates that more important than students' SES was the civic knowledge, experiences, and dispositions they had developed prior to the beginning
of class—what we refer to as the Prior Civic Exposure Index score, developed
to estimate how much civic exposure students came in with at the beginning of
the course, as determined by their answers to questions on the pre-course survey. It is a composite measure that contains information about students' political
knowledge, their concern for others, their previous civic engagement, how much
influence they believe their actions can have on the political system (political
efficacy), how often they engage in political discussion and report enjoying doing

so, and their expected political engagement in the future (see the Appendix for additional information).

There are a variety of contexts in which young people could build the knowledge, skills, experiences, and dispositions measured on the Prior Civic Exposure Index. Clearly, what happens in the home is extremely important, but we know that schooling matters too. For example, students can build knowledge in schools, may have experiences volunteering because of school (in fact, in many high schools, students are required to perform a certain number of volunteer hours to graduate), or engage in discussion about political issues. Previous research has shown that curricula and co-curricular programs in schools can influence students' political efficacy (Hahn, 1999; Levy, 2011; Morrell, 2005). Given the overwhelming power of the Prior Civic Exposure Index, we think it is generally good news that schools can clearly influence the likelihood that young people engage in the kinds of experiences that would raise their Prior Civic Exposure score.

It is not surprising that the influence of the students' prior civic exposure more powerfully predicted their post-course outcomes than whether they were in a Best Practice Discussion, Discussion, or Lecture course because we would not expect that a single course (some lasting just one semester) would weigh more heavily than the cumulaive effect of experiences over several years. Of course, to create a more comprehensive understanding of what impact school-based civic education had on students' political and civic development, it would have been ideal to start to study students much earlier—perhaps at the beginning of their first year of high school.

The Impact of Students' Prior Civic Experiences on Pre–Post Growth

Even though we did not have any way to assess what caused students to come into the classes with a higher or lower Prior Civic Exposure score (other than the strong correlation to their SES), we were able to assess whether students who came in with more preparation would show a different pattern of change between the pre-survey and the post-survey than students who came with less preparation. This was an important inquiry because it could help us assess whether the power of prior civic exposure was so strong that it would actually amplify the development of civic and political engagement. Walter Parker (2010) argues that students who have had "systematic experiences with good material" in classes year after year are more likely to learn more in subsequent classes than students without such prior experiences (p. 4). Applied to outcomes attached to political and civic engagement, it is possible that this "Matthew Effect" (i.e., the rich get richer) would give students with high Prior Civic Exposure scores a cumulative advantage over their peers with lower scores. In order to explore whether this occurred, we examined the interaction effect of time (that is, from the beginning to the end of the course) and level of prior exposure. A significant interaction effect means that the *pattern of change* was different between the groups with high and low exposure, accounting for the differences in the dependent variables from the beginning to the end of the course and other demographic factors.

As expected by definition of the Prior Civic Exposure Index, the high-exposure group scored significantly higher on all measures of civic and political engagement that we chose to examine (the four large categories and the 18 specific dependent variables shown in Table 3.2) at both the pre- and post-survey. We also found that the high-exposure students were more liberal and more politically coherent than the low-exposure group. The pattern of change between pre- and post-test, however, did not differ significantly between the high- and low-exposure group on a number of the dependent variables that we thought were particularly important: discussion score, discussion efficacy, political ideology, and political coherence. These results suggest that the high-exposure group started more engaged and remained more engaged, and the differences between groups neither diminished nor intensified. One exception did apply: when we assessed the pre-post change pattern on a variable we labeled "democratic knowledge," which assessed students' understanding of core democratic principles, the low-exposure participants started out much lower on this scale and on the post-survey, but they closed the gap between them and their higher SES peers, though by a small degree. What this means is there was no Matthew Effect in the classes—which is positive, given the tremendous advantage that exists for some students at the beginning of the classes.

Predictions and Outcomes Post-High School

Now we turn to the question of what influence the quality and quantity of engaging young people in discussions of controversial political issues has on their actual political and civic engagement—both what we are able to predict from the data we collected at the end of the courses and from the two rounds of follow-up surveys conducted in 2007 and 2009. As a backdrop, it is important to consider that many of the rationales for civic education assume that what we teach in schools can make a difference in how young people behave politically and civically as adults. As we have described, this is complex terrain because we know that in the United States a person's engagement in these realms is strongly correlated with several factors unrelated to a school's or teacher's influence, including social class, race, gender, political engagement of the parents, and political homogeneity in the community.

With the notable exception of the work by Kahne and his colleagues (Kahne, Crow & Lee, 2013; Kahne, Lee & Feezell, 2012), it is extremely rare for civic education research to capture information about what students are experiencing in school-based civic education and then follow students for years—especially after they have left high school. Thus, the best researchers typically can do if they want to assess the relationship between what students learn in school and what they do as adults is to project into the future using causal pathways drawn from the literature or to go backward, that is, to ask adults to look back on their school experiences and to describe what they experienced in classes and other co- or extra-curricular activities. The civic education literature is filled with studies that rely on each of these approaches, and they have taught us quite a bit.

Given what we have described throughout the chapter, it is reasonable to predict that Best Practice classroom students will be more civically and politically engaged as adults than they would be if they were in the other classes. To summarize what we show in Table 3.2 briefly, Best Practice Discussion students were more likely to say that they are more interested in politics because of the class, more interested in following the news, more capable and interested in political discussion and in listening to people with different views, more comfortable with disagreement in discussions about political issues, and they had increased their knowledge. As predicted, and as previously noted, Best Practice students also reported experiencing a more open classroom climate than other students—which in earlier research frequently has correlated positively with later civic and political engagement.

Of course there were also a number of ways in which Best Practice Discussion students were not different from their peers in other types of classes. Best Practice Discussion students were no different from other students in the frequency of political discussion with *family*. Best-Practice Discussion also did *not* predict a view of classroom discussions as something that all students should participate in—instead, not surprisingly, as Annette Lareau's research (2003) would predict, the students who felt that everyone should participate in discussion were more likely to be high SES. The students in the Best Practice Discussion classrooms did not differ from other students in the attitudes toward working in the community, and they were no more or less likely to feel vulnerable about expressing their opinions in the classroom.

Regarding political temperament, Best Practice students were more likely to lean left at the beginning of the study. This finding remained at the end of the course, except that the students in Best Practice Discussion and Discussion classrooms became more politically coherent over time, and, therefore, the Best Practice Discussion students overall leaned even further left by the time of the post-survey.

If our data collection had concluded with the post-surveys, we would have ample evidence to warrant the claim that students who learned in Best Practice Discussion classes were more likely to develop into engaged citizens than students who learned in the other two types of classes. Of course, our data collection did not end at the conclusion of the classes. As previously noted, we contracted with the University of Wisconsin Survey Center to do two sets of phone interviews with the students—the first shortly after the 2006 midterm elections and the second in the spring of 2009 (see the Appendix for a detailed description of how this was done and which students participated). We will use these data to examine the kinds of citizens the students would become as young adults and what relationship, if any, this has to their experiences in the classes we studied.

Five Clusters of Political and Civic Participation

Using the theoretically derived and empirically confirmed engagement composites in the follow-up data, we conducted a cluster analysis in order to classify the participants included in the study as young adults in 2009 into meaningful groups based on their scores on a set of civic and political engagement scales and an item about volunteering in the past year. For our analysis, we used the following composites from the 2009 phone surveys:

- Keeping up with news and discussing current events with friends and family;
- Thinking that it is important to keep up with news among friends and family;
- Participating in community groups and clubs (in settings such as schools);
- Using technology, such as social media, for civic purposes;
- Participating politically;
- Engaging in alternative activism, such as boycotting or buycotting;
- Participating in the 2008 presidential election cycle, such as voting in primary and general elections, watching debates, and keeping up with campaign news; and
- Volunteering in the last 12 month (yes or no).

Please note that 369 students participated in this final interview (in the spring of 2009).[7] Table 3.3 provides a short profile of each of the five clusters. These clusters were induced from the students' survey responses and clearly reflect the time in which

TABLE 3.3 Follow-Up Cluster Labels and Profiles

Cluster Name	Profile	N
Tech-Savvy Electoral Specialist	Heavily participated in the 2008 election, keeps up with the news, and uses technology as a tool for civic engagement. Shows low levels of community participation and is relatively less likely to volunteer regularly.	57
Heavily Engaged	Heavily engaged in virtually everything, but particularly notable for engagement in both political activities and group participation. Also likely to utilize technology.	65
Capital Activism Only	Relatively low engagement in all domains, except for capital activism—boycotting and buycotting. This group is more active in this domain than any other cluster.	74
(Relatively) Disengaged	Shows relatively low levels of engagement compared to other clusters in all domains; this does not mean he/she is not engaged *at all*.	95
Service Specialist	Likely to participate in groups and volunteer but shows low political participation.	78

the interviews took place, less than six months after the 2008 presidential election, which showed relatively high levels of engagement by young people—especially those who were in higher education at that time, which was the case for virtually all of our follow-up students. There are distinct differences among the clusters, and they also represent a wide range of civic and political engagement. For example, the (relatively) disengaged young adults reported very little interest or activity in either the civic or political realms, while at the other extreme, the heavily engaged cluster were the opposite. In between them is a group who were the service specialists who were primarily interested in group-based civic participation to help others, contrasted with the tech-heavy electoral specialists, a group that was very engaged in the electoral process and reported confidence in and heavy usage of technology as a tool of political engagement. Finally, the capital activists were fans of the marketplace as a tool for engaging politically—they bought products and services from businesses with political or civic stances they agreed with and did not buy from those with which they disagreed. Table 3.4 illustrates the differences between the kinds of civic and political activities that the young people reported engaging in that caused them to be placed into the various clusters.

We then proceeded to examine whether these five clusters showed distinctive characteristics in both demographics and their civic and political engagement profile *prior* to the follow-up interviews. We found that the highly engaged groups (i.e., the Heavily Engaged and Service Specialists described in Table 3.3)

TABLE 3.4 Cluster Mean Scores for Outcomes Used in Clustering (in standardized unit)

	Cluster				
	Tech-Savvy Electoral Specialists	*Heavily Engaged*	*Capitalist Activists*	*Relatively Disengaged*	*Service Specialists*
Keeping up with news and discussing events	.47	.58	−.41	−.54	.22
Perceived importance of keeping up with news among friends and family	.28	.53	−.36	−.45	.24
Community and club participation	−.71	1.19	−.58	−.56	.75
Technology use for civic purposes	.66	.71	−.41	−.53	−.08
Political participation composite	.55	1.47	−.41	−.70	−.38
Alternative activism, such as boycotting, buycotting, and environmental consideration	.07	.59	.66	−1.15	.24
Electoral participation (voting in primary and general, watching debates, and following news carefully)	.83	.31	−.65	−.72	.64
Volunteering in the last 12 months	76.9%	96.4%	77.6%	81.6%	87.0%

Note: See the Appendix for the items that went into each composite on the left column of this table.

tended to have higher SES, were more likely to be female, and had prior experience volunteering.

What Demographic and Experience Factors Are Associated With Cluster Membership?

We ran an analysis to predict membership in the two extreme clusters, which differed significantly in both their engagement profile and socioeconomic status (Heavily Engaged vs. Disengaged). We found that the students in the Heavily Engaged category were more likely to come from affluent families, as indicated by their higher average SES score. Furthermore, Heavily Engaged young adults, on average, had a significantly higher Prior Exposure Index score. Findings indicate that the effects of SES and pre-test level of civic engagement are so significant that they account for most of the predicted variance in the cluster membership (i.e., higher SES students are far more likely to end up in the Heavily Engaged cluster). We did find that "enjoying political discussion with peers," a pre-survey characteristic of the Heavily Engaged cluster, also predicted cluster membership in the Heavily Engaged cluster above and beyond the effect of SES, prior exposure index, ideology, and ideological coherence.

Which Classroom Experiences Predict Cluster Membership?

Students who ended up in the Heavily Engaged Cluster also were different from other students in many aspects of their classroom experience, especially in their attitudes toward political discussion and disagreements. When compared to students in all other clusters, Heavily Engaged students were more likely to report a more open classroom climate when they took the post-course survey at the end of the classes we studied. They also reported that they were able to listen to many sides before making decisions and enjoyed talking about politics with peers. They were slightly more likely to come from Best Practice classrooms.

The students who ended up in the Disengaged Cluster reported very different classroom experiences and efficacy around political discussions. The disengaged students reported a less open classroom climate than students in other clusters. The disengaged students were less likely to say that they were able to listen to many sides of an argument before making a decision or that they enjoy political discussion with peers. They were also less likely to report understanding political issues well or that they consider solving community issues a personal responsibility.

Even though the experiences students had in their high school classes predicted to some extent which students ended up in either the Heavily Engaged or Disengaged Cluster, it is not possible to measure what relationship, if any, this had to whether the students were in a Best Practice Discussion, Discussion, or Lecture class because of the nature of the attrition in the sample (see the Appendix for details).

Political Ideology and Cluster Membership

In Chapter 2, we described how Americans are more likely to live in ideologically homogeneous communities than in the past (Bishop, 2008). It should not be surprising that we found that sorting into like-minded communities also created relatively like-minded classes. In Chapter 7, we discuss in detail the influence that being schooled in a like-minded community has on what students experience in the political classroom and on their civic and political behavior after they leave high school. Even though the attrition in our sample prevented us from determining what relationships existed between classroom type (i.e., Best Practice Discussion, Discussion, or Lecture) and cluster membership, we were able to detect a strong relationship between going to school in a Like-Minded School and a much greater probability of ending up in one of the more engaged clusters. Specifically, students from the Like-Minded Schools were slightly less likely to be in the Disengaged and Service clusters than students from non-like minded schools, much less likely to be in the Capital Activist Cluster but much more likely to be in the Tech-Savvy Electoral Specialist or Heavily Engaged Cluster. In sum, controlling for other relevant factors (such as prior civic exposure and SES), being reared in a like-minded community had the most dramatic influences on whether the young people were engaged politically as young adults.

In addition to investigating what influence the ideological make-up of a school had on cluster membership, we were also able to determine if a student's political ideology or the extent to which their ideology was coherent influenced cluster membership. Our major finding was that student's political orientation from right to left matters. Conservative students were much more likely to be disengaged than their more liberal peers—a finding that other researchers have found as well. For example, conservative young people were more likely to sit out both the 2008 and 2012 presidential elections than more liberal young people (Commission on Youth Voting and Civic Knowledge, 2013; K. Kawashima-Ginsberg, personal communication, June 6, 2014). It is not just electoral participation that shows a relationship between one's political views and whether they participate. Conservative young people were also less likely to discuss political issues with family and friends, follow the news, or volunteer (Commission on Youth Voting and Civic Knowledge, 2013).

Conclusion

We began the chapter by describing the key questions that we sought to answer when the study was developed about how students experienced and learned in classrooms that included a focus on discussing controversial political issues (compared to those that did not) and what effect such classes had on learners in the short and long term. From classroom observations and more than 250 interviews with students while they were in high school, we learned that many, although certainly not all, students report a classroom environment that was engaging and interesting, irrespective of whether they were in Best Practice Discussion, Discussion, or Lecture classes. As we explained, we think there are many different styles and approaches to teaching that students find interesting and in which they report learning. However, that is not the case for all classes; recall that only four of the Discussion classes and four of the Lecture classes were rated as "engaging," based on our observations and what we learned from the students.

The Best Practice Discussion classes were different than the others in some key ways that accounted for differences in how students experienced the class and what they reported learning. First, in these classes the quality of the discussion was higher, which we think was largely due to the teacher's practice. In these classrooms, students prepared for discussion, the teacher structured activities so that students learned how to talk to each other, and the teacher was willing to cede center stage. Consequently, the students in the Best Practice classes did not see themselves as an "audience" for the teachers' work but as the workers. That is, they were both given more responsibility for the quality of the discussions and recognized that it took a "we" to pull them off. Second, students who experienced Best Practice Discussion become aware of the multiple perspectives of their classmates, and discussing across these differences increased their engagement in the class and their interest in politics.

In addition to the kind of pedagogy students experienced, other factors also influenced their civic and political outcomes. Most notably, we found that their social class background and the knowledge, experiences, and dispositions they reported at the beginning of the course (what we have called their Prior Civic Exposure) influenced the democratic development of the young people in our study. These factors also affected their future civic and political engagement. Drawing on the follow-up phone surveys, we used a cluster analysis to find that the young people in our study developed into strikingly different "kinds" of citizens. Again, SES and their Prior Civic Exposure were powerful predictors of whether students were more or less engaged as young adults.

While it is unlikely that schools can do much to change students' SES (especially in the short term), as we described above, many of the components that went into the Prior Civic Exposure composite are in the realm of schools. For example, the quality and quantity of coursework related to civic and political knowledge will influence the knowledge that students are able to build, and students' experiences with political discussion, when done well, will cause them to have more affinity for discussion. These findings point to the need for schools to take seriously their responsibility to construct a high-quality civic education program for students. There is clearly a strong relationship between the kinds of knowledge, skill, and dispositions that can be influenced by schooling and whether and how young people take up their citizen roles as they age.

Moreover, the strong relationship between the relative political homogeneity of the communities and schools in which the young people came of age politically and their political and civic participation after high school is a striking finding, especially given what the "big sort" predicts for the future. It is likely that in the years ahead more young people will be growing up in communities that are not very politically diverse, which presents important challenges for the project of democratic education. As we will show in Chapters 6 and 7, teachers with students whose political views align need to work very hard to make sure their students are exposed to different political perspectives. Classroom experiences in which young people are exposed to and taught how to seriously consider multiple perspectives on these important political issues become even more critical; without them, we risk a polity that is engaged but hasn't taken seriously views that are different than those in which they were surrounded as they were growing up.

Notes

1 Joe Kahne, Wendy Richardson, and Walter Parker provided very helpful guidance on the design of the study.
2 Virtually all the students graduated from high school.
3 When interviewed, students were asked how much of class time was spent in lecture, large-group discussion, small-group discussion, reading, watching films, and doing independent work. While there was some disagreement within the classes, this rough cut of "at least 20%" was usually easy to identify.
4 The post-survey classroom practice comparison findings reported in this section all control for student background (race, ethnicity, gender, and SES), political ideology, and previous experience with civic engagement.
5 In order to establish the baseline level of pre–post change, we conducted repeated measure Multivariate Analysis of Variance (MANOVA) to examine whether there was pre–post change for the students in the Lecture classes. We found no significant time effect on any of the outcomes, suggesting that the students in the Lecture classes did not show significant improvements.
6 The low SES of students in the Best Practice Discussion classes can be attributed to the high number of low-SES students at Adams High School, where all classes were rated Best Practice Discussion, and the significant number of Lecture classes in the study that were Advanced Placement classes, which generally have greater representation of high-SES students.
7 Cluster analysis is a method by which researchers identify distinct groups of people based on the pattern of their response/performance on several indicators. In this study, we first ran hierarchical cluster analysis, which identified five clusters, which were then put through a k-means cluster analysis. CIRCLE used this method in 2011 with 6,000 cases and found a similar set of clusters in their sample. See: (http://www.civicyouth.org/wpcontent/uploads/2011/11/CIRCLE_cluster_report2010.pdf)

4

EDUCATIONAL AIMS AND THE POLITICAL CLASSROOM

[T]o have an aim is to act with meaning, not like an automatic machine; it is to mean to do something and to perceive the meaning of things in the light of that intent.

(Dewey, 1916/2004, p. 104)

Sarah Potter teaches ninth-grade geography at St. John's High, an all-girl Benedictine school in a major Midwestern city. Now in her second year at St. John's and her 23rd year as a teacher, Ms. Potter explains that five values guide the school's mission: respect for the individual, respect for the community, stewardship of gifts, love of learning, and creating a life balance. These values are not simply words in a mission statement. "Every student knows [them] by memory," Ms. Potter tells us, adding that these values "are connected to everything we do." In addition, Ms. Potter explained, the school requires teachers to demonstrate how their lessons teach toward the values of peace and social justice.[1]

St. John's is truly multicultural. About half of the 275-member student body is African American or Latino, and close to 50% are first- or second-generation Americans from Pakistan, India, Thailand, China, South Korea, Ethiopia, and other countries. St. John's is a Catholic school, but it is also religiously diverse: About half the students are Catholic, and the rest represent a wide range of religious beliefs. There is also a fair amount of ideological diversity. Although 11 of the 13 students in Ms. Potter's class who participated in the study would have voted for John Kerry in 2004 (one would have voted for Bush, while the other was undecided), class members expressed a diversity of political views when we surveyed them on particular issues.[2] For example, the class is nearly evenly divided on the legality of the death penalty and abortion, and, despite favoring the Democratic presidential candidate, almost all subscribe to the politically conservative view that charity is better than welfare for addressing the needs of the disadvantaged.

We categorize Ms. Potter as a "Discussion" teacher. As explained in Chapter 3, these teachers engage students in discussion at least 20% of the time, but most student talk is directed at the teacher. There is certainly a lot of student talk in Ms. Potter's classroom, but this often happens within what we term an "interactive lecture." One student explains:

> I wouldn't call it a lecture when Ms. Potter is talking. It is more like a discussion, because . . . she will talk, and then most likely a student will raise [her] hand and just ask a question. And then that will lead into the discussion.

In addition to interactive lectures, Ms. Potter likes to engage her geography students in what she refers to as "eye-opening" lessons, such as the following demonstration activity on global poverty that we observed during a visit in 2005.

As students walked into the classroom, they noticed that most of the desks had been pushed aside, forcing almost all class members to sit on the floor. Ms. Potter proceeded to assign students to different areas of the classroom; each area stood for a region of the world. One student was told that she would represent the United States and was invited to sit in the most comfortable chair in the room. Ms. Potter explained:

> When they first came into the room, I was role-playing to a certain extent. And I was being kind of harsh on all the Third-World-country people and telling them to sit down and shut up and quit having babies and things like that. And they had never seen me be rude or mad, because I am like this really nice teacher that everybody loves, and I am very maternal and all of that. And then I was really catering to [the richer regions] and really deferring to the American. I was offering . . . a comfy chair and all that kind of stuff. And one girl, about two or three minutes into it, I heard her say, "Oh, I get it." Because they were all [thinking], "What the heck is going on?" when they first came in.

Once the students were settled into their regions, Ms. Potter distributed snacks relative to each region's wealth. At one extreme, the United States received a heaping plateful of candy; at the other end of the distribution, students representing Africa received one cracker each. During the ensuing conversation about the fairness of the situation and the geopolitical factors that contribute to it, a student representing Africa threw a piece of paper toward the United States as she yelled, "Die, Bush!" Staying in her role as The Provocateur, Ms. Potter responded by suggesting that the United States put that person in Guantanamo without a lawyer. Another student challenged the teacher by doubting that she had set up the proportions correctly. Ms. Potter went to the board to show them charts representing the global distribution and consumption of resources such as energy and food. She reflected after the class that once students saw the statistics on how much the

United States consumes relative to other countries, "Then they began to think, 'Okay, all right. This is right. This is a real accurate reflection of what is going on.'"

After students played out their roles, they each wrote a reflection on the activity and then debriefed as a class. Ms. Potter explained to the interviewer that she had carefully selected the girl who played the United States because she needed someone who "would be kind of cocky and would not be too soft and too compassionate and give all the candy away the first minute, [because] then the activity wouldn't have worked." Ms. Potter recalled that at the end of the activity, a student shared this reflection:

> Now I know why President Bush makes the choices he does and why the corporate executives make the choices that they do, because this is comfortable. I am happy. I like this. I don't want this to change. I like my tray full of candy and my comfy chair and my blanket, and I am not so upset about the fact that 17 people in this classroom have been spending 80 minutes sitting on a hardwood floor.

Ms. Potter concluded by giving background on Karl Marx and the "utopian" axiom, "From each according to his ability, to each according to his needs," as one example of an alternative to the values of capitalism and asked students in each region if they have their needs met and whether they think resources should be distributed more equally. Lastly, the teacher connected this lesson to U.S. foreign policy by stating that because the United States is relatively isolated from the world's poorest countries, it is easy to ignore these issues and instead focus on strategic interests in, for example, the Middle East. Ms. Potter's comments also indicated she was strongly opposed to the war in Iraq, believing this to be an unjust intervention in another country.[3]

Following this activity, the interviewer asked about the "political ideology" of the lesson. Ms. Potter initially responded, "There is no political ideology," and then clarified:

> The value that is underlying the lesson is one that says that people who have plenty should not sleep well as long as there are many, many who have so little and are actually hungry and in pain and in agony. We shouldn't be able to live with that. That should bother us. That should bother our consciences.

Aims and Professional Judgment

Over the years that we were collecting data for this study, we often presented cases of teachers' practices in workshops and conferences and asked educators and researchers to discuss the ethical choices related to these practices. In executing her lesson, Ms. Potter made numerous choices, including:

1. To use the simulation to demonstrate resource inequality.
2. To have students representing the developing world sit on the floor.

3. To cultivate a "cocky" character for the United States.
4. To respond to the comment "Die, Bush" by egging on the "United States" to respond with aggression.
5. To close the lesson with her own views that the United States ignores global poverty and instead chooses to use military force in the Middle East.

We open this chapter on the relationship between aims and good judgment with Ms. Potter because workshop participants had strong and conflicting reactions to this lesson. Many participants felt that Ms. Potter's lesson was well conceived and executed; she demonstrated the relative wealth of the United States in an engaging way, and they agreed with her view that this situation should "bother our consciences." Others worried that the design and execution of the lesson were unfairly biased—some arguing that the students were being indoctrinated into adopting anti-American views. Still others disagreed with some, but not all, of the choices Ms. Potter made. Someone who supported the overall structure of the lesson, for example, might nevertheless have given a different response to the "Die, Bush" comment. Others were sympathetic to trying to invoke an emotional response to global poverty but objected to Ms. Potter's decision to reveal her personal views on U.S. foreign policy.

In Chapter 1, we outlined this book's two purposes. One is to present the findings of our study on what students learn and experience in classes that engage in deliberations about political controversy. The other goal is to set forth a view about how teachers can make good judgments about the ethical questions that arise when they decide to create what we call the political classroom. Here, we return to our ethical framework for professional judgment, which requires attention to relevant evidence, the classroom and social contexts, and educational aims (see Figure 1.1).

In trying to evaluate Ms. Potter's choices, for example, it is important to consider relevant evidence, such as research about pedagogical practices, along with

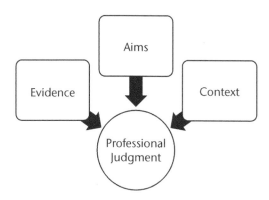

FIGURE 4.1 Framework for Professional Judgment

classroom-level realities, such as the fact that many of her students come from working-class and immigrant families who have first-hand experience with poverty. At the same time, we know from student interviews that members of Ms. Potter's class have relatives and friends who were fighting in Iraq, and some students supported their participation and others were strongly opposed; this is important for Ms. Potter to consider when deciding how to address the Iraq war in the curriculum. Evidence presented in the lesson is also relevant. If Ms. Potter had not set up the classroom as an accurate reflection of resource distribution, there would be good reason to be concerned about the lesson, but insofar as the setup reflected credible statistics, the demonstration cannot be considered unfairly biased, even if the evidence causes students to question U.S. economic policies.

Context also matters. Ms. Potter is teaching geography to ninth graders at a parochial school that promotes a certain set of values—presumably values that parents support. The stated value of "stewardship for gifts" includes developing a sense of responsibility toward God's creations (human and nonhuman), as well as a commitment to justice and peace. One could argue that aspects of this lesson are inappropriate for a public school but allowable for a private school because private schools have more leeway to promote the values that parents endorse. Even within a private school, however, students ought to be encouraged to make their own decisions about political issues, such as whether to support U.S. foreign policy. Ms. Potter's characterization of the United States as cocky and purely self-interested simplifies complex issues, crowding out and possibly silencing competing views that her students hold. Another judgment that Ms. Potter must make is how to strike the correct balance between promoting religious/ethical values and promoting democratic values within the context of her school.

The craft of teaching ought to be cultivated and developed, preferably, in our view, in collaboration with other teaching professionals. All teachers occasionally make questionable judgments; the hard part is recognizing those moments and, when necessary, thoughtfully making corrections. We argue that teachers ought to be educated about how to think about the judgments they make within the political classroom in a way that is attentive to their own contexts, considers the best evidence available, and can be justified within the aims of democratic education. Notice that in thinking about good judgment, we do not address the question "Is Ms. Potter a good or bad teacher?" In our view, this question oversimplifies the complex task of teaching.

What Are Educational Aims?

The act of aiming implies that there is a target. In archery, for example, the archer aims for a bull's-eye, and the target provides a focus for the activity of shooting an arrow. Similarly, someone discussing the "aims of education" has in mind a set of purposes and values that guide the activity of teaching.[4] This is a fairly abstract idea, but simply put, educational aims answer the question, "What do we—as a society and as individuals—hope to achieve through schooling?"

This question has many possible answers. As a society, we require children to attend school because we hope that they will acquire the knowledge, skills, and dispositions that will help them flourish as adults.[5] This might include, among other things, learning to work with others or developing an appreciation for art. Schooling is also a vehicle for promoting equality of opportunity; it is an attempt to secure a fair start in life for all children. Through schools, a society might also hope that children will be exposed to a variety of ideas, skills, and ways of living that will help them pursue fulfilling work and create a life that is interesting and meaningful. Further, schools should introduce young people to the norms and practices of academic disciplines and prepare them for more advanced work in post-secondary education. Finally, in democratic societies, schools are social institutions that prepare young people to contribute to public decision-making.

To sum up, possible aims of schools in a democratic society include

1. To develop in young people the skills and knowledge required for living well as adults (that is, to enable them to flourish).
2. To promote equality of opportunity.
3. To prepare students for the workplace.
4. To foster academic preparation (norms of disciplines, college preparation).
5. To advance democratic values and create engaged citizens.

This list of aims does not represent everything schools try to do nor is it clear that this is the set that all or most people support. For the moment, let us accept that these are at least a good starting point for discussion; if so, three considerations follow.

First, aims will be prioritized differently in varying contexts. A high school with very low college attendance rates may try to correct this by prioritizing equality of opportunity and academic preparation, while a school of the arts might prioritize flourishing through artistic expression. This does not mean that either school will abandon the other aims entirely, but school leaders will make different choices based on their priorities. Second, there are multiple paths to similar aims. One English teacher might ask students to write and perform slam poetry so that they develop an appreciation for artistic expression as a component of a flourishing life. This same teacher might also design the assignment to require students to write their poems about a political issue of concern to them, thereby promoting the aims of democratic education. Another instructor might teach toward the same set of aims (appreciation for artistic expression, democratic education) by developing a unit on Richard Wright's *Native Son* (1940), in which students study and discuss the economic, social, and political forces pressing upon Bigger Thomas, the main character in Wright's story.[6] Finally, aims often conflict with one another. Tracking students into AP courses may further the college readiness of some but interfere with the aim of equality of opportunity, because some students will be denied access to courses that are highly valued by university admissions officers. One important feature of professional judgment is developing the ability to decide which aims matter and how to evaluate their relative weight in different moments and contexts.

Before turning to the specific aims of the political classroom, it is helpful to think about what aims are *not*. First, aims are never neutral. Instead, they represent the purposes and values that undergird the project of schooling. Educating for democratic citizenship, for example, includes teaching young people to treat each other as political equals, participate in decision-making, and respect the rights and freedoms of others, and these values should shape the curriculum. For this reason, a teacher does not need to give a fair hearing to racist views, because racists do not treat people as political equals.

Second, aims are not the same as "outcomes." Policymakers often focus on educational outcomes, which are observable skills and behaviors that can be assessed by teachers. Identifying outcomes of interest is an important part of designing educational experiences, and, ideally, they will align with justifiable aims. It is indisputable that the ability to read is a necessary skill for most aims of schooling. Reading allows a person to evaluate evidence, is important for employment, and helps one engage in democratic life. But when educators focus narrowly on comprehension (by choice or by mandate) and on decoding of text without promoting an appreciation for literature or developing the skill of argumentation, then literacy has fallen short of several important educational aims.

Third, aims are different from "content." Courses usually have a particular set of skills and information that students are expected to master as part of a class. Teachers make many decisions about how they will present the content, what concepts and skills they will emphasize, and how they will evaluate students, and these decisions ought to be guided by an understanding of educational aims. To clarify, a narrow conception of a history course is to have students demonstrate that they know about key historical events and can explain their significance. But history teachers should also teach students to "think like a historian," which would require them to look at primary sources and engage in historical debate—activities that teach the norms of the discipline. Further, a teacher who believes that schooling should prepare students for democratic life will connect the study of history to contemporary debates and develop students' ability to discuss and evaluate evidence and arguments. A teacher might also structure the course around perennial questions, such as When is a country justified in going to war? What is the best course of action for addressing social injustices? What role should the government play in the economy? Engaging students in these types of questions makes the history classroom a political classroom.

Aims of the Political Classroom

The political classroom represents one approach to democratic education. It is different from other practices, such as service learning or studying the basic functions of government—though all of these activities broadly aim to develop democratic citizens. Here we outline the democratic aims most closely associated with cultivating students' ability to discuss political issues. Another way for educators to think about the specific aims of the political classroom is to ask, "What values, skills, and dispositions am I trying to encourage when I engage students in discussions of political controversy?" Because the primary practice within the political classroom is deliberation, we draw on theories of deliberative democracy, as well as the philosophy of education, to identify a set of aims appropriate for guiding discussions about political issues that ask, "How should we live together?"[7]

Political Equality

One foundational principle of democracy is the idea that the state ought to treat all adult members of the polity as equally capable of contributing to public decisions. Further, citizens ought to view each other as having political equality. Robert Dahl (1998) notes that there are two conceptions of equality embedded within this principle. First is "the principle of *intrinsic equality*" [emphasis original], defined as the belief that because each person's life is equally valuable, all members of society have "equal claims to life, liberty, happiness and other fundamental goods and interests" (p. 65). Second is a competency claim that asserts that even though people have different levels of expertise on a particular matter, adult citizens have the capacity to decide for themselves what course of action they would like for a particular policy (p. 75). Governing, like teaching, requires judgments and trade-offs, and the principle of political equality holds that all citizens should be allowed to contribute to decision-making. Deliberating as equals within the classroom is one way for students to develop an appreciation for the principle of political equality.

Tolerance

One of the central questions of political theory is, When is it legitimate to use state power to coerce our fellow citizens? All democratic decisions, including speed limits, income tax rates, and drug policies, give the state authority to enforce rules on the polity. The principle of tolerance provides the basis for an important limit to democratic decision-making. Democracy requires citizens to be respectful of people whose religious, cultural, political, or ethical views are different from their own. Political tolerance is the recognition that citizens should not use the coercive power of the state to unjustly outlaw or persecute individuals or groups for holding reasonable views that others find objectionable. Religious tolerance, for example, means that people cannot use the power of the state to privilege one religion over another, or worse, persecute people on the basis of their religion. When students within the political classroom consider policy questions, it is important that they consider their personal preferences alongside considerations about whether their views are in line with the principle of toleration.

Autonomy

Discussions in both political philosophy and philosophy of education highlight the value of autonomy or self-government. "Political autonomy" refers to the idea that adults ought to be allowed to direct their own lives, including participation in decisions about the rules of the state. This is often what is meant by the values of liberty and freedom. Autonomy also refers to having the disposition and capacity to revise one's values and commitments. In classroom settings, teaching toward autonomy helps young people develop the skills and knowledge that will help them make well-reasoned decisions about how they want to live. This requires students to learn how to weigh evidence, consider their inherited beliefs, and come to their own understanding about their political views. In the political classroom, deliberation helps students encounter views that are different from their own, to reflect and respond when their views are interrogated by others, to consider relevant evidence, and to practice argumentation. All of these are important experiences for coming to understand one's place in the political landscape.

Fairness

One aim of deliberation is to come to a policy solution that promotes the common good. Another way to think of the common good is through the principle of fairness. That is, when participants discuss a policy idea, they should enter the conversation with the intention of finding the best solution, given competing views. This requires participants to articulate reasons why they hold particular views, to listen, and to reconsider one's preferences in light of other people's concerns. This approach to democratic decision-making differs from the method of counting up individuals' preferences through voting. In deliberative theory, the process of reason-giving and seeking fair solutions often involves compromise, and this is more important than, and sometimes antithetical to, the vote (Mansbridge et al., 2010). Notice that the focal question of the political classroom is, "How should we live together?" and not, "What are my political views?" In the political classroom, students should not only evaluate policies based on personal preferences, but also consider and reflect on the views and rights of others. Students should learn to consider both fairness and self-interest when making political choices.

Political Engagement

Democratic states can (minimally) compel citizens to participate in certain aspects of public decision-making: Requiring people to serve on juries is one example, and Australia's compulsory voting law is another. But to flourish, democracies need citizens to participate voluntarily in activities such as voting, protesting, performing community service, campaigning, and many other acts that contribute to the health of the polity. One aim of the political classroom is to increase interest in political issues and democratic activities through the process of deliberating the controversies that students will confront outside of school. Further, being informed and concerned about particular issues and political outcomes is an important starting point for engagement, and teachers in the political classroom ought to encourage students to care about the outcome of current issues. For these reasons, teachers can encourage students to become politically engaged.

Political Literacy

Often when we see teachers engage students in discussions of political issues, the issue is introduced without discussion of how it fits ideologically into the political landscape; students are simply asked to consider evidence and each other's views. But just as important as weighing evidence is understanding how issues align with fundamental disagreements about the ideal democratic system. For example, opposition to extending programs that create a social safety net fits ideologically with the libertarian view that the government should be small and not use tax money to redistribute wealth. Conversely, political liberals generally believe that the government has an obligation to ensure that people have access to basic needs like food and housing. Teachers in the political classroom should help students understand competing ideologies underlying controversial issues and competing views about democracy itself. This "literacy" will help students place the arguments they hear and their own views into the larger political picture.

Note several points about this set of aims. First, while the aims are not neutral to the value of democracy, they are nonpartisan. That is, there are competing views in the public sphere about foundational issues such as the role and size of government in a democracy and what justice requires, and in the United States these ideological differences mostly align with the philosophies of the major political parties. But these very differences can and should be deliberated in the political classroom. Promoting these aims does not coerce students into a particular ideological camp, but it does encourage students to adopt a view of democracy that is more deliberative than what they see in the public sphere.

Second, the list of aims is derived from a more ideal version of democracy. As Dahl (1998) notes, democracy is "both an ideal and an actuality" (p. 26). In the ideal, democracy is a system of government that begins with the idea that members of a society ought to be regarded as political equals and as such should be allowed to contribute to public decision-making. In order to be considered a democratic society, large-scale democracies must have particular features, one example of which is "free, fair, and frequent elections" (p. 85).[8] In the ideal, people see each other and are treated as political equals and all have equal opportunities to express their views through elections. In *actuality*, democratic publics must make all kinds of decisions about how voting will take place, such as when and how people register to vote; the age at which citizens are allowed to take part in elections; the rules that determine whether people with felony convictions can vote; the type of identification, if any, required to receive a ballot; and the language or languages that appear on the ballot. Making these decisions is part of actual, or non-ideal, democracy. In practice, democracies are constantly confronting policy choices that make the system more or less ideally democratic. Teaching students to think about and experience a more ideal version of democracy should help them understand how choices can advance or inhibit the project of democracy.

Third, while the values promoted within the political classroom are more ideal than those practiced outside the classroom, this does not mean that teachers should ignore the ways in which our non-ideal democracy is flawed. For example, teaching students *to view each other as political equals* is quite different from teaching them that the United States *has achieved* a system of political equality. Nearly all societies struggle to address prejudices based on race, ethnicity, social class, gender, religion, physical ability, age, and sexual orientation. Further, those in marginalized groups may not be taken seriously when they voice their opinions and concerns to elected officials, fellow citizens, or classmates (Levinson, 2003; Sanders, 1997) and may not receive the same political education as more privileged members of society (Levinson, 2012). As discussed in Chapter 2, political polarization is negatively affecting democracy in the United States, primarily by increasing social distrust. Social inequality and polarization create two levels of challenge within the political classroom. The first challenge is how these phenomena affect what happens within the classroom. That is, how do the social composition and political orientation of a particular group of students affect the deliberative process? The second challenge is how to teach students about social inequality and polarization in a way that encourages rather than discourages further participation.

To consider how these aims and democratic flaws might help teachers make more justified professional judgments, we return briefly to Ms. Potter's practice. In the lesson on global distribution of resources, Ms. Potter touches on several aims of the political classroom, with particular emphasis on political equality and fairness. The activity forces students to experience social inequality within the classroom by assigning some to lower-status poor countries and awarding a few individuals wealth and high status. The aim (and effect) is, as Ms. Potter says, "to open [students'] eyes" to inequality while underscoring how easy it is to ignore inequities when one is relatively well off and separated from the suffering of others. This teaches the value of political equality by demonstrating to students the injustice of inequality. As the lesson and unit of study continued, students were asked to reason about global poverty, not from the position of what is best for the United States alone (self-interest), but also to think about the suffering of others and what fair and just policies might be. At the same time, Ms. Potter's depiction of the United States as "cocky" and without compassion is *a possible* interpretation of U.S. foreign policy, but not the only interpretation. Her characterization of the United States and tacit support for the "Die, Bush" comment communicates to students that there is one view—or one reasonable view—and oversimplifies complex political issues. Further, it exacerbates rather than ameliorates polarized thinking in which one political party is positioned as benevolent and the other evil. The danger with this sort of approach is that students may come to believe that there are easy answers to political issues—a belief that encourages political intolerance.

The Political Classroom in Practice

In what follows, we use data from the study to explore three cases of teacher practice within the political classroom. In all cases, we have deduced from the data the primary democratic aim of each educator. For one teacher, the central aim is to motivate students to participate actively in democratic institutions; for a second teacher, the paramount goal is to foster political friendships that transcend partisan lines; and for a third teacher, the key objective was to inspire students at an independent Christian school to reflect critically on their political values while adhering to their religious beliefs. These cases serve several purposes. First, they demonstrate the way in which aims guide (or ought to guide) teacher practice. Second, each case illustrates how the teacher's context affects the ranking of particular aims. Again, it is not that all aims matter equally in all cases, but that teachers should think about which are most relevant to their students. Third, the cases exemplify two of our principal findings: (1) Teachers often struggle with the social dynamic created when classes are heterogeneous along lines of race and social class; and (2) Political polarization affects what teachers do and are able to do within their classrooms. Finally, these cases highlight varying ways in which teachers respond to some of the ethical challenges associated with introducing politics into the classroom. In Part III, we use the cases as the basis for discussing three issues that are particularly divisive—and important—for teachers. First, which issues should be framed as controversial political issues? Second, when and how should teachers address political issues that are sensitive to a minority of students in the classroom? And finally, should teachers share their political views with students?

Notes

1 In a phone conversation discussing her reactions to this chapter, Ms. Potter explained that the school required teachers to submit lesson plans that demonstrated the ways in which their curriculum taught toward the values of peace and social justice (phone communication, October 28, 2013).

2 Students volunteered to participate in the study, with parental consent. There were 22 students enrolled in this class and 13 who agreed to participate. Four were interviewed. This is the "middle" track of a three-level tracking system.

3 In a phone conversation discussing her reactions to this chapter, Ms. Potter explained that this was not just her view but the official view of the school, which had recently used one of their regularly scheduled "Teach-in Days" to discuss injustices related to the United States' invasion of Iraq (phone communication, October 28, 2013).

4 This analogy of aims and shooting is adopted from John Dewey's discussion of the aims of education. See p. 105 in Dewey, J. (1916/2004). *Democracy and education*. Mineola, NY: Dover Publications.

5 The philosophic conception of "flourishing" has its roots in Aristotle's idea of "eudaimonia" and is sometimes understood to mean "happiness." For a more complete account of the educational aim of flourishing, see Brighouse, H. (2006). *On education*. New York, NY: Routledge.

6 Richard Wright's book, *Native Son*, first published in 1940, is about an African American 20-year-old who lived in poverty on Chicago's South Side.

7 See as examples Barber (1984), Gutmann & Thompson (1996), Mansbridge (1983), and Mansbridge et al. (2010).

8 Dahl (1998) lists six requirements for a country to be considered democratic. They are elected officials; free, fair and frequent elections; freedom of expression; alternative sources of information; associational autonomy; and inclusive citizenship (p. 85).

PART II
Cases of Practice

5

ADAMS HIGH

A Case of Inclusive Participation

What does the deliberative ideal demand of a citizen facing a vote? Ideally, that the citizen first deliberate with others in the sense of actively seeking out opposing views, listening attentively to the full panoply of those views, offering justifications for his or her own views, taking seriously the objections to those justifications, and being willing to revise his or her views on the basis of the objections of others and with the goal of promoting the common good and fairness to all concerned.

(Mansbridge et al., 2010, p. 89)

The balcony of the Adams High School auditorium is filled with students, teachers, and administrators who are skipping lunch to watch the senior class legislate. Even the local mayor is in the audience. They are observing more than 200 seniors who are dressed in crisp shirts, dresses, and suits and ties. On the theater floor there is a hum of anticipation. As the three American Government teachers walk about answering last-minute questions, groups of students huddle in deep discussion; several are clutching their prepared comments as they pace near one of two microphones standing in the aisles. Majority and minority leaders, and a bevy of more than 20 whips, are busily directing and organizing their peers. Democrats gather on the left side of the theater floor; Republicans huddle on the right. On the stage, the Speaker of the House sits at a table reviewing the docket with the Sergeant at Arms. The bell rings, and with a loud bang, the speaker's gavel signals that the session will resume.[1]

Since 1993, all seniors at Adams High School have participated in an American Government course that has as its focal point a complex simulation that uses the legislative process to immerse students in a culture of political talk.[2] Throughout the semester, students are learning about issues and deciding as individuals what position they will take. Unlike simulations in which students role-play as other people, in this activity the students pretend to be legislators, but they express their own political views, which results in a complicated interplay between the values of deliberation and the practices of legislating. Now, 12 weeks into the semester, the students have come together for a "Full Session" in which they will debate and vote on bills they have spent the semester authoring, deliberating, and shepherding through legislative committees. Next up is a bill to ban the death penalty, an especially important and timely political issue in the state.[3]

The author of the bill, a Democrat, rises to speak first. Her opening line makes clear that she believes the death penalty unjustly targets the poor. "The term 'capital punishment' is ironic," she begins, "since those without capital receive the punishment."[4] For the next several minutes, she briskly summarizes the reasons why the death penalty should be banned, while projecting onto a large screen slides that showcase the data underlying her arguments. The Sergeant at Arms warns her that her time is nearly up and she ends on the dot. The next speaker, a Republican, goes to the microphone to make his argument, which is similarly brisk, prepared, and fact-filled. Then, back and forth, students from each party are recognized by the speaker; they approach the microphone to raise new arguments and rebut others. The debate is lively, fast-moving, and covers a wide variety of reasoning, including appeals to evidence, biblical interpretation, and ethical arguments. At one point, a student talks about why people convicted of particularly heinous crimes should not be given a term of life in prison, arguing that it is "too easy." At this point, the Democratic majority leader rises and challenges him based on her personal experience: "How do you even know what it is like to be in prison? I do know. Both my father and brother are in prison, and, trust me, there is nothing easy about it."

When the 30 minutes allocated to the debate are nearly up, a motion is made to extend the session. It fails, and after a three-minute closing argument, the debate ends and the voting starts. A spreadsheet fills the screen, and students watch as the votes are entered. The mayor of the community has previously asked to address the group, and students have granted him just three minutes to do so. He gives a motivational speech about the importance of democracy and political engagement. The students listen politely as they watch the votes being tallied, and as soon as it is clear that the bill has passed, supporters erupt with clapping and high fives. But not for long, because the students have a busy afternoon ahead of them as they debate bills on immigration policy, the Patriot Act, and other issues.

Inclusive Participation

In this chapter we discuss the American Government program and teachers of Adams High. Eileen Heller, Julie Matthews, and Andrew Hempstead are the three teachers who orchestrated the simulation during the 2005–2006 academic year, when we were studying Adams. The program was established in 1993 by Ms. Heller's now-retired cooperating teacher; Ms. Heller has been teaching American

Government and other social studies courses at Adams for 15 years. Mr. Hempstead has worked at Adams for 12 years, but this is his first semester teaching the senior course. Ms. Matthews is just beginning her teaching career and is experiencing the simulation for the first time. Unlike in the next two chapters, which focus on individual teachers, here we present a highly cohesive teaching team.

Adams High is one of the more socially, politically, and economically diverse schools in our sample. Students come from six communities in the western suburbs of a major Midwestern city. As at many suburban schools, the demographics of Adams have shifted from being a mostly White and working-class community to one that is home to a large Hispanic population.[5] At the time of the study, the school had 2,100 students: 52% White, 40% Hispanic, 4% multi-ethnic, 2% Asian, and 2% African American. The Hispanic population is also diverse: Some families have been in the United States for several generations, while a growing number are more recent immigrants, mostly from Mexico. Our sample of 123 students at Adams High School was markedly different from the overall sample. Compared to the other schools we studied, Adams High students represent a lower average on our measure of social class, and our sample contains a higher representation of girls, students of color, students who were born outside the United States, and students who live in a home in which English is not the primary language.[6] Finally, unlike the schools discussed in the next two chapters, Adams High is politically diverse. The survey that students took at the start of the course showed that, had they been able to vote in the 2004 election, 66% would have voted for Democrat John Kerry and 26% for Republican George W. Bush. Further, more than 25% of students could be found on each of the opposing sides of controversial issues such as abortion, civil unions for same-sex couples, and the death penalty. In both semesters that we observed, Democrats were the majority party, but Republicans were still able to pass bills that cut across party lines, and there was enough diversity to stimulate lively debates.

The way in which students are learning how to be politically engaged at Adams High is unlike anything else we saw in other schools participating in the study. We devote attention to this *atypical* case of the political classroom because it has value as an example of a group of educators who are committed to teaching toward "inclusive participation." In democratic theory—particularly deliberative theory—a new policy can be considered legitimate only if all voices are included in the decision-making process. Inclusive participation requires citizens to see each other as political equals and to engage in the process with the intention of arriving at a solution that promotes the common good. Further, including all voices widens participants' perspectives and, it is hoped, results in decisions that all are willing to abide by, because the process allowed all voices to be heard.

The political classroom engages students in questions that address the larger issue, "How should we live together?" In this chapter we show that the composition of the "we" within the classroom matters. In Chapter 2, we discussed current trends in tracking and segregation; these policies often result in classes constituted by students who have very similar experiences and, thus, are more likely to have similar views on issues. We have previously shown that even within exceedingly homogeneous classes there is always some degree of ideological diversity that can be activated by skilled teachers (Hess, 2009), but it is both theoretically and empirically accurate that classes with diverse student populations have an important deliberative asset that can be highly educative—and also create a number of challenges. When classes of White students discuss public policy without students of color and students of color discuss policy issues without White students, all groups are forming political opinions and orientations without important perspectives present. Similarly, when schools track students in such a way that advanced and AP courses enroll the wealthiest students at the school and lower tracks are full of working-class students, democratic education suffers because students do not confront important views.

To illustrate this point, imagine a discussion of immigration policy in a class in which no students are immigrants or have relatives who have recently emigrated or immigrated. The students in the classroom would not hear from those who are most influenced by policies and may also have the most relevant recent personal experience with the immigration system. For example, young people with immigrant parents might be able to offer insights about the complexity of obtaining a work permit or how difficult it is to negotiate high school when parents do not speak English. The teachers at Adams High believe their program provides greater opportunity for students to expand understanding and to see each other as political equals because students hear personal accounts from each other. Ms. Heller explains that the simulation is more powerful than learning about differing perspectives from books and media; through this process, students learn "that there are real people behind these issues."

The legislative simulation was designed to be, and has remained, a required, non-tracked course for seniors. The teachers are committed to providing equal access to what they consider a high-quality curriculum that is intentionally structured to lead students to see one another as political equals, to teach the skills of "civil discourse," and to develop in students an appetite for political engagement that normalizes political difference and conflict. This is in line with the values of the entire social studies department at Adams, which sees tracking as undemocratic because it creates inequality of access to engaging curricula and reinforces classism. By requiring students to learn in a diverse community, Adams teachers hope to instill in students the beliefs that diversity is a deliberative and democratic asset, that students who come from different backgrounds and hold different views deserve respect, and that political issues are best addressed when public policies are rigorously interrogated and decided by a democratic body. The social studies teachers at Adams have maintained this position even when confronted with parental pressure to create honors and AP courses. Mr. Hempstead explains their reasoning:

We are all in this country together, and we are all in this government together, so we probably should learn about all of it together. Our curriculum has been designed around that. We don't feel that the curriculum of the College Board is the curriculum that is best for all of our students. This puts the onus on us as teachers to create lessons and a classroom environment that does challenge all the kids. I am not going to tell you that it works every single time, every single day, for every single teacher. But I think that is the challenge and that is the fight that we prefer to make as opposed to trying to have some teachers motivate the "low-level" or "basic" kids and other teachers try to get the AP kids to learn all the minutiae required by the College Board.

In order to assuage concerns that students are being harmed by lack of access to the AP Government course, the teachers help students who want to take the AP exam by working with them outside of class in special study sessions and by assigning supplemental reading.

Each year, there are approximately 400 students in the senior class at Adams High; half take the Legislative Semester in the fall, and the other half take it in the spring. The only section that is tracked is one "sheltered" section for English Language Learners (ELLs), which is taught by Ms. Heller. Even though these students have their own section, they still participate in the simulation with the rest of the seniors and work with nearly the same curriculum. Ms. Heller explains why their inclusion is important:

When the administration started the [sheltered] course, I was assigned to teach it, and it was my prerogative how I wanted to teach it. And I was pretty insistent that I wanted these kids to do the simulation, to experience the things that the mainstream kids do and also to give the kids interaction. A lot of times the sheltered kids . . . are segregated from the rest of the population in the school. So for these kids to be part of the simulation, take on leadership roles, [draft] their own legislation, [and] get up to speak is really powerful.

Like the rest of the seniors, the ELLs post their ideas in online forums and participate in the Full Sessions and other activities that take the course beyond their "sheltered" section. Ms. Heller explains that this makes every student's work for the Government course more authentic because participants have to write for and present to the rest of the senior class. This interaction is particularly motivating for ELLs, since it gives them the opportunity "to express themselves and to have their voices heard by the mainstream population."

The teaching team aims to achieve an authentic deliberative experience that is flexible, intellectually rigorous, and engaging enough to meet the needs of all students. By the time we began the study in 2005, the course had become fully institutionalized. Ms. Heller explains that it "has really become part of the culture of Adams High School. It is the senior experience that the kids really look forward to." It is so much a part of the school, in fact, that the social studies department works together to prepare students in the lower grades for participation in the simulation by structuring the curriculum to develop public speaking and discussion skills. Consequently, the American Government semester is the capstone experience for the entire social studies curriculum.

The activity, while clearly not completely authentic to an actual legislature (it is, after all, a simulation), gives rise to some of the same strengths and problems that are so apparent in deliberative and representative democracy, especially with regard to social differences like race and class and the reality of political polarization. In the next section, we explain the architecture of the course, the teachers' role, and the effect it has on students. Later, we explore how the course brings to the fore two core challenges in democratic education: deliberating across difference in a way that is fair for everyone and teaching young people about how the political system actually works, without reifying some of its worst attributes.

The Legislative Simulation

The Government course is organized into four phases: political identity formation, bill authorship and committees, Full Sessions, and debriefing (see Table 5.1). Unlike the way simulations are often used in social studies as end-of-unit or

TABLE 5.1 The Simulation at a Glance

Phases	Student Activities
I. Political Identity Formation (first two weeks)	• Debate on teacher selected issues • Learn parliamentary procedures • Participate in online discussions
II. Bill Authorship and Committees	• Declare party affiliation publicly • Elect party leadership • Research and draft bills • Hear bills in committee hearings
III. Full Sessions	• Deliberate in auditorium for two half-days and are excused from their regular classes • Debate on the floor and vote on bills • Sign or veto (Governor) • Possible Supreme Court (social studies teachers) review
IV. Debrief	• Revisit and possibly revise position on the political spectrum • Compare and contrast the process students experienced to what happens in actual political process

end-of-course activities, here the legislative simulation is the spine of the course, and all the activities throughout the semester are related in some specific way to the simulation. Mr. Hempstead explains, "I think the class is the simulation and the simulation is the class. I don't think there is any real distinction between the two." As a result, what is typically thought of as the content of a government course, such as the Bill of Rights and questions of federalism, are introduced when it becomes relevant to the simulation.

Phase I: A Regulated Public Space

The success of the simulation depends on making sure that all students feel comfortable participating in political discussions. To achieve this goal, the teachers use the opening weeks of the course to provide a foundational understanding of the U.S. Constitution and the two major political parties and their platforms (content) and to establish norms of discussion (skill). By the time the first phase is complete, the instructors have laid the foundation for an inclusive public space that is regulated by teachers as well as by students.

The semester begins with two weeks of in-class debates on current issues using parliamentary procedure. These debates serve two functions: (1) to help students develop their political identities by learning about key issues and assessing the extent to which their views align with the platforms of the major political parties; and (2) to teach students the norms of what the teachers call "civil discourse." Unlike what happens later in the simulation, when issue selection is in the students' domain, at this juncture the teachers select constitutional controversies that also highlight policy differences within and between Republicans and Democrats. In this way, the students are learning the Bill of Rights and the competing ideological interpretations of the amendments. During this introductory period, students are required to read common texts to connect elements of the Constitution to current events. They then create a policy resolution to debate as a class and then debrief by discussing how the major political parties differ on the issue. During this portion of the course, the teachers also model how to run committee meetings. To that end, the teachers explicitly teach the norms of "civil discourse," a modified form of parliamentary procedure that includes addressing each other as "Representative X" and using language that signals disagreement with an idea without attacking a person. After the teachers model facilitation for a few days, students are given time to practice running the in-class debates. They alternate chairing the discussions, and they take responsibility for enforcing parliamentary procedure (complete with a gavel), determining who should speak and in what order, as well as how voting will be conducted. Throughout these class sessions, the teachers are active coaches, holding students to high standards for how they chair and participate in the debates and, if necessary, entering in to ensure that multiple perspectives are fairly represented.

The Role of Teachers. During this first phase, the teachers work to activate natural political disagreement among students, and, when necessary, they play the role of devil's advocate to push students on their thinking. This is also the part of the course in which teachers play the most central, or traditional, role in the classroom. As the semester continues, the instructors slowly fade into the background as students take on leadership roles.

Our observations and interviews made it clear that the Adams teachers are skillful at ensuring that classroom discussions are thought-provoking and lively. For example, while modeling how to chair a meeting in a class largely in favor of instituting a flat tax, Mr. Hempstead makes a point of saying, "The chair would be happy to entertain any points that explain why the flat tax hurts the poor." Mr. Hempstead further explains how he addresses ideological imbalance within class sections:

> In one class I might be giving a lot of right-wing arguments because there were no right-wingers in the class. In another class I might be giving a lot of left-wing arguments. In the other class I might not be giving any, depending on the breakdown. So that really changes throughout the day.

Teachers also know when to break out of their role to ask, "What's going on?" when students do not seem engaged. Even early on in the semester, students feel comfortable responding, "I don't understand this issue," prompting teachers to provide background and context before continuing the debate.

Another strategy that the Adams teachers use to get students talking is their strict adherence to a "no disclosure policy" with respect to sharing their own views on issues (see Chapter 9 for a detailed discussion of this issue). As Ms. Heller explains:

> We, as teachers, really have a very strong opinion that to create a safe environment, we should not say what our opinions are on any issue. We don't want the kids to feel pressured to sort of brown-nose and take on our opinion. We do not want kids to feel rejected if they have an opposite opinion. We just don't feel it is our place. We will play devil's advocate every so often with questions. We will restate things just to stir the pot . . . But we will never, no, we never say what we think on any issue . . . We won't. We won't express what we think. I told the kids I will take out a full-page ad in the school newspaper the day I retire and let them all know.

The teaching team at Adams has the most explicit and consistently enforced non-disclosure policy of any educators in the study. Mr. Hempstead reasons that this policy is consistent with their goal of having students take charge of the activity: "It is not about us. It is about them, and I think the minute that we get involved, it stops being about them." Though students desperately want to know where teachers stand on issues—Ms. Heller says she is "asked all the time. Bribed. Passed notes"—the educators all feel strongly that sharing their personal views would interfere with the simulation and perhaps discourage participation.

In other courses in the study, it was fairly common for students to disagree about whether the teacher shared his or her political views with the class. Adams High is unusual in that nearly all students agreed that teachers do not share their views on political issues. An exception to this was seen in Ms. Heller's ESL classroom. In these surveys and in two of the interviews (conducted in Spanish and translated), some students said that Ms. Heller does share her views. We found that in this and other classes in the study, students with low political knowledge and limited language proficiency sometimes misinterpreted devil's advocacy for the teacher's actual views. Others in the ESL class felt the teacher did not disclose and thought this was the right thing to do because they would not want to disagree with their instructor. As one student put it: "Well, maybe if it were a student I wouldn't feel that bad [disagreeing], but because it's the teacher, you need to respect her more." This concern for respecting the teacher is common among immigrant students—particularly those from Latin America (Valenzuela, 1999). This is an illustrative example of how students are differently prepared to engage in classroom talk. Teachers who expect students to be comfortable challenging their views and the views of their peers need to be aware that this can be a culturally demanding expectation. In 2009, we shared preliminary findings with the Adams High faculty, including this information about the confusion in the sheltered course. Since then, Ms. Heller has started explicitly explaining the purpose and practices of devil's advocacy and also wearing a pair of devil's horns when she plays the role to alert students that she is using this technique and signaling that they *should* challenge her.

Civil Discourse. During these first few weeks of the course, instructors launch an approach that Parker and Hess (2001) call "teaching *with* and *for* discussion" (p. 273). That is, teachers use discussion as an activity that imparts content, but they do not assume that students already have the skills to discuss well. Instead, they scaffold the curriculum so that students develop their skills to talk with one another about important issues. As the semester progresses, students eventually take charge of the deliberations until the teachers become observers. Making the norms of discussion explicit and establishing a structure for committee hearings are important steps for creating an inclusive deliberative space, because it puts all students on a similar footing. Further, the teachers do not simply rely on students with experience to take the leadership roles. Instead, they train all class members to play the role of chair, and they see leadership development as an important component of the class.

In order to activate more ideological diversity among students and reinforce the norms of civility, students are required after each in-class debate to post at least two comments on Blackboard, a web-based discussion tool. In their initial post, class members must explain their opinion on the issue (or the reasons for which they have yet to develop an opinion). In a subsequent post, they must respond using *civil* language to a post from a student with a different point of view. The online discussions involve all 200 students from all sections offered in a semester. The discussions are carefully monitored by students and teachers alike. Mr. Hempstead explains:

> Since there are no anonymous posts, students are always accountable for their posts. And even when they post something that isn't profane, but it just might be rude, the response from the other students is tremendous: "Why don't you talk about the issues?" or "Stop insulting people." We will, of course, speak to the students, but I think the students do a very good job of policing that as well. I think they are concerned about the image of the semester. And I think that they are proud of what this says about the school. With [posts on] Blackboard, a student can read it, and any teacher can read it. It is very public. And I think they want to impress upon their colleagues that, "Hey, you have to step it up a little bit."

Ms. Heller further clarifies that when comments cross the line, teachers will remove posts and "sit down with the student and say, 'Do you understand that people can interpret it this way?'. . . And we talk to the kids about it." In extreme cases that involve ethnic or racial insults or personal attacks, teachers will suspend students from participating online for up to a week. Ms. Heller acknowledges that the forum is "not free from censorship" and explains that students suspended from online participation need to write a letter of apology before they can rejoin Blackboard. One indication of how invested students are in the activity is that Ms. Heller finds this punishment is effective because "[the students] want to get back in."

Early lessons. Maintaining the practice of civil discourse is a concept that is reinforced throughout the semester; it is also a skill that students find valuable to their learning. We interviewed 43 students over the course of two semesters of the simulation and more than 50 in the longitudinal follow-ups. In interviews at the end of the course, students often used the phrase "civil discourse" when describing their classroom debates, and they were aware that the teachers "take it very seriously." Further, they came to realize that a certain amount of discipline is required to maintain civility. A student explained what this practice taught her:

> You really need to make sure that you are being respectful [and] at the same time . . . honest. And you have to make sure that you are not attacking certain individuals, but you are more or less attacking the situation and trying to come up with a way to prove your point. . . . You want to show . . . how you feel about things because you want them to know why you are against them or why you believe the opposite [of what they do].

One might think that regulating the public spaces of the simulation could discourage participation. In our observations and interviews, however, we found that the opposite is true. Setting clear norms, giving students feedback on their facilitation and participation, modeling productive discussion across differences, and factoring participation into students' grades invited more participation. In the follow-up phone interviews in 2007 and 2009, a total of 35 former students from Adams High participated in at least one interview; of those, 26 reported that they recall participating in class discussions "every day" or "regularly." None of the students said that they never participated. The remaining answers ranged from "every other day" to "a little bit." The students noted that it was the teachers' "excitement about the issues," as well as the structure of the class, that got them engaged. One student believes it was a combination of freedom within structure that encouraged participation: "Mr. Hempstead let us have a lot of free speech in the classroom and created a good debate setting. It was very structured."

This engagement carried over to the online discussions. A Republican student explained that she "was very confident on Blackboard" and that this allowed her to engage the more vocal Democrats in political conversations she might otherwise have avoided in a face-to-face conversation:

> I remember going home during spring break and writing on Blackboard and talking to certain people because I didn't understand their views and I wanted to understand more. I would get information, and I would put that into my post and just try to make them see how I felt about things. And, I mean, I attempted it . . . I tried asking them questions. . . . Some people were scared of certain individuals, and I just talked to them because I wanted to know what they thought about that, and I was blunt about it. I would [say], "I don't understand. Explain."

In addition to the online standards, the formality of the modified parliamentary format used in the course also helps to equalize the classroom dynamic because *everyone* must learn the particularities of discussion for purposes of the simulation. In other words, all students had to learn new rules and so started the semester on a more level playing field. These rules also tempered discussions that might otherwise become uncivil. In the two sets of follow-up phone interviews, 13 of the 35 participants used the word "heated" when asked an open-ended question about what they remembered about their class discussions. All but two used "heated" in a positive way, attributing it to "exciting" discussions in which "the whole class was involved" and the discussions "never got out of hand" even though participants were "passionate." One of Ms. Heller's students explained:

> Sometimes it did get more heated up than others. There were certain issues some people didn't want to talk about, but as a group we did a good job [of] not calling people out or using hurtful words.

Of the two students who spoke about "heated" discussions in a negative way, one observed that as people got more passionate, "it turned some friends into enemies and vice versa." At the same time, this student felt the class taught him a valuable lesson: "Don't back down, and always respect others. And be courteous during discussions. That was enforced *a lot.*" The other student observed that the issue of gay rights was "very heated, and some conservative kids got pretty nasty." This student and others noted that abortion, immigration, affirmative action, and gay rights were the issues that were the most divisive and in need of regulation by teachers and students.

Phase II: A Culture of Political Talk

In Phase II, students begin forming their legislature and writing bills. Further, because students are now more engaged with all the other seniors taking the course, they also form a democratic public. That is, they work with students in other sections of the course, continue to interact online, and begin to engage with each other's ideas as political equals. As a result of these activities, the students become involved in a school culture steeped in political talk.

Once the students have become accustomed to the norms of civil discourse and have had the opportunity to think about and discuss issues and party platforms, they participate in "Declaration Day," also known as "D Day." On this day, which happens two to three weeks into the semester, all students declare *publicly* whether they will be allied with a political party or declare their independence. Prior to "D Day," the teachers explain to students that they are running a simulation of the *current political system* in the United States and that as such, the rules are written by the two political parties that dominate politics. Consequently, students who choose to declare outside the two major parties will likely experience some of the same frustrations that third parties and Independents face in real-world politics. In the state in which Adams High is located, primary elections are closed, meaning that those who do not declare within the established parties are excluded from the leadership nomination process. Likewise, Independents might find it difficult to have their voices heard by the Majority and Minority Leaders in committee hearings and Full Sessions.

Armed with this information, students publicly declare party affiliation on a political spectrum posted along a large wall in the library. Each student pins an index card containing his or her name, an explanation of his or her views on social and economic issues, and party affiliation (or Independent). Students are free to change their position on the spectrum at any time (and several did so throughout the semester). As is the case in real legislatures in the United States, the Independents often chose to caucus with one of the parties, although they are not required to do so. Students also write a "political profile" that is published on the simulation website. The profile includes a brief biography and an explanation of the "big ideas"—on the role of government, the rights of individuals, distribution of power, and related issues—that shape their political identity. They go into additional detail about the four or five issues that are most important to them. These biographies are read by students' peers during the leadership nomination and election process. They are also used to discern who might be good secondary sponsors for bills. Once students have declared their affiliations, the majority and minority parties elect their House leadership from among all 200 students taking the course that semester.

In no other school did we observe a curriculum that was so dependent on students articulating and sharing their political views and affiliations with one another. Not only must students express their views in the online discussion forum, but they must also post their political affiliation and opinions on particular issues in full view of the "school public." Clearly, the teachers do not believe that students' political views or party leanings are private matters that a public school has no business shaping or knowing about. That said, the teachers are also aware that they are asking students to take a risk. As Mr. Hempstead put it, "One of the other reasons that I feel like this class has to be a class for seniors is because we all ask them to make some big personal statements and big personal commitments. And I don't think other students would be ready for that."

The teachers report that during the many years in which the simulation has taken place, no student or parent has ever complained about the public way in which students' political views were being communicated to others. One likely reason for this is that teachers quickly establish a regulated public space that normalizes political disagreement and provides a structure that welcomes civil participation from all students, regardless of their political views.

After the leadership elections, students begin working in small groups of three or four to identify a problem they would like to tackle (for example, drunk driving); they then do extensive research on the problem and on potential solutions. They craft a bill they believe will address the problem and post it on Blackboard. Some of the issues students are working on are ripe for a federal solution, while others are more suitable for a state-based remedy. During the two semesters we studied the American Government course at Adams High School, an astonishing array of bills moved through the simulated legislature. One semester, bill topics included ending the war in Iraq, instituting immigration reform, banning abortion, and investing in stem cell research; in another, bills to increase the minimum wage, ban affirmative action, end No Child Left Behind, and decriminalize marijuana came to the floor.

Once the bills have been drafted and assigned to committees, students are released from their courses for half a school day so that they can participate in committee hearings. Each student is assigned to serve on one of nine committees, the members of which are drawn from all sections of Government that semester, to decide whether the bills before them should move forward to the full legislative session. Each committee member is responsible for posting on Blackboard questions and comments about the bills. During the hearings, the elected committee chair is in charge of the session. First, the authors present their bill and answer questions from the committee. They are also encouraged to solicit expert witness to testify on behalf of the bill. If schedules allow, community members, parents, or government officials may appear in person to share their views. More often, letters of support are sent in and read to the committee. Once presented, the committee deliberates the merits of the bill, has an opportunity to amend the wording, and then votes. A bill must receive a majority of votes in order to advance to the Full Session.

Role of the Teacher. At this point in the semester, the teachers have fully transitioned from discussion facilitators to political coaches. Student groups are given a lot of leeway to write a bill that they care about; this means that the teachers need to be ready to help students research and develop an argument for whatever topic they choose. There are, of course, topics that come up every semester, such as the death penalty and abortion, but students also pick topics like videogame censorship and the elimination of biological weapons, which keep teachers learning alongside their students. There are also issues that are more charged than others. For example, given the demographics of the school, immigration is often one of the more-heated topics. Ms. Heller argues that it is important to confront these controversial issues in the classroom:

> When I have talked to teachers at other schools, they say, "You let them talk about *what?!* You let them write a bill about *what?!* You let them express *what* opinion?!" Well, if you don't do it in a safe, structured environment here, they are still doing it at the lunch table. . . . this at least gives them an appropriate context and a structure with which to deal with some of those charged issues and maybe get an understanding of both sides of the issue.

In other words, Ms. Heller believes that the structure of the simulation provides students with tools to address sensitive issues more productively. Because the Government course is required and non-tracked, students are often surprised to learn that their classmates disagree with them and that not everyone holds the views reflected in their peer group. Similarly, Ms. Heller notes that her ELL students often discover for the first time that some native citizens are in favor of extending more opportunities for citizenship to immigrants.

One consequence of giving students the freedom to select the issues for debate is that all three teachers said that they spend two to three hours every day consuming news, so that they can stay on top of their students' projects. Mr. Hempstead describes his role:

> I would end up researching every bill along with the kids. And [I'd] say, "Have you seen this website? Have you checked out this argument?" Or they would come to me and say, "We want a statistic that says this, but we can't find it."

Once the bills are written, the teacher's role shifts again to orchestrating the simulation as bills are discussed online and move through the committee hearings. If all goes well on the day of the meetings, students are in charge. Ms. Heller describes her duties on committee day:

> Fetch paper. Give bathroom passes. Answer emergency questions if they can't figure it out: "Is it a two-thirds vote, or is it a one-half vote?" So, basically to put out fires.

A Changing School Culture. As students research their bills and discuss the issues face-to-face and online, they begin to see political discussion as an engaging activity. One student shared these reflections:

> Senior year is big. Everyone is talking about politics. On the volleyball game bus last week, we were talking about the immigration bill. It was the hot topic in class. It is just fun because the sophomores and freshmen are looking at us seniors like, "What are you guys talking about?" We were back there having a debate on the bus.

In student interviews, many spoke about how, as a direct result of taking this class, they enjoyed talking about politics in the hallways, on buses, in their workplaces, and with their families. These students were excited about how comfortable they felt speaking up. Compared to students in other Best Practice classes, Adams High students were more likely to report at the end of the semester that they frequently discussed the news outside of school, talked more about politics with their friends, and had more experiences engaging in political conversations with people who held views that differed from their own. They also felt that they had entered the world of adult talk, as this student reported:

> I am totally interested in [politics] now. The Bush [State of the Union Address] was last night. I sat there and watched it with my Mom.
> *Interviewer.* Would you have done that before this class?
> No. I would have rather gone out with the boys and shot pool or gone bowling. But she said it was on last night, and I sat down and watched it with her. And we actually ate dinner while watching it and talked about it. It was very bonding.

Another Adams student shared this observation about the impact of the course:

> I think before the class I kind of just went with my parents' views on things because you grow up in a house, a Republican household, [and] I went with my parents' views on things . . . but once I came here I started to understand

some of the issues that I have heard my parents talking about or my other relatives and friends. And it was really interesting, a lot of fun, because I never really listened to politics before this class, and now I really like it.

While several students said that their new knowledge sparked heated political discussions at home, they also reported that these talks were enjoyable. One student, for example, shared an exchange that she had with her uncle during a Sunday dinner: "[We got] into an argument about politics, because he is a Republican and we were arguing about some stuff. So that was fun."

Phases III and IV: Taking Political Stands

Two times each semester, all students enrolled in Government gather in the auditorium for a "Full Session" of the legislature. As described at the beginning of the chapter, the purpose of these sessions is for students to debate and vote on bills that have successfully made it through the committee process. During the weeks prior to the Full Session, students have been in class debating the bills they will deliberate about as a whole body. Students are required to prepare a specific number of speeches for each full session (usually two to three), which are written and turned in to the floor leaders and whips, who will decide which are presented. As the floor debate is happening, students may submit floor-speech request forms that respond to a previous point with a question, corroboration, or counter-argument. Again, the floor leaders and whips review these forms to decide who will get floor time. An observer in a Full Session will have a difficult time locating the teachers. Once the session opens, the instructors sit in the back of the viewing area and watch as students run the session. The teachers might be called on to answer a procedural question and may step in if they see misbehavior, but for the most part they observe and evaluate from the sidelines.

At the conclusion of each floor debate, students caucus with their political party and cast their votes. A bill must have a majority of votes in order to pass. If a bill does pass, the "chief executive," elected by participants in the simulation, has the option to veto it or sign it into law. If it is vetoed, then the bill is resubmitted to the legislative body, where it must pass by a two-thirds majority. If anyone from the Full Session challenges the constitutionality of a bill, a Supreme Court, comprised of social studies teachers, will rule on the bill. If the court finds the bill unconstitutional, then the bill does not officially pass.

In the debriefing at the end of the semester, students revisit the posted spectrum of political affiliations and are allowed to "set the record straight" by shifting or altering their cards. Using a marker, students have the opportunity to add issues, subtract issues, and in some cases change their party affiliation or declare themselves Independents. Ms. Heller estimates that about "25 to 30 percent of the kids make significant movements" on the spectrum after reflecting on the semester. She speculates that the simulation results in more ideological change than traditional Government courses:

> They are forced to be a part of this political animal and be a part of the House of Representatives. And that is very different than sitting in class and reading an article and debating. So when they are confronted by the personal pressures and the party pressures . . . weighing on them, then I think it makes them look even more deeply about where they are on the spectrum. And, in fact, last semester our Democratic floor leader, probably one of the more true-blue Democrats, said that . . . the Democratic Party wasn't liberal enough for her and she became an Independent.

Lessons in Democracy. For most of the interviewed students, the Full Session was their favorite part of the class. Some students found the competitive nature of the simulation exciting; others were fascinated by hearing how their peers reasoned through political issues. One student captured both these feelings:

> The Full Session [was my favorite] because of the preparation and then just having everyone get up there and give their opinion, and then having someone else on the other side shoot it down, and then someone on the other side shoot their opinion down, and just the whole debate, the controversy, the process, the seeing of all my friends and how they look at different issues.

Our data show that students who participate in this simulation experience two competing democratic lessons. On one hand, they move through a process based on an aggregate view of democracy in which interest groups try to maneuver to get political power, and the ballot box determines the winner in a winner-take-all system. At the same time, because students are not actually representatives in a legislature but are acting as themselves, they learn many of the lessons of deliberative democracy, which values reason-giving, evaluation of arguments, and solutions for the common good. Reducing a policy decision to a vote is often seen as undesirable in deliberative theory, because the ideal process is one in which people try to come to a consensus on the best (fairest) course of action. It may seem contradictory that students would learn both lessons, as democratic theorists often see aggregative and deliberative democracy in opposition to one another, but the student "legislature" is ultimately an artificial structure that allows students to engage on a very personal level with political ideas. Further, because the course is non-tracked, students encounter a democratic space that treats people more like political equals than does the democracy beyond the school.

As students move through the stages of the simulation, they learn about the American political system, including party platforms, party leadership, the legislative process, and partisan politics. These are all elements of aggregative or representative democracy, and decisions ultimately come down to the vote. In this understanding of democracy, it is often assumed that people will vote based on their individual interests. Benjamin Barber (1984) has described this as a "thin" view of democracy, because it demands very little of citizens and puts much of the decision-making power into the hands of elites. One critique of the Adams High system is that by simulating partisan politics, teachers could reify the view that democracy is something that elected officials do and could further teach young people that the "fun" of democracy lies in political maneuvering and winning. Indeed, in no other school did we see students so engaged in *partisan* discussions. During the full sessions, students sit with political parties and work with their party leadership to move bills. When we interviewed students in class, it was clear that many were developing a partisan identity. Students who did not understand what the political parties stood for before the simulation could now identify themselves as "moderate Democrats" and others as "strict Republicans." Occasionally, students sounded as if they had political conversion experiences. One "turned Republican" and another was surprised to learn that he was "actually a Democrat." These experiences have the potential to cause students to equate being political with being partisan or to see policymaking as a game of winner-take-all, rather than a "stronger" more deliberative approach of seeing democratic decision-making as something we all do together regardless of party affiliation (Barber, 1984).

Some students may in fact come away with a thin view of democracy, but the teachers see their aims quite differently and believe they are much more in line with the values of deliberative democracy. Mansbridge et al. (2010) argue that rather than looking at voting as an unfortunate necessity for large polities, voting after deliberation should be seen as an important equalizer because it "has the capacity to bring every full member of the polity into the decision and give that member's 'say' an equal weight" (p. 85). This, they claim, is "more inclusive and egalitarian than deliberation" alone, since all voices are not always heard, or heard equally, during deliberations (p. 85).

Mr. Hempstead pointed to this same phenomenon when he spoke about the challenge of discussing racially charged issues during the semester. All the teachers agreed that some students of color felt "attacked" by some arguments that their classmates made, and while this motivated some to speak out, others spoke less as a result. However, given the political and racial/ethnic demographics of the school and its non-tracking policy, voting did have an equalizing effect on students. Mr. Hempstead recalled that "a lot of the White or wealthier or more privileged kids are Republican," while most (but not all) students of color are Democrats. Even though the Republicans were the minority party in the legislature, they were nevertheless stunned when they lost nearly all of their sponsored bills in one of the two Full Sessions that semester. Mr. Hempstead shared a discussion that he had with some of them, in which the students claimed, "But we had so many good arguments!" To which Mr. Hempstead replied: "Well, they had more votes." In our observations, we saw weak and strong arguments delivered by both parties. Mr. Hempstead reflected on this exchange:

> There really was this great cognitive dissonance . . . And you can have all the arguments that you want. You can attack people all that you want. But if you don't have the votes, you are not going to get it done. But I think for a lot of kids it has sort of showed that even though somebody doesn't speak up in class, their vote matters as much as other people's. And that was reflected in the final projects that the kids wrote about their learning and the voting processes—even if the kid didn't talk ever, their vote mattered. And there were a couple of issues that came down to two or three votes. And it really showed the kids, "Wow. Maybe I need to broaden my circle and broaden my influence and maybe talk to other people."

The students of color, for the most part, valued the experience of the simulation, though many also said that they heard views from their classmates that they found offensive. However, having the opportunity to vote and speak against these views was powerful. As one example, Gabe, a first-generation Mexican American student, overheard his fellow Republicans dismissing a Democrat speaking in favor of an immigration reform bill, saying things like, "Oh man, get out of here," and, "Go back to Mexico." As Gabe explained, "It was really difficult for me to kind of sit there and be like, 'Well, I am an immigrant myself.' It was pretty difficult." Gabe decided to act. "I stood up. I said, 'I'm going to take a stand for something.'" He walked over to the line to speak, and, though he "felt very uncomfortable," he told the assembly that he was an immigrant and a Republican and that he "supported the Democrat side." When he returned to his seat, he recalls, "they knew I was an immigrant and I was sitting right behind them." Gabe didn't think his words changed their minds, but, "they kind of quieted down and they stopped making racial slurs . . . and I was happy I had made an impact on the way they were acting." Reflecting on the experience, Gabe was disappointed by those who adhered to the party line and voted against the bill: "It is unfortunate that some [fellow Republicans] that were for immigration [reform] stayed and didn't speak a single word. They just said, 'I am a Republican.'" This experience did not sour Gabe on the simulation. In fact, he felt the simulation improved his confidence:

> [I learned] I am able to stand up and say, "This is what I see" and "This is what I really understand . . ." and [I am] able to present that to other people and be respected for it instead of being rejected for it. I feel very encouraged to talk to anybody about any subject and [take a] stand on it and say, "This is where I stand."

Gabe's example illustrates the democratic values in tension during the simulation. On the one hand, students experience a highly partisan activity designed to give them an understanding of the legislative process, but students also feel person-ally invested in the issues. Further, while students are expected to treat each other as political equals, they nevertheless experience different social standing relative to the issues. Amanda was one of the only African American students enrolled in the American Government class and the one student who finished the semester with a negative view of the experience. She felt her views, which she described as further left than those of the Democratic Party, were often dismissed by her classmates. Amanda was a strong voice in the simulation and a member of the Democratic Party leadership, but she did not have other African American students to turn to when, in response to her objection to the proposed ban on affirmative action, others told her, "We don't want to hear your facts." Her experience is in line with Lynn Sanders's (1997) critique of deliberative democracy in which she argues that the deliberative ideal of discussion among political equals is impossible in a society with racial, gender, and sexual inequality, because the views of marginalized people are easily dismissed by those with more social power. This reality creates a chal-lenge for democratic education. At Adams High, the teachers have concluded that the best response is more inclusive political talk.

The competitive design of the simulation certainly helps motivate students and exposes them to the sometimes-ugly behaviors of partisan politics and a winner-take-all view of democracy. Yet when we asked teachers what they hoped students gained from the experience, they spoke about empathy and empowerment. In both Ms. Heller and Ms. Matthews's interviews, they said one of the most impor-tant lessons that they hoped students would get out of the simulation was to understand that there are "faces" behind political issues. Ms. Heller explains how discussing immigration policy in an inclusive public forum might cause students who are not the children of immigrants to think to themselves:

> Wow. I have been going to school with this kid for a long time and I didn't realize [what their experiences were], and now I kind of understand where they are coming from. And I may still be against illegal immigration, but now there is a face to it, and my dialogue is not going to be as maybe racially charged, confrontational, disrespectful.

This illustrates an important aim of deliberation: Through the practice of reason-giving, perspectives are broadened. Further, theorists argue that when a citizen stops to consider how others are affected by a policy and does not simply push for a solution that most benefits her, the entire polity moves toward a "stronger" democratic system (Barber, 1984; Gutmann & Thompson, 1996; Mansbridge et al., 2010). Recall that in the quote that opened this chapter, Mansbridge et al. (2010) argue that deliberation is an important precursor to voting precisely because it encourages citizens to consider which policy is most fair.

The simulation also counteracts some possible limitations of aggregative and deliberative democracy, because, from the students' perspectives, the most authentic and powerful part of the experience was that these were their *real* friends and class-mates, and their behavior and views affected their real relationships with others. The students do not experience a "silent counting of individual hands" (Mans-bridge, 1991, p. 122), but a multi-layered deliberative process in which they learn about each other and the diversity of views in their community. Further, the teach-ers encourage students to appeal to "logos, ethos, and pathos" (reason, ideals, and emotion) when constructing their arguments. As the death penalty debate that opened the chapter shows, many students share personal experiences as part of the debate, and their peers often found these the most persuasive arguments. At the same time, while the teachers, in our view, do an admirable job of scaffolding this experience to instill the value of "civil discourse" and making it safe for students to share their views and personal experiences, this type of student disclosure is also personally risky. Amanda, for example, explained that she was frustrated by people who did not want to speak against the Republican Party on the issue of immigra-tion, because "a lot of people are afraid to swim against the tide of their peers."

Again, it is the *inclusive* participation of the course that further broadens stu-dents' political understanding. Nearly every student interviewed spoke about being interested in learning about the diversity of views at Adams. In one of the longi-tudinal phone interviews, one student reflected on what she learned from the class:

> I think it has made me more aware of different issues, and has made me more confident in discussing issues with people that I wouldn't have even thought of before. Most of our classes were tracked by different abilities, but social studies wasn't, so there were a lot of different people in the classes. It just makes you realize that everyone has something to say, and everyone has a different opinion.

Being able to connect across classrooms also allowed students to learn from their peers. This was especially helpful to those in the Republican Party who may not have had many allies in their class section. One student recalls that the Full Session allowed her to learn from her fellow Republicans:

> It was good to see people who supported you and hear all of [their] opin-ions. They have angles you didn't even think about.

Overwhelmingly, Adams High students reported that they feel much more aware of the political issues of the day and ready to vote as a result of having taken the Government course:

> We are seniors. We are going out into the real world in a few months, a few weeks, actually, from now. And, you know, we have to be exposed to that stuff some time or another. Otherwise, you are going to be completely clue-less when you get out there and then it is like, "What is this?"

Conclusion

Since its first iteration in 1990, the Legislative Simulation has been revised extensively, not because of the desire of one teacher but because the group of teachers has deliberated collectively and made changes. Because of the committee structure and the Full Sessions, the simulation requires the teachers of the various sections to jointly plan and literally be on the "same page"— unlike the more autonomous teachers we encountered at the other schools. Even though the teachers were quite different from one another in key ways, such as the number of years of experience and their own political views, we were continually struck by the similarities with which they discussed the rationales for this unique approach to teaching government and the challenges they encountered. While the teachers were committed to their policy of non-tracking and the need to ensure that students encountered views starkly different from their own, they were not naïve about how difficult this is to actually pull off in a nation that is marked by high levels of social and political inequality.

In Chapter 8, we address the many challenges that teachers and students must confront when dealing with issues that are more personal and sensitive to some students than to others. At Adams High, this was a recurring challenge because students are given so much responsibility to facilitate meetings and to monitor discussion boards. Moreover, students are allowed to choose the issues they want to bring to the floor, and they were typically drawn to social issues that were most authentic to their concerns and to the world outside of school. Given that issues related to economic inequality, race, immigration status, and sexual orientation were attracting a lot of attention in the actual political world, it is not surprising that students authored many bills on these topics. But it was precisely these topics that posed the greatest challenges in striking the balance that allows students to discuss issues that matter to them without allowing personal attacks or pejorative arguments.

Finding the right balance between authenticity and civility is at the heart of the challenge facing teachers and students participating in the legislative simulation. While the teachers recognized this tension, they were not able to find a complete solution to the problem that some views can be disregarded even in "civil" classrooms. It is important to acknowledge that a central part of Sanders's (1997) critique is that deliberative theory is overly rational and privileges certain kinds of (White, middle-class) talk. She argues that personal testimony ought to be recognized as a valuable contribution to deliberative spaces. The teachers at Adams agree with this view and encourage students to include personal experiences when making their arguments. Indeed, part of the power of the simulation is that students do stand up in a room of several hundred peers and share deeply personal experiences, such as how their family members were treated in prison, how they have felt as a Mexican American or as a gay person, and how not having health insurance has affected their family. Valuing personal experience as a legitimate form of evidence in issues discussions is not typical.

Recall that the course in which the legislative simulation is housed is non-tracked and that students regularly engage with others whom they likely would not encounter in tracked schools (or even in other subject areas in this school in which the classes are tracked). As noted earlier, the teachers were adamant about the need to have all students in the simulation—regardless of race, religion, immigration status, social class, English language skills, or academic ability. This was not only to ensure that all students had access to the simulation, but, equally important, to create the most diverse deliberative space possible. But the teachers at Adams High were concerned not just about individual students but about the democratic community they were developing. In a time when so much discussion about education is focused on individual students' readiness for college and career, we find it noteworthy that a group of teachers is bucking this trend in the interest of preparation for democratic life.

Notes

1 Diana Hess and Louis Ganzler, a PhD student who worked on the study and wrote an excellent dissertation on it, observed the full sessions in December 2005 and in the spring of 2006. See: Ganzler, L. E. (2010). *Simulated citizen: How students experienced a semester length legislative simulation.* Retrieved from ProQuest Dissertations and Theses Full Text database. (UMI No. 3448866). Paula McAvoy went to the school to watch full sessions in 2010. Parts of this chapter also appear in McAvoy and Hess (2013).

2 The first iteration of the simulation began in one teacher's classroom in 1990. The all-inclusive senior experience described in this chapter was first tried in 1993 (e-mail correspondence with Ms. Heller, 5/14/13).

3 Five years earlier, a Republican governor established a ten-year moratorium on executions in light of a number of high-profile cases in which inmates on death row were exonerated of their crimes. Six years after the simulation, in 2011, a Democratic governor signed a bill making the state the 16th to abolish the death penalty. But now, in December 2005, the disagreement among students about whether the death penalty should be banned mirrors the red-hot debate taking place in the broader community.

4 This quote is paraphrased from the website http://www.aclu.org/capital-punishment/death-penalty-questions-and-answers, which reads, "Some observers have pointed out that the term 'capital punishment' is ironic because only those without capital get the punishment" (ACLU, 2007). The student credited this source on the accompanying slide.

5 For a discussion of the changing demographics of the suburbs, see Frankenberg, E. (2012). Understanding suburban school district transformation. In Frankenberg, E. & Orfield, G. (Eds.), *The resegregation of suburban schools.* Cambridge, MA: Harvard Education Press.

6 The teachers reported that some portion of the students born outside the United States did not have legal documents, although we do not know precise numbers because we did not ask this question on the survey. Moreover, we do not know how many of the students who were born outside the United States were citizens. Although if we extrapolate from national census data from 2005, we can estimate that 20% of the students born outside the United States were U.S. citizens. See: U.S. Census Bureau, American Community Survey. (2005). Retrieved from http://factfinder2.census.gov/faces/tableservices/jsf/pages/productview.xhtml?pid=ACS_05_EST_B05003&prodType=table.

6

MR. KUSHNER

A Case of Political Friendship

The ancient Greeks encouraged one another to be hospitable to strangers on the ground that any of them might turn out to be a god in costume. We teach our children, "Don't talk to strangers!" in order to protect them from dangers. But democracy requires vulnerability before one's fellow citizens. How can we teach children, as they begin to near adulthood, to develop countervailing habits that allow them to talk to strangers? And what should these habits be like anyway? These are important questions in a democracy where our fellow citizens are strangers to us.

(Allen, 2004, p. 49)

Joel Kushner has been teaching social studies at Academy High for 13 years. His classroom is small and charming to those who appreciate the old-fashioned feel of a 1930s school building. The floors are hardwood, the blackboard requires chalk, and students sit in a horseshoe formation at small wooden desks with attached chairs that look as though they might have been in use since the school opened. The walls are covered with a multicultural collection of posters, including images of Gandhi, Lenin, the United Nations' flag, Martin Luther King Jr., Malcolm X, Diego Rivera, Frida Kahlo, and various pieces of modern art. Though quaint, the room lacks modern-day conveniences, such as a computer projection system. If Mr. Kushner wants to show a video clip from the Internet, he has to request a projection cart and often hooks up his personal laptop to bypass the older, slower school computer.

Mr. Kushner teaches a senior-level elective course called Contemporary Controversies.[1] The class is non-tracked and enrolls a range of students, including some who have been accepted to elite colleges and others who are unsure of their post-graduation plans. The class size is usually small, between 20 and 25 students, and about one-quarter are students of color. The course places a heavy emphasis on discussion; class time is often spent moving between small- and large-group activities, watching documentaries, and doing research. At the beginning of each semester, Mr. Kushner and his students generate a list of about 20 contemporary controversies; students then vote for the ones they most want to investigate. The top vote-getters become the units of study for that semester. During one of the three semesters we were in Mr. Kushner's classroom, topics selected for investigation included gender and society, race and society, the environment, abortion, same-sex marriage, immigration, and health care. There is no textbook for the course. For each three-week unit, Mr. Kushner brings in readings that present competing points of view, along with newspaper articles, Internet resources, and Supreme Court cases. Mr. Kushner creates a seminar-like feeling in the classroom: He welcomes participation and expects students to be civil and fair with each other. Students are encouraged to be candid, but flippant remarks, such as calling an idea "dumb," are not tolerated.

Political Friendship

In this chapter, we focus on Mr. Kushner's Contemporary Controversies class at Academy High and address the ways in which he responds to two discussion challenges in the political classroom: political polarization and social inequality. We show that Mr. Kushner's responses to these classroom realities reflect the values of what Danielle Allen (2004) terms "political friendship." As the quote that opens this chapter indicates, Allen is concerned with how citizens treat each other in a democracy. Specifically, she argues that distrust among the citizenry destroys the social fabric necessary for democracies to tackle pressing problems. Allen's argument centers on the history of racial distrust in the United States, but she notes that this is just one illustration of the way in which distrust "paralyzes democracy; it means that citizens no longer think it sensible, or feel secure enough, to place their fates in the hands of democratic strangers" (p. xvi). The polarized nature of our current political climate is another example of the toxic consequences of distrust. As explained in Chapter 2, the students who took part in our study have grown up in a political culture in which politicians and the media promote a view of politics as an ideological battle between the political left and the right. This phenomenon is particularly stark in like-minded communities, whose residents live, socialize, and work with people who are politically aligned (Bishop, 2008). As Diana Mutz (2006) has shown, when people talk with others who agree with each other, their views get "amplified" and move toward the ideological extreme, an effect that causes discussants to view those who disagree as irrational and untrustworthy.

Academy High is a particularly good example of a school in which students are at risk of becoming politically distrustful—and one that struggles to effectively address racial distrust. Located in a medium-sized Midwestern city that is home to a research university, the school serves 2,000 students, many of whom are the sons and daughters of highly educated, professional parents. The school offers a rigorous college-prep program; 79% of its graduates attend four-year colleges. At the same time, about one-third of the students receive free or subsidized lunches, and about 40% of the student body are students of color (16% African American, 13% Latino, 10% Asian, and 1% Native American). In addition, students of color make up nearly 80% of the free or subsidized lunch program, which creates social-class divisions that align closely, but not perfectly, with race.[2] While the school is quite proud of its rigor and college-acceptance rate and outwardly celebrates diversity, our observations and interviews revealed that subtle divisions along race and social-class lines affect the dynamic within the classroom and throughout the school.

Regardless of their racial or class background, however, Academy students lean heavily toward the political left, as does the ethos of the school. Indeed, our survey data show that these students are the most left-leaning in the study. At Academy, we surveyed and observed students in two senior elective courses: Mr. Kushner's Contemporary Controversies class and Mr. Kuehl's Sociology course. Of the 101 Academy students who participated in the study, 94 reported in the surveys that they took at the beginning of the course that they would have voted for John Kerry in the 2004 election, four said that they would have voted for Ralph Nader, and three would have voted for George W. Bush. In addition, students' views on particular political issues reflect general agreement with liberal attitudes (see the Appendix). This dynamic puts students in danger of becoming politically intolerant and distrustful of those on the political right. We label schools such as Academy Like-Minded Schools.[3] In the next chapter, we discuss Mr. Walters's class at right-leaning King High School and address findings associated with learning in ideologically homogeneous communities.

Like-mindedness and social disparities along the lines of race and social class make Mr. Kushner's classroom a challenging place in which to engage in political talk. On the one hand, discussion is less charged in conversations that focus, as one student put it, on "exactly what should be done as a liberal." But, the reality that students are generally like-minded in their views makes them susceptible to being distrustful of those on the other side of the political spectrum and denies them the opportunity to engage with people who challenge their views. Further, the social dynamic within a school can lead students of color and students from lower social classes to speak less frequently, to question whether their views will be heard and respected, and to feel frustrated or offended by the views of their more vocal, more privileged peers (Ochoa & Pineda, 2008).

Allen argues that overcoming feelings of distrust is essential for democratic processes to be effective. Although Mr. Kushner does not refer to Allen's work specifically, we find that his aims are well-aligned with Allen's requirements for political friendship, which include being "oriented toward others" such that we consider their well-being alongside our own—a value that we label "fairness." Political friendship also includes the "knowledge that rivalrous self-interest is the basic problem for democracy" (p. 137). That is, citizens should not make democracy a winner-take-all proposition. Allen argues that this type of friendship is the central component of democratic society because it provides citizens a set of values with which to treat each other in the public sphere. For that reason, political friendship is "not an emotion, but a practice" that promotes trust among citizens (p. xxi). Acquiring the habits for this practice requires a certain type of education, and we find that Mr. Kushner has designed his class to teach students the values associated with political friendship.

In an analysis of Mr. Kushner's aims and practices, we found that he responds to his students' potential for political and racial distrust by structuring learning to promote political tolerance and fairness, both of which are key elements of political friendship. These are not the only two democratic aims that Mr. Kushner tries to advance; for example, he also wants students to be politically literate and to reflect autonomously on their political values. But promoting tolerance (by encouraging students to recognize that those who disagree can still be reasonable) and championing fairness (by helping students develop an awareness of who is being asked to make sacrifices when particular policies are enacted) are clear priorities for Mr. Kushner.

Political Tolerance in a Like-Minded School

As noted above, Academy High is home to the most left-leaning student body in the study. This was evident in the survey data, in which students' views on political issues revealed that they were more ideologically coherent and liberal than students at other schools (see the Appendix). It was also evident in the student interviews in which, without prompting, students routinely described their school and city as "liberal" or "really liberal," and as places where "it would be uncomfortable" to be politically conservative. When students described Mr. Kushner's class, they reported that it is "mostly discussion," with about "30 to 50 percent" of class time devoted to large- and small-group discussion. Several students chose the course because it is known to be "discussion-based." In their interviews, students were aware that the views expressed in Mr. Kushner's class were often "liberal" and that when students disagreed with each other, the differences expressed often reflected nuances on the left and not ideological divisions. Yet Mr. Kushner often structured activities so that conservative views would be included in the discussion. Immersing students in moot court activities was one way he did this.

A Lesson in Difference

It is the spring of 2008, and Mr. Kushner is just a few weeks into the semester and nearing the end of the course's first three-week unit, on Religion and Society. Mr. Kushner has been weaving in information about the 2008 election, and he begins the class with an announcement that the following week, two students from another class will be coming in to explain the superdelegate system and how it is affecting the protracted Democratic primary race between Barack Obama and Hillary Clinton. Next, he reminds students that their test on the first section of the course, Religion and Society, will be given on the following Wednesday. As he hands out a review sheet, he explains that students will be asked some basic questions about the Supreme Court and will write a two-page analysis of an Establishment or Free Exercise case of their choice.

In preparation for the activity that is about to take place, Mr. Kushner had taught introductory lessons on the Supreme Court and the First Amendment. Students also spent one class period doing research in small groups and wrote oral arguments as homework. Now, Mr. Kushner directs the class to the seating diagram he has drawn on the chalkboard showing the setup for today's moot court case, the first in a series of cases that will be argued in class. As students move their desks into position, Mr. Kushner reviews the procedures using Supreme Court vocabulary, with phrases such as, "The petitioners will . . .," and, "The Chief Justice should . . . ." Once the desks are rearranged, the nine students who have been assigned to play justices wait in the hallway as Mr. Kushner picks up a gavel. When he cries, "Oyez, Oyez," the students in class rise respectfully as the justices enter and take their seats at the front of the classroom. Mr. Kushner chooses a desk by the door, and the case is turned over to Mike, the student playing the Chief Justice.

Today, the Court is listening to arguments in *Van Orden v. Perry* (2005), a case about whether a monument displaying the Ten Commandments outside the Texas State Capitol violates the Establishment Clause. A young man from the petitioner's group stands to make opening arguments. He has clearly prepared and has a visual of the monument in question. He speaks for five minutes, using formal language and arguing that monuments on public property must have a "secular purpose." He tries to cite precedents, but the argument gets a bit jumbled. The Court interrupts him twice. One justice asks a question to clarify where the monument came from; another asks if it is possible for this monument to have a secular meaning. The student responds adequately to these questions. When the petitioner's time is up, the Chief Justice invites opening arguments for the respondent. A young woman stands to give her opening. She has also prepared for her role, though her grasp of the case is weaker than that of the previous student. She argues that the monument is secular because it is a cultural artifact. She is also interrupted by the justices. One asks about her cultural claims: "Are you saying that our legal system is based in part on the Ten Commandments?" Another wonders if the monument looks like state endorsement of Judeo-Christian religions and then follows with: "Do you think people would react to a Buddhist statue in the same way?" Like her classmate who sought to challenge the monument's constitutionality, she has some difficulty articulating her answers. The case continues with a rebuttal from the petitioners, also delivered by the first young man because, as one student puts it, "he did all of the research." This group decision was not in line with the assignment, and Mr. Kushner looks disappointed, but he allows this change, presumably so that the activity can continue. As the arguments proceed, the students discuss an array of issues, ranging from whether God can ever be viewed as the author of a secular message to the application of the Lemon Test, which enumerated specific conditions for deciding Establishment Clause cases (*Lemon v. Kurtzman,* 1971).

At 10:45, the Court leaves to deliberate in the hallway, while students in class discuss the case in groups of five. When the justices return, Mike announces their unanimous decision that the monument is in violation of the Establishment Clause and should be removed, a decision that reflects the liberal view that there should be strict separation between the state and religion. A student playing the role of "journalist" reads a short account of the Supreme Court's actual 5–4 ruling that the monument is constitutionally allowed. Mr. Kushner asks for a show of hands on how students would rule, and the class is split. Interestingly, members of the group that argued that the monument should be removed all end up concluding that it should be permitted to stay. The group that argued for the respondents is divided in its views. This was the first of a series of moot court cases that the class was going to discuss, and Mr. Kushner indicated that he would need to address some of the rough spots the next day.

During the activity, students were in charge of the discussion for a full 40 minutes, and nearly all members of the class were engaged—either by speaking or listening respectfully to the arguments. In Mr. Kushner's Contemporary Controversies course, discussion is both a *skill* that is being developed and a *tool* for learning course content—a practice that Walter Parker and Diana Hess (2001) label teaching "with and for discussion." In this instance, the moot court cases, which took place in the first few weeks of the semester, were an activity that used discussion to help students learn the course's content, which includes considering the place of religion in a democratic society, examining the workings and impact of the Supreme Court, and understanding the elements of a legal argument. Students were also learning *how* to discuss in this classroom, as well as what Mr. Kushner's expectations are.

This discussion of *Van Orden v. Perry* is noteworthy for several reasons. First, the structure of the moot court ensures that students will be forced to confront or defend conservative views that would likely not come up if the students discussed on their own; this is one key strategy Mr. Kushner uses to expose students to difference. Second, the activity had an interesting outcome. The students portraying the Supreme Court justices, who based their judgments on the oral arguments and a short description of the facts of the case, voted unanimously along liberal lines. The students who were on the teams arguing the case had read the actual court opinions and ended up being more divided. Further, the students who had to argue against the monument (the liberal view) all decided that they had the weaker arguments and, in the end, voted to allow the monument to remain on display. We do not know these students' views on this case prior to the activity, but it is striking that those who read deeply were less ideologically united than those who had read less about the case. Given what we know about this class, this suggests that at least some students embarked on the activity predisposed to side with the liberals but came to believe that the conservative view was more defensible. Finally, we observed that, of the three African American students playing justices on the court, none asked any questions during the proceedings, and no students of color who were members of the legal teams delivered opening arguments or rebuttals. The most vocal student on the Court was Mike, who played the Chief Justice. Mike is a White student who, we later learned, had been accepted to an Ivy League college, was the son of two professors, and had spent a summer working in Washington, D.C., as a Congressional page. These experiences made him an asset and a liability in class discussions. As the first student of several students who would act as Chief Justice during the moot court cases, Mike was able to effectively model how to interject questions into the argument, and he helped to set a serious tone to the proceedings. Mike was also one of a handful of students who often took center stage in the discussions. His comments were usually insightful and demonstrated more understanding of politics than is typical of a high school student, but the delivery was often long-winded. The field notes from one of our early observations of this class include a question about Mike's effect on other students: "Vocabulary very high, ideas complex, thoughtful, but also fairly arrogant, and I imagine might intimidate others from speaking?" (Observation notes, May 29, 2008). Mike and a few of his friends were often eager participants in the discussion, and if Mr. Kushner did not structure activities to bring others into the conversation, this small group of students could easily take up most of the class time. This social dynamic was not at all uncommon in our observations of majority-White classes with social class diversity. We will return to how Mr. Kushner addresses this later in the chapter, but for now we turn to how Mr. Kushner responds to his students' like-mindedness.

Teaching for Political Tolerance

Mr. Kushner creates a friendly atmosphere in the classroom: Students describe it as "open" and "relaxed." This ethos invites discussion, yet Mr. Kushner is aware that his students' political views make deliberating political issues challenging. He explains that he has to choose issues carefully: "It would be more interesting at Academy to have more of that [ideological] mix . . . but now I'm looking at issues that bring out more subtle differences that are significant, but they are not as peg-holed ideologically." For this reason, he did not culminate a unit of study about abortion by having students discuss whether abortion should be legal but focused instead on whether fathers should be notified. He also incorporates diversity by bringing in articles and films that present competing views. Mr. Kushner chooses materials that demonstrate that there are reasonable competing views and then defends those views by playing the devil's advocate as he guides discussion. He notes:

> With abortion, I try to make the arguments as best I can. I divide it up: today is the pro-choice view, today is the pro-life view, and I get the strongest

arguments I can. I think Don Marquis[4] has a good secular pro-life argument, and some of my very good students picked up on that. . . . So Mike and other students in the end were giving a pro-life argument and it was very interesting and it got a little heated. So that's what I do: I make the best arguments that I can, and I actually enjoy it. It's a challenge for me. There is actually a little theater involved and that makes it fun.

During these activities and throughout the course, Mr. Kushner assumes the role of neutral facilitator and does not share his views, even when asked by students. Mr. Kushner explains that this policy for Contemporary Controversies has "emerged" over time as the one he feels is best given the population at Academy:

> I think it is probably best not to [share personal views], especially at a place like Academy, because that's the last thing those three or four conservatives in the class need is to think that the teacher also is harboring judgments of them. Even if they kind of know, or think they know, that's different than knowing. It's the one gun that doesn't have the bullet; it leaves them a little room.

Students report that there is good reason for Mr. Kushner to be concerned about those in the political minority. One student who "votes Democrat" explains that in other classes at Academy, there is little to no attempt at presenting competing views, and consequently during his time at the school he has "watched every Michael Moore movie, except *Fahrenheit 9/11* . . . twice!" While this does not particularly bother him, he still feels it "gets kind of ridiculous," and that, "if I was like a Republican or a Conservative at all, there are some things [that would] just piss you off a lot."

Mr. Kushner's students report that his policy of objectively airing competing views sets the class apart from other social studies courses at Academy. It stands out as "one of the few . . . where you actually learn both sides," says one student. Another characterizes Mr. Kushner's approach as follows:

> One of the nice things is he knows what he is talking about, but he doesn't just say what he knows. He kind of expects you to figure it out yourself. And he presents the information in a good way instead of some boring lecture. He actually makes it interesting.

This view is in line with one of our general findings around teacher disclosure: Students enjoy puzzling over issues, and the process of trying to "figure it out" makes the class more challenging and, thus, more engaging. Not knowing what the teacher thinks, some say, contributes to feeling that the curriculum is open to investigation. Yet while all of Mr. Kushner's interviewed students describe him as "neutral" and as a teacher who presents multiple perspectives in a fair manner, some believe they can "guess that he's liberal" because of "a little wink-wink now and then." Students differentiate this from explicitly advocating his views. In the follow-up phone interviews, some students reported that Mr. Kushner shared "a little bit," but all also agreed that he "remained objective" and "never imposed" a view.

Mr. Kushner reasons that his policy of withholding his personal views helps develop trust among students—particularly those in the political minority—but he also realizes that when he plays devil's advocate, it is not ideal for his aims:

> It is a different experience talking to somebody who [is a] theater actor, giving a perspective, than [to] somebody who is really speaking from their heart and really giving you what they think. I think some of the humanism of a discussion is lost. . . . You interact with the person differently because you know that they are not speaking from what they really believe. And so it changes how you interact. You might not think so much about the dynamics, the interaction, and how you talk to the person. You may not be as sensitive as to how you word it. . . . When you are playing a role, arguments fly out and perspectives fly out more easily, and in some ways probably less thoughtfully *on a personal level.*

Note that Mr. Kushner's concern with the inauthenticity of devil's advocacy is that it removes the personal from the political: As he puts it, "[S]ome of the humanism . . . is lost." We take Mr. Kushner's concern for authenticity here to mean that he not only wants students to learn how to reason, but also how to see others who hold different views as having moral worth. That is, he wants students to know how to disagree in a spirit of goodwill and to talk about differences in a way that preserves relationships and respect.

To that end, in addition to shaping discussion questions so that students will naturally disagree, Mr. Kushner occasionally brings in guest speakers to expose class members to people who hold opposing views. For example, during a unit on abortion, he invited a member of a local anti-abortion group to come in and share her views. A student recalled this moment when she was explaining why it would be better if Academy had more political diversity:

> I suppose that [a teacher playing devil's advocate] is just not believable. . . . For example, when we were talking about abortion, we had a woman come in and she was from like the Christian Society of Non-Abortion [sic] or whatever, and like she was so like *abortion,* you know? She was very, very, very passionate about what she was saying. And in our class—you go to Academy High, we live in University City—most of us are pro-choice. Most of us are saying, "You are crazy, out of your mind! What are you talking about?" But Mr. Kushner . . . was trying to say, "But some people feel this way. And you need to understand what they are saying." But it was not the same because he was being so nice.[5]

We interpret this last comment—"it was not the same because he was being so nice"—to mean that the conversation would have been far more heated if Mr. Kushner had not been setting a tone of civility and countering the prevailing view that those who disagree are "crazy."

This reaction shows that Mr. Kushner successfully communicated his aims to this student, who understood why the speaker was brought in and supported the decision because, as she put it, "[W]e got to see how people really respond." We also note that Mr. Kushner was not trying to change students' views by inviting the speaker to address the class (though that could have happened); instead, he wanted students to have an authentic political experience of engaging in discussion with someone who advocates a different view and to practice listening and responding in a way that promotes goodwill and respect.

Student Reflections

The follow-up phone interviews asked students to recall what they remember about the discussions they had in class. Many students who took Mr. Kushner's class reported that the discussions were often "pretty one-sided" but that there were also issues on which there was a lot of disagreement. Students also noted that Mr. Kushner gave alternative viewpoints a fair hearing. As one student explained, "Even if everyone in the class had the same opinion, he made sure that he presented other sides to the issue, and did so in a way that was very easy to understand how people would think that." Confronting these differences of opinion (both natural and manufactured) helped students see "that when two people have different views on a topic or issues, it's not bad because you can learn from one another." Appreciating that reasonable people can hold different views is essential for the development of political friendship and "non-rivalrous" political relationships because it encourages democratic participants to enter into discussions with humility and, as Allen advocates, goodwill. As one of Mr. Kushner's students explains, he learned "that it is not effective to go into a conversation with your mind made up on a position."

When students reflect on whether and how the course influenced them, they spoke about being more informed and interested in current events. They also pointed to developing discussion skills. One student in Mr. Kushner's course reported that "high schoolers don't tend to hang out and talk about current issues," but after taking this course, his behavior changed:

> I have some friends in this class and even in other classes, [and when we talk] it is like, "Yeah, I learned this, what do you think about that?" And I feel like I have more basis to talk about these issues. Before this, I used to kind of jibber-jabber about the issue. And now I can actually look toward the things that I learned in the class.

Another former Kushner student shared how Contemporary Controversies influenced her:

> Before taking the class, I tended to avoid any political or controversial discussions, and now I don't mind talking about those kinds of things with my friends occasionally. I became more comfortable with the structure of a conversation and with being able to have my own views, whether they were the same or different from the people around me.

This evidence suggests that students understood and appreciated Mr. Kushner's commitment to political tolerance. Overall, students reported that they found value in seriously considering other perspectives, and while very few felt that their views changed as a result of taking the class, they felt more able and willing to engage in discussion with others.

While students found value in Mr. Kushner's strategies to make discussions more ideologically diverse, we still noticed a fair amount of social imbalance in the discussions. Mike's interview showed that he was aware of both the liberal ethos in his school and the effect that social class has on discussion:

> Yes. I would say that mostly the class does disagree on various points, but there are not huge, ideological divides in the class that come up. There are many people who do disagree that don't speak. But the majority of the people who speak are fairly liberal, fairly affluent, fairly well educated. And fairly, you know, agreed upon most of the issues.

Next, we look at strategies Mr. Kushner used to address racial and social class distrust.

Fairness in Conditions of Social Inequality

Allen (2004) uses the idea of sacrifice to argue that democracy requires one to shift one's orientation from self-interest to fairness. Democracy, she contends, forces participants to deal with the "losses one experiences at the hands of the public" (p. 30). Allen shows that civil rights activists who sat at lunch counters and walked through the doors of Central High School in Little Rock, Arkansas, sacrificed their safety in the pursuit of a better, more equitable democracy. Similarly, if Congress votes against extending unemployment benefits during a recession, some families will be required to sacrifice so that other government programs can be saved or so that budgets can be balanced. Citizens also experience feelings of loss when their candidate does not win or when causes they believe in do not move forward into policy. Democracies require us to give of ourselves and to learn to lose, but Allen adds that sacrifice needs to be for the common good and reciprocal. When the least advantaged in society are regularly required to sacrifice so that the most advantaged can maintain their social positions, then a culture of distrust in the system grows. Trust, Allen argues, "consists primarily of believing that others will not exploit one's vulnerabilities, and that one's agency is generally secure, even when one cedes some elements of it to others" (p. 132). Ideally, political friends will enter into policy discussions with a spirit of goodwill and an understanding that, while some will win and others will lose (and sacrifice), we must try to preserve relationships over time (p. 137). Unlike rivalrous political relationships,

> Friendship introduces a different technique for solving this problem [of pursuing self-interest]. Friends know that if we always act according to our own interests in an unrestrained fashion, our friendships will not last very long. Friendship teaches us when and where to moderate our interests for our own sake. In short, friendship solves the problem of rivalrous self-interest by converting it into equitable self-interest, where each friend moderates her own interests for the sake of preserving the relationship.
>
> (p. 126)

Getting students to understand power differences across race, class, gender, sexuality, and ethnicity is an underlying theme in Mr. Kushner's class, and highlighting these is one way of helping students recognize who is sacrificing and who has historically sacrificed in American democracy. In addition to this sociological orientation to the class, Mr. Kushner also has an interest in political philosophy, and together these influence how he thinks about the aims of his course. In one of his three interviews, Mr. Kushner explains that he wants students to practice "public reasoning" that is "not subjective" but moves toward "ethical truths." By this he means that he wants students to think about policy issues from a position of fairness and not self-interest. This is clear when he talks about why he likes to use moot court activities:

> A lot of kids think of issues in terms of themselves, and I want them to make those distinctions where you are reasoning and coming to policy decisions that are binding on the rest of society, [and] that may be different than your personal opinion. . . . What I love about moot court is that it forces them to do the role-play as judges or audience or whatever and think about the arguments . . . in terms of the Constitutional issues. That teaches them a kind of public reasoning . . . and then you can apply that to the policy, too. This isn't about you.

While Mr. Kushner believes that some policy choices are more morally defensible than others (because they reflect ethical truths), he also believes that rational deliberation enables students to identify viable solutions to modern problems. Ideally, he would like students to move from holding views based on self-interest to considering how fellow citizens are affected by various policies. When we base decisions on fairness and the public good, policymaking becomes a negotiation about how to make choices involving tradeoffs among competing interests:

> So you talk about that and how different interests play out in society and how you negotiate those—and all of that interplay is very complex and very interesting and fun. And that is what we do in Social Studies.

Mr. Kushner's desire to have students think about policies as "binding to the rest of society" helps students think about what costs they are passing on to others when they hold particular views and advocate particular positions.

Yet the social dynamics in Mr. Kushner's class can make this challenging. In one of his interviews, he explains that unlike his philosophy course that typically attracts "scholarly kids," students with a range of academic abilities enroll in Contemporary Controversies. On one hand, this is a great asset when students share their varied experiences and really hear each other, but it is also pedagogically challenging to get all students similarly prepared for discussion. For example, in the moot court activity that we described earlier, some students would likely need a lot of support to read and analyze a legal brief, while others might be quite familiar with this type of writing and argumentation. Students might have ceded the assignment to their classmate "who did all of the research" because they felt less equipped to contribute. A Southeast Asian student who stated, "I really like this class," touched on this when she explained why she finds the discussions "hard for me, a little bit" and why she thinks she deserves a lower grade because she participates less than others:

> Like sometimes when we have student discussions, they use a lot of hard words that, I mean, like when I talk, I like to use just simple words. But since they talk really professional, I don't want to, you know, talk to them. I think that is kind of why I feel I should just get a B [in this class].

This student is expressing both a concern that she is not as academically prepared to use "hard words" and noting a social class difference between "professional" students and her own background, an observation that leads her to believe she deserves a lower grade. Social class differences can create an additional imbalance in the classroom. As we showed in Chapter 3, tracking can structure a student's day so that he or she is learning with students from the same social class; arriving in Mr. Kushner's non-tracked classroom may, in fact, be a new social environment for many Academy students. Race adds yet another layer of complexity. Scholars such as Lynn Sanders (1997) and Meira Levinson (2003) have long theorized and observed that in majority-White settings, the norms of deliberative democracy can disadvantage or harm those in the minority, in part because their views are often ignored or dismissed by those in the majority, a reality that contributes to public distrust.

Allen's call for political friendship aims to combat this dynamic by identifying the disposition that adults should assume when acting in the public sphere—one in which people are habituated to be open to the views of others and enter with a willingness to find a fair solution. The classroom is a different type of political space: it is one in which students are often actual friends, but they also can be strangers or enemies. A classroom is also not an ideal public space in which people are equally seen and heard, and it is typically a space that reflects the very different social statuses that students occupy within the school. These differences in academic preparation, social class, and race require teachers in the political classroom to artfully create a climate that fosters trust within a complicated set of relationships.

Because Mr. Kushner wants to address some difficult issues in the class, and because he is aware of these social dynamics, he takes great care to create a culture conducive for discussion. In order to promote trust and open communication between himself and students, Mr. Kushner tries to meet individually with each student for a "check-in" two times per semester, usually during free periods and after school. Mr. Kushner also explains that given that the class is majority White, he thinks it is especially important for him as a White teacher to meet individually with students of color to discuss how they are feeling in the class: "With so few minorities, the biggest thing is [that] you really have to build the trust of the African American kids and the other kids in the class who are a statistical minority." In these conversations, he wants them to know that he is "not an adversary" and discusses with them:

> What it means to have a minority viewpoint and also what it means to be a spokesperson for a group, [and that] just because you statistically represent that one group in the class, we all know that is a flawed model. So I think that takes some of the pressure off the kids, like "You are not speaking for all Black people or Latinos, or whatever."

In addition to these conversations, he organizes a "social day" once per semester in which students bring in food to share, and he tells them, "Your assignment is to go and talk to [a classmate] you don't know." He then has students circulate and post discussion topics on the board. All of this preparation work occurs throughout the semester so that students have time to develop a relationship with him and friendships with each other. This allows him to arrange the units of study so that more heated topics, such as those related to race, come at the end of the semester, when students are more comfortable with each other.

Students overwhelmingly agree that Mr. Kushner "is really respectful of his students" and wants to know "what we think." This attitude is communicated daily in his interactions with students and also through these extra efforts to build honest relationships with them. But even with all this preparation, there is no guarantee that a particular configuration of students will "gel" in the way that

Mr. Kushner would like, and he is aware that there are always factors beyond the teacher's control:

> You know, it's interesting. It seems like every year, even though I kind of do the same things, it seems like things turn out so differently every semester. Like not only the issues, but how you work with the class. I think about [how] sometimes [a] class was just really strange, like strange dynamics.

It is more typical, he goes on to explain, for the climate in the classroom to be unpredictable than predictable.

Race and Distrust

Mr. Kushner's unit on Race and Society introduces students to a variety of issues and controversies surrounding race and racism in American society. In 2008, the class watched and discussed Senator Obama's speech, "A More Perfect Union," which was his response to the racially charged controversy surrounding statements by Obama's former pastor, Jeremiah Wright. This was followed by small-group discussions about a collection of newspaper editorials responding to the speech. Using lectures and films, Mr. Kushner also introduced students to a variety of concepts that complicated their understanding of race and racism, such as institutional racism, critical race theory, the social construction of race, and the different ways that liberals and conservatives understand "equality." In addition, students read and discussed arguments made by Black scholars from across the political spectrum, including John McWhorter and Shelby Steele.

In both years that we visited Mr. Kushner's classroom, he ended the unit on Race and Society with a deliberation about affirmative action policies. The first year, the discussion was structured as a moot court hearing on *Gratz v. Bollinger* (2003) and the undergraduate admissions policies at the University of Michigan. Mr. Kushner explains that this activity sparked tensions:

> In one of the most intense moments of the whole year, a student—a well-meaning, liberal student—was trying to figure out [how to respond] after reading a conservative statistic about the dropout rates for African American students in colleges. [He] suggested that maybe, for some, they could go to kind of a prep college beforehand, before they go to the university. And it came off, kind of like *(using an arrogant voice),* "Maybe they should go and get more training." There was an African American student in the class who started talking. And she [said], "Do you have any idea what that feels like?" She started crying, and she was very upset. The boy was very well-meaning, and he was like, "Well, I didn't mean, you know, da, da, da." Now, they agree on the fundamental principles of higher achievement. He actually supports affirmative action.

In the second year, Mr. Kushner decided to change the format to a graded roundtable discussion, also about *Gratz*. The focal question for the discussion was, "Does the University of Michigan's use of racial preferences in undergraduate admissions violate the Equal Protection Clause of the U.S. Constitution's Fourteenth Amendment?" Preparation materials for the discussion included a three-page reading developed by Street Law, a non-profit organization that produces curriculum about law and human rights; a reading about the facts of the case; legal precedents and arguments for and against affirmative action; a one-page explanation of the point system used for University of Michigan admissions and the role of race within this system; and a 12-page chapter on the Equal Protection Clause from a textbook typically marketed to undergraduates.

We observed two periods of this discussion. In both classes, Mr. Kushner begins by explaining that this graded discussion will be considered part of their test on this unit, with the second part being a writing assignment due in the next few days. A graded discussion, he explains, "means that if you are not being attentive and participating, and staying with the flow of the discussion," your grade will be affected. Next, Mr. Kushner hands out a sheet to students with discussion criteria, topics, and room for note-taking. He goes over some of the discussion criteria, explaining, for example, that "drawing another person into the discussion is not randomly calling on someone, but building off of someone's comment or asking for clarification." He also reminds them that active listening is an important discussion skill, and, for encouragement, shares with them that when he was in high school he had to overcome his own fear of participating in discussions. Finally, Mr. Kushner tells students: "What we are trying to do here is promote democratic participation by encouraging you to think through various issues so that you develop arguments for when you are talking to people this summer and fall leading up to the election." Mr. Kushner asks class members to move their desks into one big circle, which the 25 students do without difficulty. He then takes a seat within the circle and reviews the *Gratz* case and the points-based admissions system under question at the University of Michigan. The discussion begins with the opening question, "What are the constitutional issues in this case?"

The discussion in the first class quickly moves away from the constitutional issue to students' views about the concept of affirmative action; the class lands on a discussion centered on whether race or social class should matter more in admissions. At no point does a student take the view that affirmative action is wrong or unconstitutional, but many question whether race is really the most relevant issue. Students draw upon a variety of evidence, including some of the readings from class and their personal experiences. Many of the White students are leaning toward caring more about social class, but Tonya, an African American student who had participated in a college access summer program at the nearby university for the past several summers, argues that racial considerations matter:

People just don't understand—they just won't understand what it is like to live as a Black person. The great thing about [the program I did] is that there is support. There is still racism here [in University City]—when we are [at the university] in the summer, we walk around in big groups and people yell all kinds of things at us—the n-word and "What are all you Black people doing here?" Then people not from [University City] don't want to go here, and I try to tell them, "It is not all like this, we are mostly downtown and that is mostly White, but there are other parts of [the city]." But it is really hard.

Following this comment, others continue to defend the view that social class matters more than race in admissions, but the discussion also pivots to talk about the value of diversity and what all schools can do to help students learn to talk about race.

Throughout the discussion, Mr. Kushner listens intently and occasionally asks students to expand or clarify a comment; otherwise, students direct their comments to each other and do not need much facilitation. The field notes from this visit indicate that we felt this was a productive session:

> This was an interesting discussion. The students of color (about 6 present) were more vocal, White students respectful, and asking some good questions. The students seem to have internalized the idea of social class and White privilege—not just from this class, it seems. Teacher said he was happy with the conversation—happy also that Mike checked himself and didn't say too much, but what he said was good (I agree—had thought perhaps the teacher had talked to him before; he said no). It is too bad their classes are not longer; this could have gone on longer.
>
> (Field notes, June 5, 2008)

The following hour, the class is smaller (20 people present), and there appear to be a few students of mixed race and one African American girl, Anna. Mr. Kushner talks through the same opening, and again the discussion quickly turns to whether social class or race should be taken into consideration. But unlike in the previous class, nearly all the students who participate in the discussion are White. Some predict that they would not feel "angry or resentful" if they lost a spot on the basis of affirmative action, but one White girl is firmly against affirmative action, reasoning: "[W]e all have friends who are minorities who don't try because they just assume they'll get in." This comment leads to a discussion about whether students of color abuse the system and "don't try as hard." Mr. Kushner interjects, telling students: "This conversation makes me a little uncomfortable, because I see mostly White students talking about 'they' and 'letting them in.'" He tries to redirect the conversation to previous readings and how minority students experience school quite differently and asks whether an admissions policy should consider that. The conversation does not go much further, because Mr. Kushner notices that Anna, who had not participated, has tears in her eyes. Mr. Kushner asks students to write for the last few minutes of class and later shared that he did this to give the student "a little privacy." Mr. Kushner was visibly concerned afterward and made an appointment to talk with Anna in the last hour of the day.

These two discussions illustrate how the composition of the class can greatly affect the discussion dynamic. In the first section, there were more students of color and nearly all had been accepted to college. Further, about five students, including Tonya and Mike, were members of a student group that strives to promote multicultural awareness on campus and teaches students to engage in these types of discussions. Finally, as noted previously, Tonya had participated in a summer college-access program for several years that gave her considerable practice talking about race with many different types of people and in groups that were nearly all people of color as well as groups in which she was in the minority. Tonya later noted that part of the reason she "really enjoyed the [affirmative action] discussion" was because she could draw on these prior experiences and felt comfortable sharing her views with her classmates:

> I mean, I enjoy hearing other people's opinions and point of views. [But I still feel], "You don't know how it is because you are not Black. You aren't mixed. You don't know how it is." So I think they should be able to provide their opinion, but they can't really know how it is and tell you what is right, if affirmative action is right or wrong, because they don't know how it is.

Tonya felt it was important for her classmates to hear her point of view, and in fact, several other students said in their interviews that they wished she had talked more. She left the discussion feeling that it had been productive.

In the second class, there were far fewer students of color and they were in conversation with White students who either did not support affirmative action policies or were more skeptical that it was effectively addressing social inequality. Further, Mr. Kushner later shared with us that Anna had missed quite a bit of class this semester and was a student who was struggling to finish high school. This left her less prepared to engage in the discussion. When we interviewed students about this discussion, their views varied. White students expressed feelings of guilt, surprise, discomfort, and confusion. One Asian student felt that Anna had "ruined" the discussion by being overly "sensitive." Anna did not agree to be interviewed.

One thing is certain: These are difficult conversations. An easy response to this story is to conclude that this is an issue of teacher skill: If the teacher had done a better job managing the environment and preparing the students, then tensions would not escalate. Teacher skill certainly matters, but our data show that even with teachers (like Mr. Kushner and the teachers at Adams) who set clear norms for respectful discussion, model those norms, and explicitly teach and enforce them, students still make comments that offend and anger others, and students will come away from the same discussion with very different experiences. As a result, White students sometimes report that they hesitate to speak, for fear of "sounding like a jerk," while students of color say things like "I bite my tongue" when listening to White students talk about issues around race.

Another response might be that these conversations could be improved if we encourage students to be less emotional and more rational in political discussion—a "stick-to-the-facts" approach. Danielle Allen and Mr. Kushner disagree with this view. Allen argues that "reason, interest, and emotion cannot be disentangled" from political deliberation (p. 56). The reality, she contends, is that

> Debates over these issues (unemployment, welfare, taxes, affirmative action, monetary policy and other social-justice issues) are politically divisive not only because they are substantively difficult but also because they give citizens superb opportunities to reveal what their fellow citizens are worth to them.
>
> (p. 96)

The solution for Allen is to recognize that feelings of loss and distrust are unavoidable when we talk about politics, and democratic education ought to teach people to "learn how to live with them" (p. 102). To that end, Mr. Kushner spoke with Anna privately to see how she was feeling afterward:

> I asked her, "Was this an incident that makes you grow and makes you think, 'Wow, this really affected me, and this is how I deal with this,' or was this just hurtful and damaging?" She said, No, it didn't make her feel bad about herself, but she learned that this is a deeper issue than she thought, and that she came out supporting affirmative action much more strongly because of that dynamic and how that played out.

In this conversation, Mr. Kushner recognized Anna's sacrifice during the class discussion and helped her think about her own feelings and responses to political talk. Once Mr. Kushner had Anna's approval, he raised the issue with both classes the next day, first explaining what had made *him* feel uncomfortable about the way students were addressing the issue. We did not observe this discussion, but Mr. Kushner recalls:

> A good number of kids said, "I missed all sorts of stuff in that discussion because I was intellectualizing it and I was just discussing it and I had no idea that a student would feel so bad that she'd cry." So those kids, they really, really thought about how to talk about the issue more than like *[using*

nerdy voice], "Is it an Equal Protection argument?" It was much more like, "Wow, this is intense." And so I talked to Anna about that, because in a way she became this sacrificial student who had to go through all this so that the White liberal kids could see it. . . . So those benefits were pretty great. Hopefully they learned how to talk about the issue. And hopefully they didn't learn that you shouldn't talk about [controversial issues] because you are going to make someone cry, but hopefully they came away from it thinking, "Well, when I do talk about it, how does my language frame the conversation? How are these words different for me than for other people?" . . . So those things were really good.

It is striking to us that Mr. Kushner's response to such an "intense" class discussion—in which a student ended up crying—is that the outcome was "really good." Some might argue that it is wrong to put students of color in a position to be "sacrificed" for the good of White students. Indeed, when we asked Mr. Kushner which students usually vote for Race and Society as a course topic, he responded, "White kids, for sure"—a fact that further complicates the ethics of discussing race in majority-White classes. We address this concern in Chapter 8, but for now we simply note that Mr. Kushner's response to these emotionally and racially charged issues is in line with the aim of political friendship. A sacrifice was made, but Mr. Kushner also made sure that it was recognized by him and by the class. Further, it was a sacrifice made for the "common good" of teaching students—White and Black—to better respond to the emotional aspects of political talk.

Moving From "Me" to "We"

One of the essential elements for developing the disposition of political friendship is that citizens see themselves as part of a democratic community concerned about the common good and not acting on pure self-interest. As we have noted, this was one of Mr. Kushner's aims for the course. It is difficult for us to know to what extent students' political reasoning changed in this way, but our evidence does suggest that Mr. Kushner was effective in getting his students to create a democratic community in the classroom.

In the follow-up interviews, administered after students had graduated from high school, students were asked the open-ended question, "What do you remember about the course?" In analyzing these answers, we were struck by how many times students from Mr. Kushner's classroom used "we" when describing the course. For example, they began sentences with "We talked about . . . ," "We had a lot of discussions . . . ," and "We tried to look at both sides. . . ." Students described him as "an amazing teacher" and the class as "one of my favorites," but it was notable that most of the comments did not focus on Mr. Kushner but on what they did in the class. Students spoke about debates and group work and named specific issues that they talked about, including same-sex marriage and abortion. They also remember learning about multiple perspectives and that the class was "open." We were curious to see if the students were saying something unusual, so we compared Mr. Kushner's students to the responses from another teacher at Academy High, Mr. Kuehl. Mr. Kuehl was labeled a "Lecture" teacher because other than the occasional film, this was the only pedagogy he used. In looking at the responses from both follow-up years, only three students in Mr. Kuehl's class used the word "we" when answering this question (out of 37 responses), and almost all the comments described what the teacher did and not what the students were doing. In Mr. Kushner's class, 28 of the 62 responses included the word "we" when reflecting on the class.

This evidence suggests that there was a different dynamic in Mr. Kushner's classroom. Students in his courses felt that they were learning more than just the content. They were learning from their peers as well as their teacher, and as a result they experienced political talk within a democratic community that, while mostly like-minded, was nevertheless structured to encourage discussions across social differences. Finally, in a testament to Mr. Kushner's skill in creating a climate conducive to discussion, one student recalls, "I also learned that you *can* have constructive discussions in high school settings."

When we analyzed the follow-up data from Mr. Kushner's class, we found evidence that students do learn to value political talk and recognize the importance of thinking about policy issues from multiple perspectives. It is less clear whether as adults they feel a generosity toward those on the political right. The follow-up surveys show that Academy students continue to hold views firmly on the political left; none identified as a member of the Republican Party, but a few said that they are Independents, and one described herself as a "social anarchist." It is striking that students from this school voted at a higher-than-average rate: In the second follow-up survey, 94% said that they voted in the 2008 presidential election. All but one voted for Barack Obama.

Conclusion

Danielle Allen asks, "Can we devise an education that, rather than teaching citizens not to talk to strangers, instead teaches them how to interact with them self-confidently?" (p. 165). To do so would require educators to teach toward particular habits: (1) a willingness to talk to others (strangers) as political equals; (2) reasoning about public policy with a concern for the public good; and (3) holding a view of politics that obligates winners to maintain a relationship with those who lost a particular political battle. The students in this study have grown up in a politically polarized time, and, as noted earlier, students in Mr. Kushner's and other like-minded classes are particularly at risk for viewing those on the other side of the political spectrum not as friends but as enemies.

In one of his interviews, Mr. Kushner reflected on why he sometimes asks his students to discuss issues on which he knows there is general agreement:

> *Kushner:* I like to make the point over and over that socialization is not a good enough backing for one's viewpoint. I mean just repeating what your left-wing parents say is not good enough: Why do *you* think that? You know, I had this girl, two years ago actually, who went home and decided she was against affirmative action and she started having more conservative views and her parents called her a fascist. And she came in and said, "I can't believe it, my dad called me a fascist last night!" *(laughs)* And you know, she was using arguments she was getting in my class, and I was kind of happy actually. "That's great," [I said.]. "Good for you."
>
> *(laughter)*
>
> *Interviewer:* That's great. Wait, what is the greatness in that?
> *Kushner:* Well, the greatness is that it's not necessarily my view, but she's figuring out what *she* thinks, and who she is, and what she believes. . . . I don't have the answer about which one is right on the issues that I teach the kids, so if that makes sense to her and that's what she's figuring out, then that's good. That's what the course is supposed to help them do.

The exchange between Mr. Kushner's student and her father illustrates how distrust erodes democratic progress. If one cannot consider an alternate view (for example, that a particular admissions policy might not be effective or fair) without being labeled a "fascist," then it is difficult to find productive ways to address the very real problem of access to higher education. It also shows how racially charged policies, such as affirmative action, are particularly divisive. Finally, this exchange illustrates why the practice of political friendship is a transformative idea. That is, young people do not see many models of political goodwill playing out in the public sphere—or, in some cases, in their own families. Educators like Mr. Kushner, who seek to develop the habits of political friendship, are teaching toward a civic *ideal,* with the hope that over time, goodwill can transform the political sphere. The transformation that Mr. Kushner aims for in his classroom is a political culture in which citizens can productively disagree with those they know—and with strangers—but still trust that their sacrifices will be recognized and their interests will be considered.

Notes

1 Mr. Kushner participated in the study for three semesters. Two semesters were during the 2005–06 school year ($n = 34$, 3 periods) and the third was in the spring of 2008 ($n = 32$, 2 periods).
2 In 2013, the free and reduced lunch program was 34% African American, 34% Hispanic/Latino, 13% Asian, and 12% White.

3 See McAvoy, P., Hess, D., & Kawashima-Ginsberg, K. (in press). The pedagogical challenge of teaching politics in like-minded schools. In T. Misco (Ed.), *Cross-cultural case studies of teaching controversial issues: Pathways and challenges to democratic citizenship education*. Tilburg: Legal Wolf Publishers, for more on how schools were labeled "like-minded."

4 Mr. Kushner is referring to philosopher Don Marquis's (1989) paper, "Why abortion is immoral." *Journal of Philosophy, 86*(4), 183–202.

5 In later conversations with Mr. Kushner, he clarified that this speaker was from a conservative organization focused on promoting family values. She was brought in to discuss their views on same-sex marriage, an issue that was being voted on in the state. The speaker ended up giving an overview of all of the policies the organization cares about, including abortion (personal communication, May 14, 2014).

7

MR. WALTERS

A Case of Bounded Autonomy

I define autonomy as a person's ability to reflect independently and critically upon basic commitments, values, desires, and beliefs, be they chosen or unchosen, and to enjoy a range of meaningful life options from which to choose, upon which to act, and around which to orient and pursue one's life projects. To say that a person is autonomous is to say something about the individual and about the broad social and institutional environment in which the individual lives.

(Reich, 2002, pp. 91–92)

I am trying to help them constructively navigate this transition into becoming their own selves when it comes to engaging important issues without just turning them loose and doing the whole Dead Poets Society, "Think for yourselves. Go wherever you want. There are no boundaries. Follow your heart." And so I like to think . . . that I am giving them some rope, but I am trying to show them the consequences of going too far with the rope. "Where is that going to hang you at some point?"

(Interview with Tom Walters, social studies teacher at King High)

Tom Walters teaches 12th grade U.S. Government at King High School, an independent Christian school located in a Midwestern university town of fewer than 80,000 people. Although King is one of the two most conservative schools in the study, it is located in a county that is politically heterogeneous: It voted for Democrat John Kerry in 2004 by a narrow 2% margin.[1] The school was founded in the early 1980s and enrolls students from kindergarten through 12th grade. During the two semesters that we were observing, the high school (grades 9–12) was composed of about 100 students. Each year, King accepts about 10 international students from South Korea; these students account for a large part of the school's cultural diversity.

Walking down the hallways, a visitor will find the student body friendly, orderly, and modestly dressed. The values of the school reflect a Christian faith that Mr. Walters describes as "traditional evangelical." According to its mission statement and website, King High was established with the core beliefs that parents are primarily responsible for their children's education, the Bible is the word of God, and the school ought to be an extension of the home. To enroll, students and their parents have to sign a statement declaring they have "been saved"—meaning they have dedicated their lives to Jesus and trust that He will guide them to heaven and "save" them from hell.[2] These characteristics place King High within the modern evangelical movement, which is defined by several related beliefs: the Bible is the literal word of God; the only path to salvation stems from Christ's message and guidance; and encouraging others to devote their lives to Christianity is vitally important (Noll, 2002).

In this chapter, we look at the case of Tom Walters, who teaches toward what we call "bounded autonomy" or autonomy within certain limits. We show that Mr. Walters wants students to reflect critically on the political values they hold (autonomy) while maintaining their religious beliefs. We begin with a discussion of how the aim of developing students' autonomy is controversial within a multicultural and multi-religious society. Next, we discuss the ways in which developing a disposition of autonomy is difficult at King High. Specifically, we show to what extent the school is religiously and politically like-minded and how this set of conditions makes critical reflection challenging. Mr. Walters is aware of these challenges and, in response, teaches toward bounded autonomy. We explain how he thinks about his aims and the ways in which these ideas play out in his classroom. Finally, we report findings that compare the Like-Minded Schools in our study to the Politically Diverse schools in the sample and show how growing up like-minded is both a democratic asset and a liability.

Religion and Autonomy

In the fields of democratic education and philosophy of education, it is common to talk about the educational aim of autonomy. This idea has its roots in classic democratic theory (e.g., Locke, Rousseau), which begins with the premise that individual liberty is an essential prerequisite to living a "good life." This is the starting point for establishing a theory of government that aims to secure individual rights and liberties while creating a just social order. It follows from this that the government ought to be accountable to the people, who should democratically decide the policies and laws that will be enforced by the state. To live well under this system, however, requires a certain type of upbringing—one that teaches young people, as Rob Reich (2002) states in the epigraph to this chapter, "to reflect independently and critically" on values and principles so that they may live the life they feel is best (p. 92). Moreover, because decision-making in a democracy depends on active participation, citizens should be taught to reason well, weigh options, deliberate with each other, and think both individually and collectively about issues of fairness and the common good. In short, autonomy is a disposition that helps people flourish within a democracy, and democracies flourish when people are sufficiently autonomous.

This may sound straightforward, but the idea of educating toward the development of an autonomous self is controversial, especially within a society that has cultural and religious diversity. If teaching toward autonomy means that educators encourage students to "reflect independently and critically" on their religious values and to question the beliefs their parents have tried to instill, then educating toward autonomy has the potential to conflict with the views of parents who want to raise their children to be culturally and spiritually connected to their families and communities. The consequences of too much independent thought are quite high for certain groups, particularly those—such as evangelical Christians—who believe that stepping too far away from cultural practices can result in eternal suffering in the afterlife. It is this concern for the well-being of their children's spiritual health that causes some parents to opt out of public schooling and to enroll their children in private parochial schools, such as King High School. Yet, moving children into a school where they will be surrounded by classmates and teachers who have a similar worldview can be potentially harmful to the development of the autonomous person. As Reich explains, becoming autonomous says something "about the broad social and institutional environment in which the individual lives" (p. 92). That is, autonomy is only meaningful when people have choices available to them. Some philosophers worry that if a child's family has a particular set of values (including religious, political, and cultural beliefs), and the child attends a place of worship and a school that promote those same values, and if the child socializes with peers who also hold those views, then the child may not encounter enough difference to make well-informed choices about how he or she wants to live as an adult.[3] Further, autonomy requires that one's views are developed without coercion, and religious beliefs often include the threat of hell or other conceptions of a torturous afterlife that, when internalized, deter dissent. So while a democratic state recognizes the right to religious expression, it must also be concerned that children are raised so that they eventually possess sufficient autonomy to evaluate (and either recommit to, alter or reject) the values they learned at home.

Some readers may infer that the aim of autonomy is anti-religious. There are certainly conceptions of autonomy within moral philosophy that place a high value upon rational thought and are deeply skeptical of institutionalized religion. For our purposes, we are interested in a less-demanding conception of self-government that promotes living well within a democratic society—an idea that is similar to what Reich (2002) calls "minimalist autonomy" (p. 92). This conception of autonomy requires an upbringing with certain experiences and the development of particular skills and habits of mind, but it does not require one to critically examine *all* aspects of one's life, nor does it exclude people who hold religious views. This is the line that Mr. Walters tries to walk at King High School by teaching toward "bounded autonomy."[4]

The central concern in discussions of autonomy as an educational aim is the question of whether children become adults who have reflected on why they hold the views (political and moral) that they endorse and are able to revise those views in response to changing circumstances. Critics of private religious schools worry that children who attend schools like King are not encountering enough diversity to make informed decisions about their own ethical views or political issues. Recall, however, that in the previous chapter we looked at Academy High, home to students whose left-leaning parents have moved to a left-leaning city in which their children attend school with teachers and students who, for the most part, think as they do. If these children do not encounter difference and do not question the views they have inherited from their parents, they too may be insufficiently autonomous. It is true that at King the only religion represented within the student body is Christianity, and nearly all of the students identify as Republicans. Still, we found that there is a range of views within the school, which, while narrow, may cause students to engage in some autonomous reflection.

King High is not associated with a particular church, and as a result there are a variety of Christian views represented within King's classrooms, ranging from students who belong to the fundamentalist right to a few who come from what Mr. Walters describes as "progressive" Christian churches. Mr. Walters explains that the school also enrolls students from families that are interested in private schooling but

> who are maybe nominal in their real commitment to Christian values and principles. But they see this as a nice alternative to public school. And they are willing to sign on the dotted line and say, "Well, yeah, I know my kids are going to be taught in a Christian atmosphere." But kids who come like that, it only lasts about a year because they find this atmosphere way too restrictive.

As a result of this variation, students and Mr. Walters report some disagreement over biblical interpretation and what it means to be a "good Christian."

This diversity of views at times causes conflict within the school. For example, in the past, the school community had to decide if it would allow dancing (the first prom was held in 2004, after years of discussion) and whether the girls' volleyball team would be allowed to wear spandex shorts (the proposal was rejected). The outcome of these deliberations caused some families to leave the school because they felt the decision did not align with their values. Those who left represented multiple camps, with some leaving because they could not support dancing and others because they felt the ban on spandex shorts was overly restrictive. These differences may seem minor, but they nevertheless communicate to students that there are competing views about what is allowable within the Christian faith. So even though parents are attracted to the clearly defined values of King High, the institution is nevertheless a school—which means it is a place where parents, students, and teachers sometimes disagree about "how we want to live together."

These differences of religious belief are certainly much narrower than one might find at, for example, a public urban high school, but certainly many communities in the United States have students attending public schools with students who are primarily of the same (likely Christian) religion. The difference at King is that the curriculum, school culture, and teachers are able to be much more directive in promoting and enforcing Christian values.

Politically Like-Minded Schools

The modern evangelical movement is politically aligned with the Republican Party, and the party's values are reflected within the school culture and curriculum. A picture of then-President George W. Bush was displayed in the school office and Mr. Walters explains that most teachers "would be supportive of President Bush and the Republican Party in general and James Dobson and Focus on the Family as an articulation of traditional Christian viewpoints on political and social issues."[5]

Politically, King High is one of three schools in the study that we label Like-Minded Schools (LMS). Students were surveyed at the beginning and end of their courses on eight political issues and were also asked for whom they would have voted in 2004 had they been allowed to vote. We label schools "like-minded" when: (1) at least 80% of the surveyed students reported that they would have voted for the same presidential candidate had they been able to vote in 2004; (2) they had average Political Orientation and Ideological Coherence scores that showed the class's views leaned heavily to the political right or left; and (3) interviewed students, without prompting, described their schools as places were "everyone" is ideologically alike. Table 7.1 below shows that four teachers at three

TABLE 7.1 Like-Minded Schools

Teacher	School	Students (n)	Course Sections (n)	For Bush in 2004[a] (%)	For Kerry in 2004 (%)	Class Political Orientation, Average	Class Ideological Coherence, Average
Kushner	Academy	66	5	0	96	1.93	1.04
Kuehl	Academy	35	2	9	91	1.97	1.02
Xander	Church	38	4	84	8	3.52	1.13
Walters	King	19	2	89	.05	3.58	1.31

Note: The Class Political Orientation number is an average of the individual orientation scores based on eight survey questions that asked students about their views on particular political issues. This is a measurement of whether students' views lean liberal or conservative. Averages above 2.5 (on a 5-point scale) indicate conservative views and scores below 2.5 indicate liberal views. The Class Ideological Coherence score measures the extent to which students' views align ideologically with one side of the political spectrum. On this scale, a 0 indicates "perfectly consistent" and scores closer to 2 indicate that students have views that are an even mix of liberal and conservative.

[a] Some students declined to answer this question, and as a result percentages do not add up to 100.

schools taught in "like-minded" environments. Mr. Kushner and Mr. Kuehl teach at Academy High, the left-leaning school discussed in the previous chapter, while Mr. Xander at Church High and Mr. Walters at King High both teach at private Christian schools that lean heavily to the right.

The numbers in Table 7.1 are based on surveys conducted at the beginning of the semester and reflect the views that students held prior to the course. We collected data in Mr. Walters's 11th-grade Government course during the spring of 2005 ($n = 8$) and again in the fall of 2005 ($n = 11$). Of Mr. Walters's students, 17 of 19 said that they would have voted for George Bush over John Kerry in the 2004 election; only one would have selected Kerry. All of them said they were against legalizing civil unions for same-sex couples, and the class had an average Political Orientation Score of 3.58 (out of 5); thus, their views and the views of the students at Church made their schools the most conservative two schools in the study. Further, they are politically coherent, meaning student views mostly align with conservative ideology, as indicated by their coherency score below 1.5 (a lower coherency score indicates greater coherency). It is important to note, however, that there is still some disagreement among King's students. The students in both semesters are nearly evenly divided about the death penalty, and there is a range of views about whether welfare or charity is a better response to poverty. As was the case with many of the 1,001 students in the study, there were many "don't know" responses to questions about economic issues, such as taxation and the government's role in regulating the economy.

This ideological disagreement and uncertainty explain why the conservative schools have weaker coherency scores (as seen in their higher averages) than the liberal LMS. In other words, in our sample of LMS, the liberal students are more ideologically aligned and in greater agreement than are the conservative students. One reason may be that unlike the ideology of the Democratic Party, the Republican Party platform has competing underlying principles. Beginning in the 1970s, Republicans formed a coalition between social conservatives and fiscal conservatives, and as a result, Republicans identify with the party for strikingly different reasons. We see this reflected in the data. Of the 57 students who attended King and Church, there was nearly unanimous opposition to civil unions, general agreement that abortion should be illegal, and strong identification with the Republican Party. (These views persist in the follow-up surveys.) However, on economic issues, 42% of the students marked "don't know/undecided" when asked to respond to the statement "the rich are too highly taxed" (compared to 21% at Academy High). In addition, of the 33 conservative LMS students who had a view on taxing the rich, 66% chose a liberal view (disagree/strongly disagree). Only five of the 98 students who answered this question at Academy High made a fiscally conservative choice.

We want to be clear that these classes are unusual compared to the sample as a whole, and it would be inaccurate to conclude that private schools in general are conservative and public schools are liberal. In fact, of our 35 teachers, nine teach students who tend toward conservative views, with Political Orientation Scores above 3.0 (at seven public schools and two Christian schools). Academy High is the only place where students had a Political Orientation Score below 2.0. All other political orientation averages were between 2.0 and 3.0, meaning that (1) the students are in the process of forming their political views and do not have opinions that clearly line up with one political camp; and/or (2) students are in Politically Diverse Schools. And, as we showed in Chapter 2, the ideological views of the teachers in the study were varied, and we had liberal and conservative teachers in public schools, and liberal and conservative teachers in private schools.

Mr. Walters is a moderate conservative with some liberal views. He explains that his political beliefs are similar to those outlined in Rod Dreher's (2006) book, *Crunchy Cons: The New Conservative Counterculture and Its Return to Roots:*

> I am tempted by this new phenomenon, this kind of "Crunchy Con." It [refers to] people who are genuinely conservative in that they do feel like there are foundational principles—of right and wrong, good and bad—that truth [is] built on. But they are more open-minded and liberal because [for example] they listen to National Public Radio. I listen to NPR all the time. But I read journals and periodicals that . . . would be described as conservative-right. So I am not sure what I am. I generally vote Republican, because I think that for the most part, Republican candidates best reflect my values. But there is a race in local politics coming up in which I feel like the Democratic candidate best reflects what I feel to be Christian principles on certain issues. And I will probably vote for him instead of the Republican candidate, who I think is more of a [*trails off*]. I guess if I were to define myself, I am . . . personally opposed to the two political establishments and the way in which they don't . . . reflect what I think is good governing. They reflect what will advance their party interests. And I am opposed to that. I am really genuinely committed to—I love anybody who is willing to say—"Let's govern in a way that reflects standards and principles and tries to do something for the common good instead of just establishing a position of power for my particular party or political agenda." But I don't see a whole lot of that going on.

Mr. Walters's views reflect a fairly unusual American citizen: He gets news from sources across the political spectrum, and he is not committed to one political party or ideology. In short, Mr. Walters values his political autonomy and seems to reflect continually on his political views. At the same time, like many other Americans experiencing these polarized times, he is frustrated with politicians who put their party first.

Mr. Kushner at Academy High and Mr. Walters at King High are ideological opposites, yet they share several important values. First, both approach ethical and political issues from the position that there are "foundational principles of right and wrong." For Mr. Kushner, reasoning well helps us grasp those truths; for Mr. Walters, the conduit is Christianity. Second, both are aware that they teach in LMS environments, and both find this educationally and socially problematic. Third, both aim to counteract the downsides of like-mindedness by encouraging students to reflect upon their community's values. Whereas Mr. Kushner wants students, at the very least, to see the reasonableness of those who disagree, Mr. Walters seeks to create political independence (autonomy) while maintaining religious devotion.

Bounded Autonomy

Down the hall from Mr. Walters's classroom is Mr. Whitman, a history instructor who also allowed us to observe his teaching. During the visit, the school day began with a prayer over the loudspeaker asking for a speedy recovery for a teacher who was out with the flu. Mr. Whitman is also a coach and spent several minutes taking care of various pieces of team-related business and chatting with students about issues he recently read about in *Sports Illustrated*. He eventually brought the class to order with a prayer for the local college football team and its victory over their next opponents. Students then spent the rest of the class period completing a chapter quiz, which asked them basic recall questions about the Great Depression.

Mr. Walters's government class is an entirely different learning experience. The office that is attached to his classroom is home to Mr. Walters's personal library, an impressive collection of books on history and political science, including some rare first editions. Students' desks are arranged in traditional rows, but one corner of the classroom has been made into a sitting area, with cozy chairs and a coffee table. The room is decorated with historical posters, a map of their city, and the American flag. The atmosphere in the class is welcoming, engaging, and focused.

On one observation day, Mr. Walters was using materials from the Choices for the 21st Century Education Program to prepare his 16 students for their upcoming trip to the Capitol Forum, a statewide deliberation among high school students that focuses on issues of foreign policy. Mr. Walters participates in this program because he wants students to interact and deliberate with students who hold very different political views. This experience, Mr. Walters believes, is valuable because it prepares students for democratic life and for the kinds of opinions they will encounter in college. As part of the preparation, participating classes create a poster that represents their views about a particular issue that will be discussed at the forum. One of the focal issues for this year's Capitol Forum is immigration policy, and classes are asked to include on their poster an answer to the question, "What is an American?" Mr. Walters begins by posing three questions for the day: (1) How did American attitudes toward immigration change in the 20th century?

(2) Is the process for deciding who is an American different than the process for deciding who is an Englishman? (3) How do you define an American?

Mr. Walters begins with the last question and asks one of the three Korean students how she defines "Korean." She says, "It's cultural," and Mr. Walters continues calling on students using a provocative line of questioning that leads them to puzzle about how the United States should define nationality given its multicultural population. He then moves to a short lecture about the different ways in which the United States has defined citizenship over time and how these shifts have affected immigration policy. Next, he distributes a handout that explains different ways in which ideological groups in the United States have viewed immigration. After students have looked over the sheet, Mr. Walters again engages the class with a series of questions designed to check their understanding ("What does 'assimilation' mean to you?") and to evaluate competing views ("What do you think labor leaders would think about immigration quotas?").

We label Mr. Walters's pedagogy "Interactive Lecture." That is, the teacher primarily holds center stage and blends lectures with provocative questions and short discussions designed to keep students engaged and thinking about the material. There were five teachers in the study who primarily use Interactive Lectures, and all of their interviewed students had a difficult time distinguishing between lectures and class discussion. When students in Mr. Walters's class are asked how often the teacher lectures, they respond with statements like,

> Instead of the lecturing, maybe you could say that lecturing was a large-group discussion. So . . . maybe the lecturing would be more like 30 percent and the large group would be more like 60 [percent].

Students see this technique as different from standard lectures, which are "just the teacher talking and giving you all this information and you have to take notes. There is not conversation between you and the teacher." In Mr. Walters's class, in contrast,

> It is more like just talking and we give our opinions and he will ask us questions and see what is going on in our minds so he can better teach us, because he will know what we are having problems with. And it would be about material and what we believe, not necessarily what he believes, but he will represent all the different options so we can make an informed decision.

Overall, students were supportive of this teaching method. Students describe an engaging and intellectually challenging classroom, but there is not as much student-to-student talk as we found in Best Practice classes. Instead, most of the student talk is directed at the teacher, who holds center stage while he moves back and forth between lecturing and playing the role of Socratic questioner.

Mr. Walters's teaching style is in line with the idea of bounded autonomy, because when the interactions move through the teacher, he is able to place limits on the discussion so that it does not become a "go-wherever-you-want" conversation. As an example, at one point in the lesson described above, Mr. Walters asked the class to consider what business leaders would think about immigration policies, and one student answered, "Well, you have a business leader sitting in a penthouse office saying, 'You work for me!'" Mr. Walters replied to this seemingly anti-capitalist comment with "Now, now," then turned to the observer in the room with a smile and said, "That's one of my lefties." He went on to direct the class back to the handout. This subtle redirect was done with kindness, but it also communicated to the student, "We're not going there."

Aims of the Course

In Mr. Walters's class, we interviewed nine students over the course of two semesters, and it was clear that Mr. Walters is greatly admired. Many describe the class as either their "favorite" or "definitely one of the top two." There is general agreement that Mr. Walters is "very knowledgeable" and "knows almost everything" about history and social studies. Further, his impressive intellect is balanced with the ability to make ideas and the content of the class accessible. "He gets down to our level," said one student, "and talks to us like we are normal people just going to school and trying to learn it for the first time." Mr. Walters is also clearly respected as a man of principle who has been an important mentor for his students. A student explains how he thinks the class will influence him in the future:

> I think not only learning about the issue, but the history of the issue—the Christian perspective—can radically help in the future. I think that is being done throughout [the] history [course]. And I think that is basically his mission. I don't have the statistics, and I don't have a clear example of former students, but I know when we went in there at the beginning of the year, most of us didn't know the basics of government. . . . And I know at the end of the year most of us know not only the basics but little things. And not only that, but why they are important . . . so I think just from my own perspective, which is obviously part biased, I have been very impressed with my class, because you just get this understanding. I have seen a very big change in all of the students.

This student notes two important features of Mr. Walters's class. First, the curriculum emphasizes understanding the foundations of the United States government, and discussions of current controversial issues happen later in the semester—though they are also inserted throughout to illustrate particular concepts or tensions. Second, teaching students to consider issues *as Christians* is part of Mr. Walters's educational aim. Mr. Walters coined the term "behindness" to describe this approach to political thinking:

> The most basic Christian conviction that drives everything about my worldview and what I feel to be a Christian worldview is that there is a God and that He created everything including us, and that we are not our own, and that we are responsible to live our lives in a way that acknowledges, honors, and glorifies Him. So that is the "behindness" of every other issue I will ever engage, every other situation that I will ever find myself in. . . . I confess, I think that the role of a teacher is to help students understand that single big important truth. That no matter what they may choose to adopt or pursue for a particular political persuasion or even religious denomination identity, that there is something greater behind all of that. And that is where their true self is. And that in the end, they are never going to be able to live confidently in the conviction of whatever values they are going to choose to embrace without finding some firm foundation to stand on that is outside of them.

As is the expectation at a parochial school, Mr. Walters openly shares his faith with his students and uses Christian values as a moral framework through which students should evaluate public policy. All of the interviewed students also agreed that Mr. Walters sometimes shares his political views, but "he doesn't volunteer them." Students feel that he fairly presents multiple views on political issues and encourages students to think for themselves, within the boundaries of a "Christian worldview." A student explains:

> We are a Christian school, [but] I think he has done an excellent job of presenting an unbiased view. He obviously believes in strong convictions, and he will publicly open up to you if you ask him. I think he has done a very wonderful job of just keeping those to himself for a time to make sure we have an understanding. . . . I have been very impressed with that.

Students are supportive of Mr. Walters's occasional political and religious disclosure and see it as a normal part of the private school experience. However, one might conclude that in light of his view of "behindness," Mr. Walters is not teaching toward autonomy at all. Instead, he is teaching students to see themselves as spiritually interconnected with God, and that cannot be autonomous, because young people are learning that their lives are not theirs to "self-govern" but that they are to act according to laws and principles given to them by God. In our view, what Mr. Walters describes is not inconsistent with a democratic conception of autonomy. Most people, we hope, have a set of ethical principles that help direct their lives; they seek advice from others or engage in moments of quiet reflection when making decisions. It is also consistent to see oneself as self-governing and to believe that we have ethical obligations—to others, to a moral law, or to a divine being—that place some limits on our choices. Further, in Mr. Walters's view, acting "in a way that acknowledges, honors, and glorifies" God is not straightforward and requires one to question and deliberate on present-day interpretations of correct behavior. So while he approaches his social studies courses with an eye toward a "Christian worldview," he also wants students to examine whether their political views are truly in line with their values. He explains:

> So I think what I have to do with students is first of all get them to see that truth [of behindness]—that reality—and then get them to see, "Here is how many evangelical conservative Christians would think about this issue—but not all. There also is an emerging kind of evangelical socially conscious, social-justice-minded left that is beginning to have more of a voice in politics [and] is beginning to challenge the constant association of evangelical Christianity with the political right." So I want them to see not just, "There they are, but here is why they think the way that they think. Now let's take this back to our understanding of what it really means to think and live and act Christianly, and do they have a point?" I guess I would say that my hope [in] teaching . . . social issues, political issues, even cultural issues [is for students to examine] the ways in which a Christian worldview throughout history has been challenged and . . . to recognize that [the] challenge wouldn't have been there if there wasn't some justification for it. Let's figure out what that was. And let's figure out if that was an example of an expression of Christianity connected to a particular culture or political time and space.

As this statement of goals indicates, Mr. Walters wants students to grow in their Christian faith, but he also aims to help young people develop skills to evaluate the political messages and social norms they have inherited and to evaluate whether these norms are "an expression of Christianity." Further, Mr. Walters is conscious that his students are growing up in politically polarized times and perhaps are the sons and daughters of parents who hold much more extreme political views. Like nearly every teacher that we surveyed, Mr. Walters thinks it is appropriate to have students question the political views they may have unreflectively adopted:

> We have a lot of very right-wing, Rush Limbaugh fans . . . here, which is really kind of funny. And without offending them, I try to point out to some of these kids how funny it is that they are so committed to extreme right-wing political attitudes when they really don't know what they are talking about.

Mr. Walters is concerned that he does not "have the right to step on these [more conservative] parents' toes" and undermine their religious values, but he also wants to challenge their political views just enough so that students will question the messages they hear in the public sphere.

Mr. Walters explains that walking this line is not easy. For example, he explains that the association of Christian schools to which King belongs is "the epitome of . . . why Christian schools exist." The organization promotes these views:

> "Public schools are full of secular humanists. You don't want your kids going there and being brain-washed. It is your duty as a parent to have your child in a Christian school because that is where they are going to be taught the values that you teach them at home." And that is certainly our roots. And it certainly is what we would articulate as who we are.

Yet, Mr. Walters also believes that King students should eventually be exposed to views that "push the boundaries" a bit. In addition to promoting some critical reflection about how Christians may disagree about particular policies, Mr. Walters also wants students to be exposed to the political views that exist beyond their community. This is, in part, why he has students participate in the Capitol Forum. As explained earlier, the forum is a convening of students from around the state, who come together to discuss foreign policy issues. Mr. Walters sees value in having his students interact with others who hold very different views. He also has an assignment in which he requires students to select a book from a list of political fiction that "pushes" them to think outside of their "worldviews." These are also books that he knows the English teacher would not include in the curriculum:

> They are reading *Brave New World,* and they are reading *1984,* which—that shouldn't be an issue—but, there are some things on that list that a senior getting ready to go off to college should know. [They should know] what this is and what is in it. I may be overstepping my bounds a little bit by making that assumption. But so far I haven't had to suffer the consequences really of pushing somebody too far.

He reports that the students do find some of the content shocking and say things to him such as "Do you know some of the stuff that is in here?!" Mr. Walters believes that knowing these stories is an important part of being educated, and while he would not let them read anything they chose, and he believes an assignment like this is most appropriate for seniors, he nevertheless wants students to learn to consider ideas that are quite foreign to them.

What Students Learn

It is striking how closely the students are able to articulate the same principles that Mr. Walters identifies as his teaching goals. When interviewed, they make observations such as "A Christian perspective on voting isn't particularly looking at a certain party. I think if a Christian aligns himself too closely with either party, he is doing something wrong." Another student explains, "You can't just vote for somebody because they are Republican, you have to see behind. You have to see their character." Further, while all of the interviewed students felt that for the most part the students were in agreement about current issues, Mr. Walters was still able to cause some political reflection. "I think I have thought more about stuff, [including] the Second Amendment," said one student. "I used to be like, 'Oh, everyone should have guns.' And now that I have re-looked at that, I am not so sure, but I kind of still would like that to happen. I don't know." This student is leaving Mr. Walters's class with less certainty about her views on gun control. From the perspective of autonomy development, this is an important educational outcome. Just like the young woman in Mr. Kushner's course who became unsure about her position on affirmative action, there is an educational and democratic value in considering the question "Could I be wrong?"—even if in the end students reaffirm their initial views.

Mr. Walters's students feel that the class was valuable for their development as citizens; most spoke about the importance of being an informed voter and noted that after taking the course, they feel more confident making political decisions and discussing political issues. There also is evidence that while hearing liberal views was often shocking to them, they still found value in thinking about alternative points of view. This was seen in interviews with two of the students who attended the Capitol Forum. One girl reported that she "like[s] to hear different people" but also was surprised when someone thought her "isolationist" views were "selfish." She thought to herself, "Whoa, I don't think I'm selfish," but still she "liked to hear what they said." Another student, who was passionate about international relations, was excited to encounter others equally interested and willing to discuss. He reflected in his interview:

> And when you get people who are extremely well informed . . . that disagree fundamentally, there is going to be a little bit of head butting. But what I did see [at the Forum] is a lot of mutual understanding, which is something that you don't see very often. Typically it leads to anger. I think it led to understanding. And I was very impressed with not only the professionalism but the kindness.

In the longitudinal follow-ups, students again expressed appreciation for the effect that the class had on their attitudes about citizenship and the importance of voting and staying informed. Students remember an open classroom climate where "we were able to state our opinions, [and] nothing was forced upon us." Although students in Mr. Walters' class agree in principle that it is better to be politically independent, in practice participants in the follow-up interviews continue to support the Republican Party. In 2007, nine out of 10 of Mr. Walters's students identified as Republicans and one as an independent. Six of the seven students who participated in the second longitudinal survey voted in the 2008 presidential election: Four voted for McCain, one voted for the Constitution Party, and the sixth declined to state.

Learning in Like-Minded Schools

There are striking similarities between the cultures and students at Academy High, the students at King High, and the students at our other evangelical school, Church High. Politically, our three LMS are lacking in diversity, and this greatly affects the ethos of the schools. This is not to say, however, that students are not encountering any difference at all. Academy High is racially, ethnically, and socially diverse, while also being politically like-minded. Because it is a smaller, private religious school in a place with less racial diversity, King High is more homogeneous overall, but there are still disagreements about religious interpretation and school policies, as well as some ethnic diversity. This was also true at Church. Here we discuss our analysis of the three LMS and how these students compared to the rest of the sample of Diverse Schools. We find that there are significant democratic benefits to attending a LMS; most importantly, growing up in this context greatly increases the likelihood that young adults will be politically engaged. Yet, there are also reasons to be concerned that these students are not getting sufficient exposure to political difference, making them susceptible to becoming politically intolerant.

Political Engagement

In *The Disappearing Center: Engaged Citizens, Polarization, and American Democracy*, Alan Abramowitz (2010) studied the relationship between political polarization and the "engaged public." Using data from the American National Election Studies, the "engaged public" is a measure of "citizens who care about government and politics, pay attention to what political leaders are saying and doing, and participate actively in the political process" (p. 4). Abramowitz finds that the percentage of the United States public who count as "engaged" has increased steadily over the last few, polarizing, decades (pp. 19–20). Additionally, he finds that the two strongest predictors of those who are "highly engaged," when using a scale of six measures of engagement, are (1) identifying as a "strong partisan" (identifying with one of the two major parties); and (2) possessing a "strong" ideological orientation (liberal to conservative) (p. 24).[6] Lastly, Abramowitz shows that as the two parties polarize so that the Democrats embrace a set of issues more solidly liberal and the Republicans advocate for a solidly conservative agenda, the engaged public has responded by becoming more ideological and more partisan—what Abramowitz calls "ideological-partisan polarization" (p. 37). This research shows that the more ideologically consistent one's views are "across a range of issues, the stronger their preferences will be with regard to political parties, candidates, and officeholders" and the more likely they are to be politically engaged (p. 7).

Our analysis of LMS aligns well with Abramowitz's findings. When we look at the students from LMS as a set (n = 158) and compare them to the rest of the study sample—students learning in Politically Diverse Schools (n = 841)—we find that at the *pre-survey stage,* these students already look like engaged young people. Holding SES, gender, and race/ethnicity constant, the like-minded students had significantly higher scores on our index for pre-exposure, meaning they were more likely to volunteer, discuss politics with family and friends, participate in class discussion, express feelings of political efficacy, and have high scores on political and democratic knowledge. In short, these students are growing up being groomed for democratic participation—though much of it involves engaging in discussions with people who are ideologically alike. We should note that the like-minded students also are significantly higher in SES than the rest of the group, and SES also predicts many of these same behaviors. Yet these findings held for the like-minded students when controlling for SES (see the Appendix). In the post-survey, we held prior civic exposure constant to see if like-mindedness would have an effect above the prior-exposure variable; in this analysis, these students had significantly higher measures of ideological coherence and reported more political talk with friends. As reported in Chapter 3, the Prior Civic Exposure Index is a powerful predictor of outcomes like intention to vote, political talk, and knowledge, and because the like-minded students began the class with high levels of pre-exposure, they are likely to have similar outcomes.

The benefit of growing up in like-mindedness is more apparent in the follow-up surveys, where they report more political engagement than their peers. Again, holding SES, gender, race/ethnicity, and pre-exposure index constant, the like-minded group was significantly more likely to keep up with the news, report that their family and friends believe it is important to follow current events, and engage in non-electoral political activities, such as contacting a government official or participating in a demonstration. Further, they seem to retain their ideological-partisan polarization. The follow-up surveys asked respondents if they identified with a particular political party and, using a five-point scale, indicate how strongly they identified with that party. Not surprisingly, like-minded students were more likely to report identifying as a member of one of the two major parties (and not as Independents) and had significantly stronger party affiliation compared to others. They continue to be significantly more ideologically coherent and more likely to report that they hold political views similar to their family and friends.

Students from LMS also are voters. The follow-up surveys showed that during the 2006 mid-term election, 71% of the like-minded students voted, compared to 30% for the rest of the sample. This is even more remarkable when compared to the 2006 national turnout rate of 40% and a youth (voters under the age of 30) turnout rate of 24% (Kirby & Marcelo, 2006; McDonald, 2006). In the 2008 presidential election, 88% of young people in our study who grew up in a like-minded community voted, compared to 66% of the non-like-minded group. Further, the like-minded voters continued to have a markedly different voting pattern. In the non-like-minded sample, 28% voted for John McCain and 69% voted for Barack Obama. Of the 16 students surveyed from the conservative Like-Minded Schools who voted, 12 cast their ballots for McCain (75%) and two went for Obama; of the 55 students at Academy who voted, all but one voted for Barack Obama (98%).[7]

Being raised in a like-minded political community is clearly an asset if the goal is to foster awareness of current events and participation in the electoral process. Yet there are also reasons to be concerned.

Tolerance/Intolerance

In *Hearing the Other Side,* Diana Mutz (2006) found that people who discuss politics mostly with like-minded others are less likely to acquire the benefits of deliberation. Specifically, when respondents were asked to give reasons for their own view on a political issue *and* reasons that someone would give who disagreed with that view, Mutz found that people who usually talk in like-minded groups are more aware of their own rationales (they are able to give more reasons for their point of view), but this type of talk had no effect on their ability to explain the arguments advanced by those with opposing views. She concludes:

> Highly partisan environments pose a paradox: on the one hand, the existence of large numbers of people who hold readily identifiable political preferences would tend to suggest a vibrant, active political culture. On the other hand, it appears that many citizens in such an environment will isolate themselves among those of largely like-minded views, thus making it difficult for cross-cutting political discourse to transpire.
>
> (p. 53)

This paradox poses a problem for promoters of deliberative democracy because people who talk in like-minded groups rarely discuss the ideas held by their opponents, and they likely do not consider the question "Could we be wrong?" Instead, they reaffirm each other's views and move opinions within the group toward polarized extremes (Mutz, 2006; Sunstein, 2009).

Table 7.2 shows that students in LMS are aware of the political climate of their schools. The table juxtaposes excerpted comments from two student interviews—one from Mr. Kushner's left-leaning class and one from Mr. Walters's right-leaning class.

These quotes reflect remarkable symmetry in the students' views of their school climate. Both are well aware that the student body is politically homogeneous, that a person with views that differ from the majority would likely feel silenced, and that their classroom discussions lack natural diversity on many issues. Both are also completely comfortable with their school culture, though other students speculate that "it would be better" for their learning if there were more political diversity.

TABLE 7.2 Learning in Like-Minded Schools

Observations	Mr. Kushner's Student	Mr. Walters's Student
Like-minded climate	"I guess if some students never really thought about [politics] or talked about it and then came to Academy, I think it would just be . . . implied that you think [about] most things a certain way."	"You know, coming from a small Christian school, you usually have conservative views."
Those with minority views would feel uncomfortable	"I think if I was like a Republican or a conservative at all, there are some things that just [would] piss you off a lot." The student added . . . "And I guess [conservative students] probably just get used to it [the liberal culture]. I think it is pretty common at Academy. And I think there is also such a left-wing student body that it's fine."	"Let's just say if there was a really hardcore liberal that came here or something like that . . . as a student, it is kind of like going into like a totally different society where people believe the opposite of what you believe. . . . I am not saying that there are a ton of them here, but there could be some that don't want to express their opinion because they know that there are a lot of conservatives here."
Classroom discussion affected by lack of divergent views	"Even there, it is not like the class itself is politically diverse. It is just like everyone is on one side and [Mr. Kushner] will just, I think, pretend to be other things [by playing devil's advocate]."	"I believe on big topics in general that we usually, mostly, have the same belief—like [on] terrorism [and] immigration. That is a big topic right now. But there are also some other topics—like the environment—where people have different views. Like the [debate] in Alaska [over] whether they should drill up for oil or just leave it be and then find another way to fuel our cars and stuff like that."

One of the essential components for becoming autonomous is developing the capacity to reflect on and consider different ways of living well. Philosophers suggest that in order to develop this capacity for reflection, children ought to encounter people who live differently. For example, in *On Education*, Harry Brighouse (2006) argues that the ethos of a school is an important component of an "autonomy-facilitating" education:

> I suspect the composition of the school and the ethos are more important than the formal curriculum. We probably learn more about how different ways of life are articulated, and about whether they would be well suited for us, through encounters with other people who live differently from us. An autonomy-facilitating school will be composed of both children and

adults who come from a diversity of backgrounds, and who have differing outlooks on the world and how to live their lives.

(p. 21)

We have shown that both Mr. Kushner and Mr. Walters are concerned about the problems associated with their politically polarized student bodies and actively try to counter the dominant political views in their schools by putting students in contact with others who hold different points of view (e.g., guest speakers, attending the Capitol Forum); assigning readings that express views that do not naturally come up in discussion; using structured activities, such as moot courts, that require students to role-play alternative points of view; and questioning students about their reasoning through the use of devil's advocacy. Our data cannot say definitively that Mr. Kushner and Mr. Walters were, in fact, able to counteract their students' tendency toward intolerance, but the qualitative data presented in these two cases suggest that they were both effective at teaching their students that considering the question "Could I be wrong?" has educational and civic value.[8]

Conclusion

We began this chapter with a discussion of the educational aim of autonomy, or self-government, and argued that Mr. Walters is teaching toward a bounded version of autonomy, or autonomy within limits. We end by making a distinction between *aiming* toward autonomy and actually *being* autonomous. Certainly one cannot look at the longitudinal outcomes of students from these schools and conclude that all these young people independently and autonomously ended up being highly partisan and in the same political camp as their classmates. To engage in a quick thought experiment: It seems quite likely to us that, if we went back in time and took Student A from King High and Student B from Academy High and switched their families before each started kindergarten, by the time we interviewed them in 2009, each would hold the political view opposite to their current belief. Without a doubt, these young people are being raised to adopt a particular political ideology, and for the most part, their upbringing is quite effective.

Consider, for example, how this student responded when she was asked why she thought all her classmates in Mr. Walters's class would have voted for President Bush:

I would say definitely it comes from your influence of being a Christian, growing up in church, your moral values, what you feel is right. It is just . . . a matter of what you believe as a person. You grew up in a certain area, and you accumulate different beliefs and different moral values . . . and those are going to help you decide what you vote for or even if you vote at all. So I would think that the Government class . . . gives us a [tool to] think about government and how we can vote and stuff and then [it influences] our moral values with it and what we can do.

This student sees her views coming from a combination of "being a Christian," "[growing] up in a certain area," and "what you believe as a person." To be sure, all people come to their political beliefs by a similar calculus of family beliefs, education, political context (including the location and era in which one comes of age), life experiences, and one's own reflection. And there is no denying that being political is inherently relational: Things get done when we act together. At the same time, democracies regard people as individuals who, to some extent, ought to think for themselves. There is no litmus test to measure "enough autonomy" and "insufficient autonomy," but there are better and worse contexts for becoming a person who can weigh evidence, consider competing values, and tolerate fellow citizens who think differently.

What is important for our discussion is not that Mr. Walters and Mr. Kushner are actually able to produce autonomous thinkers (or that any single teacher is able to do this), but that Mr. Walters and Mr. Kushner see the potential downside to their students' upbringing and try to counteract the negatives by modeling critical reflection about one's political views. *Aiming* toward autonomy is a reflection of what a teacher values and how those values shape curricular choices. Further, aiming toward autonomy does not mean that students should become unmoored from their belief systems; instead it is the intention that students should develop into citizens who have the tools and dispositions to re-evaluate their beliefs in light of new information and experiences.

Notes

1 Note that in Hess (2009) there is a short discussion of Mr. Walters's class that incorrectly reported that this county voted 62% for Kerry, making it a "very 'blue' county" (p. 88). In fact, it was a much closer election.
2 This is reflected in the school's "Statement of Faith," which reads, "We believe in the resurrection of all persons; those who are saved unto the resurrection of life, and those who are lost unto the resurrection of damnation (John 5:28–29)."
3 Philosophic debates about the tensions between autonomy and multiculturalism are on-going. Some examples of philosophers concerned about autonomy and religious upbringing are Callan, E. (1997). *Creating citizens: Political education and liberal democracy.* New York: Clarendon Press; Clayton, M. (2012). Debate: The case against the comprehensive enrolment of children. *Journal of Political Philosophy, 20*(3), 353–364; Dwyer, J. G. (1998). *Religious schools v. children's rights.* Ithaca, NY: Cornell University Press; Feinberg, J. (1980). The child's right to an open future. In W. Aiken & J. LaFollette (Eds.), *Whose child? Children's rights, parental authority, and state power* (pp. 124–153). Totowa, NJ: Littlefield, Adams, & Co.; Maxwell, B., Waddington, D., McDonough, K., Cormier, A., & Schwimmer, M. (2012). Interculturalism, multiculturalism, and the state funding and regulation of conservative religious schools. *Educational Theory, 62*(4), 427–447; Okin, S. (2002). Mistresses of their own destiny. In K. McDonough and W. Feinberg (Eds.), *Citizenship and education in liberal-democratic societies* (pp. 325–351). New York: Oxford University Press.
4 We draw a distinction between Reich's view of "minimalist autonomy" and Mr. Walters's aim of "bounded autonomy." In Reich's (2002) discussion of religious views, he argues that "what matters for minimalist autonomy is that the decision to lead a life of

any sort—liberal or traditionalist, agonistic or devoted, cosmopolitan or parochial—be reached without compulsion from others and always be potentially subject to review, or critical scrutiny, should the person conclude that such a life is no longer worth living" (p. 102). Mr. Walters does not see his role as teaching students to critically reflect upon their religious views, and as we show later in the chapter, he believes parents have entrusted him to help them raise their children as Christians. As a result, he wants to protect students from "going too far" with their thinking.

5 James Dobson is an evangelical Christian who founded Focus on the Family, a nonprofit organization that promotes and supports traditional family values. They produce a wide array of informational books and materials that range from self-help books for married couples to textbooks for Christian schools and homeschooling families to travel guides. Focus on the Family also advocates for social issues, such as promoting abstinence-only sex education and opposing abortion rights.

6 These two predictors are followed closely by age and education.

7 Again, one student from Mr. Walters's class voted for the Constitution Party and one declined to answer.

8 Much of this discussion of the findings of LMS can also be found in McAvoy, P., Hess, D., & Kawashima-Ginsberg, K. (in press). The pedagogical challenge of teaching politics in like-minded schools. In T. Misco (Ed.), *Cross-cultural case studies of teaching controversial issues: Pathways and challenges to democratic citizenship education*. Tilsburg: Legal Wolf Publishers. We note that in the quantitative findings reported in that chapter we did not hold prior civic exposure constant and so some findings look slightly different.

PART III

Professional Judgment

INTRODUCTION TO PART III

In the next two chapters, we build on the cases of teacher practice to focus on three dilemmas that are likely to arise within the political classroom. They are

1. How should teachers decide what to present as a controversial political issue?
2. How should teachers balance the tension between engaging students in authentic political controversies and creating a classroom climate that is fair and welcoming to all students?
3. Should teachers withhold or disclose their views about the issues they introduce as controversial?

In these discussions, we return to the idea introduced in Chapter 1 that these are questions that require teachers to use professional judgment; there is not, we argue, a single answer that ought to apply in all cases. Still, there are better and worse responses to these dilemmas, and our purpose is to model the type of reasoning that will lead to good professional judgments about these issues.

In Chapters 1 and 4, we introduced this ethical framework for professional judgment:

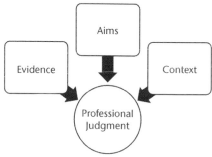

FIGURE 8.1 Framework for Professional Judgment

Professional judgment is the practice of weighing context, evidence, and aims when confronted with the question, "Why do this rather than that?" (Peters, 1966). In each of the three case study chapters in Part II, we identified the primary aims of each teacher or teaching team and discussed how the school context and relevant evidence informed their professional judgments. To review, the teachers at Adams prioritized the value of inclusive engagement within a politically and socially diverse school. Mr. Kushner responded to the like-minded, liberal student body of Academy High by emphasizing the values associated with political friendship (tolerance and fairness). At conservative King High, Mr. Walters wanted his students to think critically about their political views while holding onto their Christian values, an aim we labeled, "bounded autonomy." In Part I, we presented the major findings of the study and what students experience and learn from deliberations within the political classroom and also how the political, economic, and social realities affect what happens within classrooms. In what follows, we continue to draw on this evidence as we discuss what good judgment looks like for these particular dilemmas. Finally, recall that in Chapter 4, we identified the primary aims of the political classroom. Table 8.1 reviews and summarizes these (see Chapter 4 for a more detailed discussion).

As discussed in Chapter 4, the art of professional judgment requires teachers to keep these aims in mind, consider which aim/s ought to take priority in particular

TABLE 8.1 Aims of the Political Classroom

Aim	Summary
Political Equality	Students should recognize each other as political equals. They should deliberate with an understanding that members of society have equal claims to life, liberty, and happiness.
Tolerance	Political tolerance is the recognition that citizens should not use the coercive power of the state to unjustly outlaw or persecute individuals or groups for adhering to values that some find objectionable.
Autonomy	This aim represents both the *democratic idea* that adults ought to be allowed to direct their own lives and the *educational aim* of helping young people develop the skills, disposition, and knowledge to make well-reasoned decisions about how they want to live.
Fairness	Students should approach political deliberations with the intention of finding a solution that promotes the common good. Students should habitually weigh self-interest against the interests of others and seriously consider who is being asked to sacrifice within each policy option.
Engagement	Young people will become more interested in political issues and more willing to engage in activities associated with democratic life.
Political Literacy	Students will not just become knowledgeable about issues, but will understand how issues map onto competing ideologies about what a more just, more democratic system requires.

circumstances, be aware of how research and evidence bears on the situation, and consider options as they relate to the particular context. This may sound like an incredibly high standard, and we recognize that teachers make hundreds of decisions each day and there is often no time to stop and reflect. Nevertheless, there are times when teachers reevaluate their practice, think deliberately about curriculum design, give thoughtful consideration to their classroom policies, and sometimes disagree with each other about their professional judgments. It is in these moments that this framework will be helpful. Our hope is that by making explicit what this type of reasoning looks like, teachers may develop the habits of mind to reflect upon their practice, productively discuss these dilemmas (and others) with their colleagues, and make better decisions about how to bring politics into the classroom.

8

THE ETHICS OF FRAMING
AND SELECTING ISSUES

Enlightened political engagement is desirable in societies that are attempting to be liberal-democratic polities, but it doesn't appear without cause or context. It is constructed, and some portion of this construction work occurs in schools at the intersection of curriculum and a diverse student body, with instruction that orchestrates these two on a civic mission.

(Parker, 2011, p. 4)

Throughout the study, the question of whether same-sex marriage should be legalized became increasingly controversial. It was clear that even while public opinion was shifting rapidly, there was a robust debate in the political sphere, which, not surprisingly, entered the curriculum as well. As one student told us, "Gay marriage is a new issue that is coming up. It is going to be around for a while. It has just popped up now. But it is probably going to affect the way we are citizens for the rest of our lives. So if it is relevant to us, I think we should talk about it." We know that at least 11 of the 35 teachers in the study included same-sex marriage in the curriculum. Some of these lessons on same-sex marriage we observed ourselves; others we learned about through interviews with students and teachers. As we were analyzing the data, we often wrote up short case studies for use at professional development workshops with teachers, as a tool to open up discussions of professional judgment.

One of the same-sex marriage lessons we described took place in the spring of 2005 in Mr. Dunn's Modern United States History class at a charter school in a major Midwestern city. It focused on the question Should same-sex marriage be legalized? In the first half of the class, students read materials representing competing points of view and then deliberated in small groups of four about whether marriage should be defined as between one man and one woman. In the second half of the lesson, Mr. Dunn asked members of the class to stand along a continuum that ranged from "strongly agree" to "strongly disagree" and to explain the reasons for their views. In his interview following the activity, Mr. Dunn expressed his belief that students in the class represented the full spectrum of opinion on this issue, a belief confirmed not only by our interviews with students but also by our pre-survey, which showed that approximately half of the students were opposed to legalizing civil unions. But interestingly, when students took positions on the continuum in class, the range extended only from "undecided" to "strongly in favor." No students expressed opposition to same-sex marriage. Typically, Mr. Dunn facilitates discussions and does not "take a stand" himself. But in this instance he did, by standing on the "against same-sex marriage" side of the continuum even though that did not represent his personal position on the issue. "I wish that I did not have to place myself on the spectrum," he told us, "but I felt it was important to the conversation. . . . I didn't agree with anything that I said . . . but I hope the effect leads them to understand their own opinions better and to question why they are making the decision they are making."

Mr. Dunn's lesson took place in 2005, by which time Massachusetts was the only state that had legalized same-sex marriage (in 2004), and 13 states defined marriage as between one man and one woman. In 2009, when we finished collecting data, a total of three states had legalized same-sex marriage and 27 had passed "defense of marriage" policies. What we found from the professional development workshops we taught on controversial issues was that Mr. Dunn's case study provoked a lot of disagreement among teachers. One point of contention centered on Mr. Dunn's choice to frame the issue of same-sex marriage as controversial. Instead of treating same-sex marriage as an open question, some argued that it should be presented as a human rights question for which there is a correct answer: Same-sex marriage should be legalized. Others agreed that it should be treated as settled but in the opposite direction: Marriage, they reasoned, should be defined as between one man and one woman, a position that the federal government took in 1996, when it passed the Defense of Marriage Act.[1] Other teachers agreed with Mr. Dunn's choice to present same-sex marriage as an open issue, noting that it was still an authentic political and legal controversy, as evidenced by its prominence in federal and state legislatures and courts and, in some states, on ballots for a direct vote. Still other teachers felt that same-sex marriage was not an appropriate topic for the classroom, either because homosexuality does not belong in the curriculum, or because it was not right to put gay students in the position of having to listen to the potentially offensive views of their peers. Some responded to those who felt this issue did not belong in the curriculum by defending the classroom as a deliberative space. The teacher's role, other teachers argued, is to create a climate in which even the most difficult issues could be discussed and that removing genuine political controversies from the curriculum to protect some students is patronizing to them and would rob everyone of the opportunity to learn about many important issues facing contemporary society.

What is apparent from the teachers' reactions to the same-sex marriage lesson in Mr. Dunn's class is that engaging students in discussions of controversial political issues presents a number of challenging pedagogical questions that teachers must address, many of which are rife with ethical dilemmas. Moreover, the teachers we studied recognized that the content of the curriculum and the students in their classes interacted in powerful ways. While many aimed to orchestrate the two on a civic mission as Walter Parker recommends, the challenges they encountered along the way illuminated the importance of two pedagogical and ethical issues that we address in this chapter: How should teachers decide which topics to frame as open (by this we mean controversial) or settled (by which we mean non-controversial)? And, how should teachers balance the tension between engaging students in authentic political controversies and creating a classroom climate that is fair and welcoming to all students? These questions have important ethical underpinnings and consequences for what students learn, as well as for how people outside schools perceive what is happening in classrooms.

To address these questions, we begin by clarifying two central aspects of this conceptual terrain: We define what we mean by empirical and political issues, and we discuss the difference between presenting an issue to students as open or settled. We describe why decisions about whether to frame empirical and political issues as open or settled are so controversial. We then describe and evaluate various criteria that a teacher could use to determine whether an issue will be included in the curriculum as open or settled. Next, we turn to a second problem: Even when there is considerable agreement about whether a particular issue should be presented as a matter of genuine controversy (that is, an open issue), teachers and students still are confronted by the reality that discussions of some issues will be especially sensitive for some students in ways they are not for others. We will explain and evaluate different choices that teachers make when introducing sensitive issues and describe the reasons for their practice. Throughout our analysis of these ethical dilemmas, we hope to illustrate how the careful analysis and evaluation of teachers' aims, the context in which they are teaching, and empirical evidence from existing scholarship can help educators develop better professional judgments about the teaching of controversial issues in the political classroom.

Types of Issues

When teachers select issues for discussion in the political classroom, they will need to be clear about two sets of classifications. The first set of classifications addresses the difference between empirical and political questions. The second set of classifications addresses the presentation of an issue as settled or open (see Table 8.2).

TABLE 8.2 Types of Issues

Types of Issues	Definition
Open Empirical Question	Question that can be answered with evidence, but for which there is a scholarly debate happening, because the evidence is conflicting or insufficient.
Settled Empirical Question	Question that has been sufficiently answered with evidence.
Open Policy Question	Question about a policy for which there are multiple and competing views.
Settled Policy Question	Question for which the choice of appropriate policy is considered non-controversial.

Defining Empirical and Policy Issues

Empirical questions are those that can be answered through systematic inquiry requiring observation or experimentation. These are questions for which there conceivably could be a "right answer," even if one has not been arrived at yet. Such inquiry can come from a variety of disciplines, including (but not limited to) history, sociology, economics, or biology. Many empirical questions are matters of live controversy, while others are questions for which it is generally accepted that there is a particular answer. The other kind of issue is what we call a policy or political issue. To be explicit here, policy issues are grounded in larger political questions that address public policy. This is why, given the symbiotic nature of this policy/political relationship, throughout this chapter we alternate our usage, sometimes referring to them as policy issues and other times referring to them as political issues. These policy/political issues are questions about how we should live together. While empirical questions have an important place in decision-making about policy, virtually all policy questions require much more than empirical evidence to answer. For example, many policy questions raise important moral questions or need to be evaluated based on a rigorous cost–benefit analysis. Consider the political question of whether to ban genetically modified foods. This question requires more than empirical evidence to answer, although clearly such evidence would be important to consider. Similar to empirical questions, some policy questions are matters of live debate, while others have been settled.

Defining Settled and Open Issues

The difference between a settled and open issue is whether it is a matter of controversy or has been decided. Settled issues are questions for which there is broad-based agreement that a particular decision is well warranted. Open questions, on the other hand, are those that are matters of live controversy.

Looking at Table 8.3, we see examples of settled questions: two empirical and two political. The first empirical question, "Are women biologically less capable than

TABLE 8.3 Settled Empirical and Political Issues

Empirical Issues	Political Issues
Are women intellectually less capable than men of making a reasonable choice about an election?	Should women have the right to vote?
Are people more likely to get into a car accident if they are under the influence of alcohol?	Should driving while under the influence of alcohol be illegal?

men of making a reasonable choice about an election?" is a settled empirical question: We know that women and men are equally capable intellectually of making decisions about candidates and public policy. During the Women's Suffrage Movement, there were spurious scientific reports claiming that women were simply not as reasonable as men and thus should not have access to the ballot box. A *New York Times* editorial from 1914 outlines the views of those opposed to woman's suffrage:

> The objections . . . are many and weighty; the chief among them is the danger of increasing the electorate by a body of citizens who have shown no special aptitude for dealing with the kind of questions that are submitted to voters . . . that the consequences of such an enlargement might be disastrous is a fact too plain to be waved aside.
>
> (McClure, 1916, p. 107)

These views and the faulty evidence on which they were based have since been debunked and are now viewed as examples of using pseudo-science to maintain social power relations.

In the United States, the question "Should women have the right to vote?" is an example of a settled political question. There may be subgroups within the United States that do not believe women should vote, but at this time there is no movement to revisit the issue, and it is largely accepted as decided. Notice that there is a relationship between the empirical question and the political question. If it were true that women are less reasonable, that could persuade some people that women are less deserving of the vote; however, it does not necessarily follow that reasonableness is a prerequisite for voting. So, while empirical questions can inform political issues, evidence alone does not usually settle a political issue.

Teachers occasionally ask students to reexamine a settled political issue by having them investigate documents from the era and perhaps role-play the debate by representing different interest groups. The aims of these activities are usually to introduce students to historical thinking or to use the role play as a way of teaching historical content (Wineburg, 2001). This is certainly good pedagogy for the history classroom, but these discussions are different than discussions of controversial political issues, which aim to engage students in deliberations about how we should live together now and into the future.

TABLE 8.4 Open Empirical and Political Issues

Empirical Issues	Political Issues
What effect do voter ID laws have on voter turnout?	Should states require citizens to produce a valid photo ID before being allowed to vote?
Is it safe for humans to drink raw (unpasteurized) milk from cows?	Should it be legal to sell raw milk for human consumption?

Looking at Table 8.4, we can see examples of open empirical and political issues. The top row offers two questions related to electoral policy. Leading up to the 2012 presidential election, 34 states introduced laws to require photo identification (ID) for voting, and eight were passed into law, making this an open political question that is continuing to play out in many states (Brennan Center for Justice, 2012). Those opposed to ID requirements often argue that the laws will depress voter turnout—especially among young voters and African Americans. While there are studies that find some small decreases in turnout, others find no effect, and overall the evidence is not solid enough to consider this a settled question (Silver, 2012). As with the last example of women's suffrage, answering the empirical question does not completely provide an answer to the political question. In this case, if young people voted less as a result of the law, this does not necessarily mean that there are not other valid reasons for requiring identification but depressed turnout would be an important consideration.

Framing Empirical Issues

Even though it is relatively easy to define the broad differences between open and settled empirical issues, it is much more difficult—and often contentious—to apply those definitions to specific issues, in part because there is disagreement about what criterion should be used to determine if an empirical issue is still a matter of live controversy (that is open) or is actually much more settled (non-controversial). As an example, in May 2014, about 2,000 eighth-grade students in a school district in Rialto, California, were assigned to write an argumentative essay about whether the Holocaust actually occurred or was "merely a political scheme created to influence public emotion and gain wealth" (Rocha, 2014, para. 7). School Board President Joanne Gilbert explained that the assignment was designed to meet Common Core standards for developing students' critical thinking skills but apologized for what was clearly a "horribly inappropriate assignment" (Rocha, 2014, para. 6). One middle school student demanded an apology from the district because the assignment planted an idea in young people's minds that was both empirically incorrect and perpetuated an offensive stereotype about Jews being manipulative and greedy. Appropriately, the lesson created a furor in the community, in large part because it presented an empirical truth (the Holocaust happened) as a question that could conceivably be open to interpretation. If a teacher, or district curriculum writer, introduces a question as controversial, the implications are that there is more than one way to interpret the evidence and, relatedly, it presumes that the teacher is open to students holding and articulating multiple views. In this case, the assignment implies it is reasonable for students to conclude that the Holocaust did not happen and that Jews created the story to gain sympathy from the world community. In an editorial in the *Washington Post* regarding this assignment, Michael Gerson (2014) remarks, "the assertion of two-sidedness is a victory for one side. Holocaust denialists crave academic validation above all else, hoping to gain legitimacy for pseudo-history" (para. 7). This is a clear example of why settled empirical questions should be taught as settled.

In the United States, climate change is another particularly powerful example of how the question of whether to frame an empirical issue as open or settled can generate controversy. There is an overwhelming consensus in the scientific community (comprised of experts who publish their results in peer-reviewed journals) that the primary question of whether climate change is occurring is settled. More than this, the secondary questions of whether it is caused, at least in part, by human behavior, and whether this change is damaging to the earth's ecosystem and to the future of human life also are settled. In other words, scientists believe there is ample, reliable evidence to conclude that the climate is changing and that this shift is due in large measure to human activity, causing harm to human beings and to the planet. Others, however, challenge this evidence. For them, the question of climate change might also be settled—because they believe the evidence "proves" that the climate is not changing in any new or remarkable way, is not caused by human behavior, or is not harmful. Still others frame these central climate-change questions as open controversies, arguing that a well-warranted debate is currently (and legitimately) happening in the scientific community. A teacher's decision about whether to present the existence, cause, and effects of climate change as settled or controversial has important implications for whether policy issues about climate change come into the curriculum for deliberation. After all, why should society seek solutions to problems allegedly caused by climate change if such problems are not actually occurring?

Climate change is a strange case because though it is settled in the scientific community, many Americans are climate-change deniers and these beliefs often align with partisan affiliations. Republicans are much more likely than Democrats to deny that climate change is occurring or that any global warming is caused by human behavior. In a 2013 survey conducted by the Pew Research Center, 84% of respondents who identified as Democrats or Democrat-leaning said there is "solid evidence the earth is warming," compared to 25% of Tea Party Republicans and 61% of non-Tea Party Republicans (Pew Research Center, 2013b, p. 1). As a result, treating climate change as a settled empirical question has political consequences. Consider the following situation: A teacher would like her students to discuss whether their state should enact a policy to reduce carbon emissions as a way to combat the effects of climate change and improve air quality. Some students in her class may be climate-change deniers and believe there is considerable, reputable evidence that human activity—such as the emission of carbon caused by the burning of fossil fuels—has no effect on climate change, or they may not believe these questions are still a matter of debate among scientists. If the teacher takes the position that climate change is a settled empirical question, it is quite possible that she will be accused of being biased and staking out a partisan position on the issue. To avoid such an accusation, it may seem wise to "teach the controversy" by presenting the empirical issue as a live controversy. As Casey Meehan (2012) learned from his study of how high school science and social studies teachers frame climate change, teachers often think that this approach respects students' autonomy by allowing them to "make up their own minds" about the issue (p. 168). We believe that adopting this approach is a mistake. It is irresponsible for schools to present questions as empirically controversial when in fact they are not.

An important aim of the political classroom is the development of autonomy, which includes the ability to critically reflect and revise commitments in light of evidence. When teachers treat a settled empirical question as if it is open to interpretation, they undermine this aim by suggesting that students should seriously consider evidence known to be false. An assignment that points out the differences between history and pseudo-history or science and pseudo-science is valuable for learning to recognize and evaluate false arguments, but the purpose of such a lesson would be to show false evidence as false and good evidence as good. This is quite different from telling students to "decide for themselves" what to believe about known facts.

What makes this distinction particularly challenging for teachers in the political classroom is that one feature of our polarized public sphere is that it is politically advantageous to confuse the facts. As in the case of climate change, when the public is dumbfounded by an onslaught of information and misinformation, it is more difficult to gain traction on policies that might address a pressing social problem. One effect of this is that both teachers and students may come to doubt what is otherwise reliable information. One way out of this problem is to rely on actual experts in the scholarly community. When wondering if a question is appropriate for the classroom discussion, teachers should first ask themselves which questions related to the issue are *political* and which are *empirical*. When empirical, teachers should investigate whether there is a well-warranted "right" answer to the question. If yes, then the answer should be treated as settled and can be used to inform discussions of controversial political issues.

To sum up, empirical issues are those that can be answered through observational inquiry. It is important for teachers to identify and teach settled empirical questions as settled, so that the corresponding political questions are considered from a foundation of good information. We note, however, that many empirical questions that press upon political issues are not settled and that the aims of autonomy and political literacy are furthered when students learn to weigh evidence, competing values, and likely outcomes under conditions of uncertainty. In these cases, teaching students to identify what is empirically unsettled and what is empirically settled will make for more productive discussions.

Criteria for Framing Political Issues

We have identified the political classroom as one that engages students in questions that ask, "How should we live together?" Another way to think of this is that controversial political issues are the primary focus of the political classroom. But as the story of Mr. Dunn illustrated, there is often disagreement about which questions should be presented to students as controversial. Same-sex marriage, some argued, had only one reasonable answer (and there was disagreement about what that answer is); others thought that the reasonableness of views had no bearing and that what matters is that people disagree. This ethical debate about issues selection shows that the salient issue for teachers is not just what a controversial question is but also the centrally important follow-up question: Which issues should be *treated* as controversies? As we saw with the examples of climate change and the Holocaust assignment, treating settled empirical issues as open is miseducative, but there is often more grey surrounding what is settled or controversial about political issues. Moreover, framing an issue as controversial implicitly communicates that students are invited to make up their own minds about the issue.

We identify three possible criteria for determining controversiality drawn from both the philosophic literature as well as from our data about how teachers used these criteria in practice. They are *behavioral, epistemic,* and *politically authentic.* We will define each and identify its strengths and weakness for deciding what should be treated as controversial. As we will explain, we find politically authentic to be the most promising criterion for the political classroom, but it also has its weaknesses. As a result, deciding which criteria or criterion to use will require teachers to attend to context, evidence, and aims.

Behavioral Criterion

Charles Bailey (1971) defined a basic starting point for identifying a controversy: Something is controversial if "numbers of people are observed to disagree" (p. 69). He notes that controversies are "largely social phenomena" and that people might disagree about any number of matters, including those that are scientific, religious, historical, and moral (p. 69). Thus, the question to ask about an issue using the behavioral criterion is, Are people in society currently disagreeing about this topic? The strength of this criterion is that it takes seriously what is actually under dispute in society, which, on its face, seems to adhere to the general democratic notion that what "the people" think and believe is what society should care about.

Robert Dearden (1981) argues that the behavioral criterion is not a good standard for deciding which issues should be included in the curriculum because it is overly broad. The Holocaust assignment described earlier, for example, could be justified using this standard, since all that is required is that some people hold opposing views on a particular topic, regardless of whether these views are empirically warranted. Moreover, given that controversial political issues are taught in schools in part to develop and sharpen the reasoning skills of young people, Dearden argues that we need to be able to apply some truth standards—such as what counts as historical evidence—in order to decide if an issue is indeed controversial. Otherwise, students receive the message that all types of evidence and reasons are equally valid.

Even without these critiques, the behavioral criterion is hard to implement because of its inherent vagueness. How many people have to disagree to reach a level of controversy that matters? What *level* of disagreement? For example, there are a variety of issues in the United States that people believe are effectively settled: the legality of interracial marriage, voting rights of women, and the illegality of race-based discrimination by private employers. A small minority of citizens disagrees with these views, but treating these issues as genuinely open would serve to validate these fringe views, sending the message to students that these outlier views are far more prevalent and credible than they in fact are.

Epistemic Criterion

Dearden (1981) rejects the behavioral criterion as a tool for deciding curricular issues and instead offers the epistemic criterion. He defines this as "a matter is controversial if contrary views can be held on it without those views being contrary to reason" (p. 38). Clearly, the key here is how to identify which views are "contrary to reason." Dearden argued that reason is "not something . . . timeless and unhistorical," but a standard that encompasses the "public knowledge, criteria of truth, and critical standards and verification procedures which at any given time has been so far developed" (p. 38). In contrast to the behavioral criterion that seeks to privilege that which the public actually disagrees about (irrespective of the reasons that undergird or warrant the articulated reasons), the epistemic criterion draws attention to the existence and quality of reasons that could be used to support different perspectives on an issue. Thus, if a teacher determines that an issue does not have multiple views that fulfill academic standards of reasonableness, then this issue would not be appropriate for classroom deliberation.

Michael Hand (2007, 2008) is one of the strongest advocates of the epistemic criterion. Hand (2008) argues that if the aim of education is to "equip students with a capacity for, and an inclination to, rational thought and action," then teachers have a responsibility to expose students to issues for which competing views can be warranted (p. 218). Put another way, it is extremely challenging to teach young people how to form well-reasoned views about a policy if they are focused on a controversial issue in which one position has the only defensible arguments. Similar to the Holocaust assignment, framing political questions as controversial when rational thought points in one direction invites students to adopt the unreasonable view. In Hand's view, that would constitute a form of miseducation.[2]

The strength of the epistemic criterion is that teachers engage students in deliberating issues that are buttressed by reasonable arguments from different perspectives. Presumably, this trains students to develop and hold reasonable views. Using this standard, Hand (2007, 2013) argues that policy issues about gay rights should not be treated as controversial issues because, in his view, none of the reasons against granting equal rights are morally defensible. A few teachers in our study agreed with this view, believing that opposition to marriage rights was "akin to racism." However, others argued that there are reasonable views against same-sex marriage. For example, note that 11 of our 35 teachers in the study included same-sex marriage as a topic for class discussion. This, of course, does not mean that they made the right decision, only that for most in this group this was an issue that they thought students should decide for themselves.

The epistemic criterion is quite helpful for deciding whether an empirical issue is controversial because there are academic standards for empirical inquiry that for some issues are clearly settled. However, identifying reasonableness and unreasonableness about controversial political issues is problematic for democratic education. Hand wants teachers to use standards of moral and political philosophy to determine whether views are sufficiently reasonable, but this is a much higher standard than is used in the public sphere and would require teachers to exclude discussions of important political issues. A teacher in a state with a defense of marriage amendment on the ballot, for example, does not prepare students for political engagement by asserting that there is one right answer. While the behavioral criterion is critiqued for being too broad, the epistemic criterion is too narrow for the political classroom. Moreover, reasonableness is *an* aim of the political classroom but not the only aim. Teachers also want students to learn to treat each other as political equals by deliberating across their political, moral, cultural, and religious differences. Toward that end, students need to learn to respond to views that appear unreasonable (and to be open to the possibility that their own views do not hold up under scrutiny). Further, political literacy is advanced when students are exposed to the actual views in the public sphere. Certainly some views ought to be excluded at times—hateful speech, for example—but teachers should be cautious about deciding there is only one reasonable view on a political controversy.

Politically Authentic

Recall that the behavioral criterion had the broadest definition of controversy: Do people disagree? The politically authentic criterion distinguishes between what is bandied about in general society as a matter of controversy and that which has entered the authentic political sphere of democratic decision-making. Using this standard, political issues are controversial when they have traction in the public sphere, appearing on ballots, in courts, within political platforms, in legislative chambers, and as part of political movements. According to the political authenticity criterion, if these issues are included in the curriculum, they should be presented to students as controversial. This aligns with the aims of the political classroom, which seeks to develop in students an understanding of the political world in which they live, a willingness to deliberate issues with an eye toward fairness, a capacity to develop their own (reasonable) views, and an orientation to and preparation for active engagement in the political debates of their time. Using the political sphere as a guide to identifying controversial political issues is a helpful way of determining which issues should be presented as controversial in the political classroom.

However, as with the behavioral and the epistemic criteria, using political authenticity as a criterion is not perfect and, therefore, creates its own set of challenges. One is the question of how much traction an issue must have in the public sphere of political decision-making to be considered legitimately open for the classroom. If a lone state legislature deliberates a bill that other states are clearly not taking up, is that sufficient traction? Perhaps if that legislature is in the same state in which a teacher's school is located, that would be good enough. But teachers clearly need some standard to determine which questions are getting enough attention in the political sphere to merit designation as open issues; otherwise, the same problem that we previously described regarding the behavioral criterion would apply, raising the strong possibility that a vocal—and perhaps ill-informed—minority of policymakers could open up an issue that should remain settled. A second problem with this criterion is that even when issues have political traction, they are sometimes framed and deliberated in the political world in a manner that subjects them to the worst excesses of manipulation and political polarization. Often the reasons used to support positions are incoherent, poorly reasoned, buttressed by empirically shady evidence, or downright hysterical. Volume, repetition, and passion masquerade as relevance and reason. Consequently, teachers need to use judgment when deciding which issues to introduce to students as authentically political. Not only should they be clear about the relationship between empirical questions and political questions, they need to think about which political issues are live in the public, are likely to be controversial in their own classroom (recall that in Like-Minded Schools teachers had to work harder to identify issues that would activate disagreement), and further their aims. To demonstrate how to weigh all of these factors, we return to Mr. Kushner's classroom to ask, "Should the United States use torture in times of war?"

The Case of Torture

In Chapter 6, we described Mr. Kushner and his left-leaning, like-minded students at Academy High. When we interviewed him at the end of the school year in 2008, the United States had been at war with Iraq for five years. We asked Mr. Kushner whether he had taught about the Iraq war during the semester. "No," he shared, but then he mentioned that the topic of torture had been included in the curriculum the previous semester. In response to the question about whether he framed torture as a controversial issue, Mr. Kushner explained, "[The U.S.'s policy around torture] is still a live issue . . . a lot of people would say, '[Torture is justified] if you were going to save 1,000 lives,' you know, a utilitarian argument." Note that Mr. Kushner's reasoning here uses the authentically political criterion: He argues that it was included because there is a "live" public debate. He also drew upon the epistemic criterion; that is, he articulated the belief that there is an argument that could be used to justify torture that is not contrary to reason (utilitarianism). Mr. Kushner further asserted that including the issue had democratic value:

> [Discussing torture] is almost like inoculating the population before it becomes something we might have to discuss. You know, if we had another 9/11 and we started capturing people, and the fear was ratcheted up again, to have [students] really [think] that through beforehand, I think that would be a useful thing.

Because so few teachers in the study reported teaching about torture and because Mr. Kushner had taught it only one time, we were especially curious about why he had included it. He explained:

> Well, the fact that our government has been torturing people for six years is probably big. I mean, this has become a part of the Bush Administration's policy, and it's out there and being discussed. I mean, after 9/11 there were [pieces] in *Time* magazine [about the issue].

Mr. Kushner also pointed to the treatment of people labeled enemy combatants in the U.S. prison in Guantanamo, Cuba, as well as the scandal at Abu Ghraib, in which U.S. soldiers were exposed for sexually humiliating prisoners of war in Iraq, as evidence that torture had become a public controversy.

As Mr. Kushner described the content of his students' discussions about whether torture is ever justified, he began wondering aloud whether opening the issue for deliberation might have had the effect of convincing his students that torture was wrong. He described how his students reacted to some of the materials he used:

> When you really look at waterboarding and stress positions and sensory deprivation, all of those things, I mean when you get the accounts, there's a very powerful human revulsion, and I think the issue itself leads people, many people—now maybe it's just my blue-state class—to reject it, or at least start questioning it, or at least seeing it with a sort of reverence. . . . So I think looking at the issue humanizes it to some degree. And McCain has been useful on this. . . . He was asked in one of the debates, "How did we get here?" And he was like, "I don't know, but it's not where we want to be."

Interestingly, in talking through the issue with the interviewer, Mr. Kushner began to question whether he did, in fact, teach government-sanctioned torture as an open issue. He reflected:

> I present Dershowitz's argument [in defense of torture], which is to go through the courts [by issuing torture warrants].[3] I mean I still make those arguments available, but I think I use materials that create an emotional response. I mean, I had [one student] who had no idea about what [the United States was] doing and she said, "Of course they hate us! My God, look at what we are doing to these people!" I'm doing a little soul-searching as I'm thinking about it, and I'm wondering if I do teach it more as a settled issue. I mean, I might be a little bit more disingenuous with this one.

Mr. Kushner's reflections on how he approached the issue of government-sanctioned torture illustrate his profound discomfort. He invoked the political authenticity criterion arguing that because torture was being debated in the public it could legitimately be debated in schools. He did not see the issue as settled, but it was clearly morally abhorrent to him. In contemplating his use of materials in combination with his students' articulated political views, he realized that he might be framing the issue as a controversial issue but in reality was trying to steer his students to the conclusion that he himself had made: Government-sanctioned torture is categorically wrong. His use of materials may have represented multiple positions and perspectives on the issue, but on a more micro and even non-verbal level, there may have been something about the materials themselves or his (unconscious) orientation to the discussion that steered students to particular views.

How should we think about Mr. Kushner's choices? First, in 2008 torture was indeed an issue being discussed in the public sphere. More specifically, it was an issue that had "tipped" from being settled in U.S. policy (prior to 9/11 there was wide agreement that it should not be used) to being a live controversy. In *Controversy in the Classroom*, Diana Hess (2009) describes how issues that are "in the tip," that is, moving from open to settled or settled to open, create challenges for teachers because it is simply not clear whether they should be taught as open or as settled. In this example, Mr. Kushner's hesitation to treat torture as a policy question that is open for deliberation was motivated by his belief that torture is morally wrong and a violation of basic democratic values of respect for human life. Clearly, Mr. Kushner believed that the question of torture had tipped open but he wished it had not. Consequently, he was torn between two competing aims: the desire to develop a curriculum that was politically authentic and did not dodge especially hard issues and the competing desire of wanting to help develop students' understanding of and respect for core democratic values. This tension is one reason why a teacher might identify an issue as authentically political but decide not to include it in the curriculum or to do so in a way that violates the first principle of the deliberation of controversial issues, which is aim for a "best-case, fair-hearing of competing points of view" (Kelly, 1989, p. 368).

When reflecting on the materials he used and his students' reaction to them, Mr. Kushner worried that he had been "disingenuous," believing that he had actually steered toward a particular answer. Michael Hand (2013) defines steering as "guiding participants by means of strategic prompts, questions, and interjections, toward a predetermined conclusion" (p. 499). In our experiences, this is not an uncommon practice, and it is particularly tempting to do so with issues that have strong moral underpinnings, such as torture, same-sex marriage, or abortion. Hand (2013) argues that steering is appropriate if, after applying the epistemic criterion, teachers or policymakers determine that there is only one justifiable answer to the question. But note that Mr. Kushner did not believe this applied to the torture issue because he felt that there were reasonable arguments to justify torture (even though he personally was not persuaded by them). Of course, Mr. Kushner had another option as well—he could have included the topic of torture in the curriculum as a current event so his students could learn about the controversy but not ask them to engage in deliberation. This was not an attractive option to Mr. Kushner because he believed that what made the torture issue important was that it was actually being deliberated in the political sphere. Moreover, using the current events frame as a way to dodge controversy is antithetical to the overall aims of the political classroom, which is to invite students into the nation's challenging debates.

Was Mr. Kushner justified including the issue in the curriculum as open but actually steering his students to a particular conclusion? We think not. If the issue is being presented to a class as a political controversy, then the teacher is necessarily saying that this is an issue that students should figure out for themselves. To steer when the issue is framed as open is, as David Bridges (1997) argues, "manipulating the whole process to your own ends" (p. 114).

Steering the issue was a violation of Mr. Kushner's well-articulated commitment to create a classroom in which his students are developing their own views. But, while not steering respects the autonomy of the student, it may also undermine a traditional (and we believe, highly justifiable) democratic value of respect for human life. The potential for undermining is a risk worth taking if the issue is clearly important, actually authentic to the political sphere, and developmentally appropriate for students (a concern raised by Mr. Kushner).

We recognize that many readers will disagree with our critique of Mr. Kushner's decision. We know this because when we ask teachers to deliberate which issues should be taught as open or settled, this example of torture provokes a lot of disagreement. In our experience, teachers who have been in the military are almost always the strongest advocates for teaching torture as a settled issue (that it is wrong for a government to torture, regardless of the circumstances) and typically have a much more sophisticated understanding of existing international treaties and U.S. federal laws that ban torture. We have considerable respect for their opinion and do not suggest that our opinion on how Mr. Kushner should have taught the issue is one that cannot or should not be critiqued. In fact, we believe just the opposite. As we have argued, decisions about what issues to include in the curriculum and whether to include them as open or settled are themselves highly controversial *pedagogical* issues that should be deliberated.

Balancing Authenticity and Inclusivity

The decisions teachers make about which issues deserve classroom time and how they should be framed for their students are complicated and often quite controversial both within and outside the school community. But we learned from teachers that the ethical and pedagogical challenges of determining what is a matter of legitimate and genuine controversy for students to deliberate is often accompanied by another challenge, which is that some issues are much harder for students to discuss than others. This is true even with issues that meet very sound criteria for inclusion in the political classroom and even in classrooms with teachers who are skillful and concerned about the need to create a learning environment in which all students feel welcome, challenged, and safe.

Recall that in two of the previous chapters, students who were ethnic and racial minorities were stung by the comments of their peers. At Adams High, Gabe stood up against his Republican colleagues when they made offensive remarks against Mexicans during a discussion of immigration policy. At Academy, Anna was the only African American in a discussion of affirmative action, and this put her in a difficult position when the conversation turned to students of color who "don't try as hard." Clearly, even when a classroom conversation focuses on political issues, it is inextricably linked to the social circumstances of the students, making issues sensitive to some.

On the pre- and post-course surveys, we asked two questions to investigate who feels less comfortable talking in class discussions. The first question asked whether students were afraid that their teachers would criticize or judge them based on their comments in discussion; the second question asked whether they hesitated to speak in class because classmates would think their ideas were unworthy of consideration. Notably, the vast majority of students did not agree that these statements applied to them at either the pre- or post-course reflection points, and the number that *did* feel vulnerable to their teachers and classmates decreased at the end of the course. Specifically, 28% of students agreed with at least one of the statements in the pre-course survey (the correlation between the two items was .71), while just 17% did on the post-course survey. However, English Language Learners, immigrants, and low-SES students were significantly more likely than other students to hold these views.

We are concerned that it is distressingly easy to predict who will feel silenced in class discussion, and we wonder whether it can possibly be fair that students who are already vulnerable in U.S. society are being asked, once again, to make a sacrifice for others who occupy a more privileged status. While we are not romantics about the capacity of schools to transform society, we are convinced that schools, at the very least, need to interrupt the most damaging trends in U.S. society that are creating such clear and, in our view, damaging cleavages. So a challenging question stands before us: Should teachers include issues that are especially sensitive to some students? And if they choose to do so, what can be done to mitigate harm?

The teachers we encountered recognized the challenges of creating a safe climate for the discussion of controversial issues, especially if they had been teaching for a number of years and had been a part of discussions in which some students were especially vulnerable. We have identified two ways these teachers typically respond to this challenge: avoidance and deliberation. To evaluate these very different approaches to dealing with the challenges caused by sensitive issues in the political classroom, we consider how aims, evidence, and context interact to inform decision-making when it comes to this challenge. Again, our goal is not to suggest that there is a single, ready-made approach to negotiating the socio-emotional, intellectual, and curricular dilemmas inherent in teaching sensitive issues. Rather, it is to illustrate how different approaches present both opportunities and costs and to argue that the approach to the complex work of teaching open issues demands a case-by-case analysis.

Avoidance

Teachers who avoid issues that may be especially sensitive to some students typically do so for reasons of safety, fairness, or personal discomfort, as well as from a desire to create an environment that is as safe as possible for all students. They do not believe that students need to tackle highly sensitive issues in order to learn how to deliberate; they contend that the skills necessary for civil discourse are probably best developed by discussing issues that do not set up some students to defend themselves or their choices or cause so much controversy that they create more heat than light. Thus, their primary aim is not to replicate the contemporary political climate through the inclusion of hot-button issues of the day but to create a classroom environment that is as safe as possible so that students can build important skills and sensibilities related to civil discourse.

Erring on the side of caution, however, does not allow avoiders to capitalize as fully on the many deliberative assets that exist in most schools. Even with all their inherent challenges and structural defects, schools are still most likely the best place in the United States for young people to grapple with difficult and authentic issues. In the literally hundreds of interviews we conducted with students in discussion-rich classes (while the students were in high school, and two and four years after they left high school), we heard time and again that the classes we studied were the places where they had learned to discuss authentic political issues "civilly" and that these discussions were the most memorable and appreciated elements of the class. Many of the issues that were likely sensitive to some students were also extremely important in the political sphere. For example, during the years of the study, abortion, same-sex marriage, affirmative action, and immigration policy were being acted on by legislatures and courts and, as a result, dominated many political campaigns. If students did not talk about these issues in school, it was unlikely they would build the political literacy needed to weigh in on them when called upon to make decisions as participants in the political sphere.

Moreover, avoiders tend to underestimate the ability of their students to engage in meaningful discussions and overestimated the sensitivity of their students. As a case in point, consider what we learned from Gabe, a Mexican American student at Adams High School (see Chapter 5) who was rightfully offended by some of his classmates' bigoted comments about immigrants but proud of his ability to stand up for his views. Gabe also reminds us that banishing issues from the classroom would not do anything about the problem of what is said in the hallways and out of earshot from teachers. Learning to voice his opinion in the simulation helped him to respond productively to offensive views. In another example, Letty, a Puerto Rican student, spoke enthusiastically about Mr. Kushner's class at Academy High, even though she recalled a number of discussions in which she heard views that she found insulting. When asked to explain what she would say to a friend considering enrolling in Mr. Kushner's course on controversial issues, Letty said,

> You have to take it. It is a really important class. And it brings out the part of you that you kind of cover up and keep quiet and the part of you that says, "Don't say anything," that you kind of mute and silence until you get home. And you have to be able to get that out some time. Because what it usually turns into is either fear or anger. Whatever opinion you have, if you don't get it out, then that is what it is. It is usually negative. So you have to hear it. You have to discuss it. You have to force yourself to feel uncomfortable. And you take the best out of it that you can.
>
> *Interviewer:* So, simultaneously, you are saying that it is a good class to take, that it is important, but you also felt like there were times when you were not very comfortable.
>
> *Letty:* Yeah. I think that is society.

We interpret Letty's comment, "that is society," to mean that she believes it is valuable to confront the ideas that actually exist in the public sphere, even though such confrontations are sometimes uncomfortable or difficult. Notice that both Letty and Gabe were enormously positive about the classes they took and would recommend that their fellow students do the same. In other words, we think they were telling us that they are not fragile, vulnerable, or unaware but that they have important contributions to make, especially to the "majority students" who, from their standpoint, needed a lot of educating.

Not all students agreed with Gabe and Letty that the cost of avoiding sensitive issues would be too high. Other researchers have documented this as well. Terence Beck (2013) studied how discussions about same-sex marriage played out in the classrooms he visited. After describing how LGBTQ students were marginalized and often put on the defensive during these discussions, Beck concluded,

> At the end of this study, I still see the potential of controversial political issues discussions of same-sex marriage to engage a significant civil rights issue, but I am less sanguine about its potential to communicate to LGBTQ students that they count. Around the country, people engage in often-hostile debates about same-sex marriage and the associated arguments are likely to enter classroom discussions. As Hess (2009) argued, it seems that schools have a responsibility to introduce students to the discussion. Yet, striving for a safe classroom and structuring the discussion around an issue of policy is unlikely to be enough. This study suggests that teachers need to consider carefully their own students and contexts and work to create spaces that, while not perfectly safe, invite in a wide range of Discourses where dominant and destructive narratives can be challenged.
>
> (p. 27)

We share Beck's concern about how to balance the importance of engaging students in deliberations of politically authentic issues while simultaneously building a classroom environment in which all students "count." We also agree with Beck that striving for a safe climate and providing appropriate structure around some issues is unlikely to prevent the kinds of troubling discussions that caused the avoiders' wariness. So it is crucial to consider whether the possible advantages of including such issues are important enough to mitigate these concerns.

Deliberation

The deliberators in our study believed that the cost of avoidance was simply too high, in large part because they were convinced that the very issues that could be most sensitive for some students had a high payoff in terms of important educational aims: engagement, fairness, and political equality. Many of the deliberator teachers made the case that the most troubling aspects of discussions that were especially sensitive to some students could be reined in with exemplary materials, strong pedagogy, and enforced norms for civic discourse. These teachers knew that bad behavior could occur, but they viewed correcting students about the civility of their comments as part of their educational responsibility and part of the learning process itself. That is, instead of shutting down discussions that were not going well or avoiding hard issues in the first place, these teachers felt it was up to them to address the problems head-on by encouraging vulnerable students to stand up for themselves and by helping students who make insensitive comments learn how to express themselves in ways that do not exact such a high price from others.

Teachers who favored the inclusion of sensitive issues also argued that in many cases it was simply impossible to know which issues would be especially sensitive for which students and that exiling all issues that could conceivably be problematic would be overly censorious. While it is relatively easy to predict that some issues, rather than others, have more potential to be sensitive to some students, it is often unclear to the teacher who is vulnerable and why. This is not necessarily because teachers have inadequate knowledge about their students; it may be due to students not wanting (often for very good reasons) to disclose the factors that make them vulnerable. Recall the student at Adams High who disclosed during a debate about the death penalty that both her father and brother were serving terms in prison. We have reason to believe that the teachers and other students were completely unaware of this important fact in her family background—a fact that profoundly shaped her response to the claim that "the death penalty is needed because life in prison is not enough punishment." What is striking about this story is that this student chose to disclose this information in the heat of a full session of the legislative simulation.

The deliberator teachers often felt that sensitive issues had educational impact. Recall that Ms. Heller at Adams High School reported having discussions with teachers from other schools who were shocked by some of the issues students discussed in the legislative simulation. She argued that sensitive issues are important for the aims of democratic education, because if students learn how to talk about them in a way that is productive, it furthers the aim of teaching people to deliberate as political equals:

> bout people who have abortions as murderers, but then
> in the simulation and confides that she had an abor-
> hink, "Wow, I am not going to talk like that anymore
> to that." Or, you know, the immigration issue: "Wow,
> chool with this kid for a long time and I didn't realize
> es were], and now I kind of understand where they
> I I may still be against illegal immigration, but now
> d my dialogue is not going to be as racially charged,
> ectful."

> eration that Ms. Heller is addressing makes a clear
> er in which an opinion is expressed (as racially
> disrespectful) and the opinion itself (views about
> is that bringing sensitive issues into the classroom
> students to learn how and why their words can affect

others. Further, teaching students that "there is a face" behind issues reflects the aims of fairness and tolerance. The teachers at Adams want to habituate students to recognizing that people are differentially affected by policies and to communicate the point that the value of fairness expects citizens to weigh self-interest against the interests of differently positioned others. This type of political thinking also addresses tolerance, which expects citizens to be cautious about using the power of the state to persecute ways of living that are allowable but objectionable to some.

Teaching young people how to talk about highly controversial political issues in a way that is respectful and furthers the aims of the political classroom is itself a challenge. But the problem of sensitive issues is much greater and harder to solve if it is the *content* of the views expressed—and not the language or tone—that is offensive to other students. Remember, for example, that in the difficult discussion about affirmative action in Mr. Kushner's class, what was offensive to the lone African American student in the class was not the way in which a view was expressed but the content of the opinion. And there are many other scenarios in which the content shared during a discussion might be offensive or hurtful. Imagine a discussion about abortion in which a student argues that abortion should be illegal because she believes life begins at conception and the value of life should always outweigh other values. This is not an uncommon argument, and, regardless of whether one agrees with it, most would probably find it well within the bounds of civil discourse on this controversial issue. But now imagine there are students in the class who have terminated a pregnancy; they could hear this argument as an accusation that they have committed murder. Or imagine a discussion about same-sex marriage in which a student says she believes homosexuality is a sin. The gay students in class would likely hear this statement as an indictment of their very personhood. Or imagine a discussion of whether federal money should be used to fund school vouchers for religious schools in which a student argues that the government should not subsidize religious education because organized religion is a destructive force. Again, it is likely that students who hold strong religious views may interpret this argument as a personal insult.

Comments like those described above are exactly what many teachers fear hearing uttered in their classroom. While they recognize that such views may be part of mainstream political discourse, they do not want students who might be personally offended to have to endure the indignity of hearing such utterances. At the same time, they are not comfortable policing the content of arguments that students make, especially when the way in which a view is voiced is not meant as a personal insult to another student. Many teachers in our study reported both a willingness and a commitment to monitor (and sometimes punish) speech that was framed as a personal attack on another student. But it was less clear to them how to protect students who were vulnerable to the views of other students that did not, in their words, "cross the line."

Mitigating Negative Effects

We have described and evaluated two different ways in which teachers negotiate the challenges presented by sensitive issues. Teachers make different decisions for sound reasons, and competing aims undergird these decisions. "Avoiders" are less concerned with political authenticity than deliberator teachers are and are more concerned about making sure that their classrooms are spaces where all students feel safe. Our data suggest that a wholesale adoption of the avoidance strategy is highly problematic because the aims of engagement, fairness, and tolerance are furthered when students discuss the issues they are likely to encounter in the public sphere. Moreover, even though we encountered many examples of discussions that were extremely difficult for some students, in the literally hundreds of interviews we did while students were in class and in the follow-up calls after study participants had left high school, very few students thought it would be wise to strip the curriculum of these issues. Notably, what clearly emerged was students' view that the curriculum ought to include these issues.

That being said, we have considerable respect for the argument that schools are special places that should at times temper political authenticity rather than emulating it. After all, the vast majority of teachers in our study were unhappy with the quality of political discourse in the world outside school, so replicating that world within the classroom was certainly not in line with their aims. Moreover, it is hard to argue that every issue deserves classroom time, so teachers have to employ some criteria to decide which topics should be included and which should not. We think the context in which students are learning is an important criterion that should be considered and that in some circumstances keeping an issue out of the curriculum in order to make the environment less threatening is not only justified but perhaps essential. For example, Lawrence Blum (2012) argues that when teaching a high school course about race, he felt ethically obligated to work with the school administration to make sure the class was at least half students of color. This was not the same as avoiding an issue but reflects the concern that teachers ought to be aware that they are not creating an unfair set-up within the classroom. Blum had the luxury of this choice, but this option is typically out of teacher's hands and not available at highly segregated schools. Nevertheless, we have noticed that Best Practice teachers are aware of potential problems within the classroom dynamic and work to mitigate the costs to particular students.

First, teachers who know a lot about their students will have more data to draw upon when deciding which issues to include and in what ways. While we are not arguing that teachers ask intrusive questions about the private lives of students, it is possible to capture ideological information anonymously through class surveys, enabling an instructor to determine how much agreement and disagreement exists within a class. Not only would this help a teacher identify the issues for which there will be naturally occurring diversity in the class, along with those for which some perspectives will need to be deliberately inserted, but it could also reveal differences of opinion on sensitive issues, which may mean that students will have ideological allies in the class.

It is also important for teachers to establish and enforce strong norms for what constitutes civil discourse. Even though we have explained why civility norms will not on their own prevent students from encountering ideas they may find offensive, a classroom in which personal attacks are tolerated or in which the use of hateful and aggressive language is not dealt with appropriately will become a hostile, counter-productive, and even harmful environment for students. In many cases, it is wise and appropriate to engage students in co-constructing the civility norms, and in all cases it is important to teach these norms explicitly and to enforce them consistently and rigorously. Many teachers in the study believed that one key reason for violations of civility norms was that students had not learned what is and is not appropriate in a public setting. This is unsurprising, given the vitriolic nature of most "conversations" in the public sphere. These educators went to great lengths to teach students the norms and how to adhere to them instead of immediately punishing a student for breaking them.

Timing is also important when including issues that are likely to prove especially sensitive for some students. It is generally not a good idea to include such issues at the beginning of a course before students know one another well, understand the norms of civil discourse that have been established, and have developed the skills to create high-quality discussion. We were also struck by the different and more constructive atmospheres in classrooms where students knew and used the names of all their classmates compared to those in which it was obvious that students did not possess this basic knowledge about their peers. Moreover, some teachers quite consciously crafted groups so that students would have opportunities to work with as many other classmates as possible, not only ensuring that students would get to know one another but that stereotypes could not form that would contribute to an unwelcoming atmosphere in the class.

Fourth, and often overlooked, is the importance of the teacher's content knowledge. To make informed decisions about the curriculum requires that the teachers know a great deal about the political issues they introduce. Teachers can stumble onto landmines when they are not sufficiently informed to be aware of how an issue might differently affect students. The empirical/political distinction matters here as well; a well-informed teacher will be able to correct students who appeal to questionable evidence to defend offensive views.

Finally, just as teachers should gather evidence about their students on the front end, we believe that teachers benefit from getting enough information from their students throughout and at the end of courses to obtain feedback that would help them think about the choices they made about these controversial pedagogical issues. From the post-course surveys and interviews with students, we learned a lot about how they experienced and learned from the class. While it would not be possible for teachers to routinely gather the amount of data we did for this study, it is not difficult to ask students for feedback, ideally anonymously through exit slips or surveys.

Conclusion

This chapter has focused on two central questions that are controversial and important: In the political classroom, what issues should be introduced to students as controversial? And, how should teachers balance the tension between including issues that are politically authentic and establishing a classroom environment that is fair to all students? It is clear that these questions present ethical dilemmas for teachers and that there is not a clear best answer for either one of them. We urge teachers to think carefully about these questions—ideally, in advance of when they arise in practice. Deliberating these questions with others is helpful, as well. In the professional-development workshops we lead, we treat these topics as controversial pedagogical issues in which teachers grapple with questions of aims, analyze and interpret evidence about them, and think critically about how the context in which they and others are teaching could and should matter. These discussions tend to be rich and interesting because teachers realize (often for the first time, they report) that their views on what should constitute a matter of legitimate controversy and those of their colleagues are not one and the same. While teachers will answer these questions in different ways, we think it is likely that their answers will be stronger if they come to them deliberatively.

Notes

1   DOMA was repealed by the U.S. Supreme Court in 2013, see *United States v. Windsor* (2013).
2   There is a lively philosophic debate about the epistemic criterion. See Hand (2007, 2008, 2013); Gereluk (2013); Nocera (2013); Petrovic (2013); Keys (2011).
3   Alan Dershowitz is a lawyer and political commentator who argued that courts should review requests to torture and issue "torture warrants" if the state can make the case that it is justified. See Dershowitz, A. M. (2002). The case for torture warrants. Retrieved from http://www.alandershowitz.com/publications/docs/torturewarrants.html.

9

THE ETHICS OF WITHHOLDING AND DISCLOSING POLITICAL VIEWS

To be conscious is to be aware of what we are about; conscious signifies the deliberate, observant, planning traits of activity.

(Dewey, 1916/2004, p. 104)

In the previous chapter, we addressed two questions that are central to the political classroom: How should teachers decide which topics to present as controversial political issues? And how should teachers balance the tension between engaging students in authentic political controversies and creating a classroom climate that is fair and welcoming to all students? In this chapter, we build on this work to ask, How should teachers make sound professional judgments about whether to share their own political views about the issues that they introduce as controversial?

First, we continue with the example of Mr. Dunn that was introduced in Chapter 8. Mr. Dunn's case illustrates how issues selection and the teacher's decision to include or not to include his views in the discussion are a) interrelated; and b) affected by evidence, aims, and context. Second, we discuss what we found when investigating how students and teachers think about whether teachers should share their views. From this research, we have concluded that teachers ought to think about disclosing and withholding their political views as pedagogical tools that should be used intentionally and with good judgment. We recognize that "disclosing" and "withholding" are both words that have somewhat negative connotations; disclosure implies that something that was to remain secret is being revealed, and withholding suggests that someone is refusing to give over something another wants or needs. For the most part, we use "share" to avoid these more loaded terms, but we will also use "disclose" and "withhold" because we want to emphasize that teachers ought to be making conscious choices about their practice, and these terms connote that a purposeful decision is being made. Finally, we argue that these professional judgments will be better made with attention to evidence, context, and the aims of the political classroom and present several cases of teachers' practice to demonstrate how this framework can be applied.

The Case of Mr. Dunn, Continued

Chapter 8 opened with a description of Mr. Dunn's lesson on same-sex marriage at Charter High, a small urban charter school. Recall that Mr. Dunn had engaged his class in small-group deliberations about whether same-sex marriage should be legal and then asked students to stand along a continuum of "strongly agree" to "strongly disagree" as a way of moving into a larger class discussion about the issue. When no students stood to defend the view that marriage should be defined as between one man and one woman, Mr. Dunn took that position on the continuum, though he explained to the interviewer, "I didn't agree with anything that I said."

In an interview following the same-sex marriage activity, Erica, who was relatively new to the school, shared that she began the lesson holding views against legal recognition of same-sex marriage, but after hearing her classmates' arguments said, "[now] in a way I don't know." Later, she told the interviewer, "I don't believe [same-sex marriage] is right, because that is what the Bible says," but for "no special reason," she did not make that argument to the class. Interestingly, Erica had placed herself in the middle of the same-sex marriage continuum and believed that Mr. Dunn, who stood in a position more in line with her actual views, was genuinely expressing his own opinion. After explaining that she thought that Mr. Dunn was sharing his views with the class, the interviewer asked Erica if she supported what she believed to be Mr. Dunn's policy and she replied,

> I think it is good because we get to understand what they think, and they might think the same thing that we think. So we don't feel that we are alone in what we are thinking. It just gives us a better understanding and helps us out, and I think it is nice that they share with us.

When we interviewed other students from Mr. Dunn's class, there was some confusion about whether Mr. Dunn shared his views. Most knew that "he's not a Republican," but some thought he never told his views, others said that he was primarily "objective" but would occasionally answer honestly if students asked what he thought at the end of a project, and still others felt they had a "sense of how he feels about [the issues]" because many had been his students for several years but "he is not going to tell you straight out." Despite these differences, students overall liked that Mr. Dunn "gives us both sides" of an issue, which "allows us to discover on our own . . . how we feel about these issues." The story of Erica and the other students' responses illustrates how complicated this issue is, in part because students interpret differently what teachers say and do.

The Relationship Between Issues Selection and Sharing

Mr. Dunn structured his U.S. History class around compelling questions and often used material from Facing History and Ourselves, a curriculum that Mr. Dunn described as focusing on "issues of fairness and equality," "civil rights," and "government power." The curriculum, he explained, teaches students to look at questions like the legality of same-sex marriage primarily "as an issue of personal freedom." He admitted that it "doesn't take a political analyst to figure out that [the curriculum] is created by people interested in [the rights] of the underdog." He explained why he has chosen to use these resources to shape his courses:

> I guess the other defense or justification or apology I would make for being one-sided as a whole, is that there are two competing goals for me. One is to educate my students about politics. The other is to inspire them to care about politics. And those are not the same thing, and too much attention on educating about politics can kill the inspiration about politics and how you do it. And so part of my goal is to model for them a person who cares, and personal involvement, and [someone who] is aware, and to do that I have to be pretty genuine about that. . . . Many of my students come from families who are [or] . . . who have been made to feel disenfranchised. So they don't perceive themselves as even having an option [to] . . . participate in all sorts of ways.

Notice that Mr. Dunn teaches toward two aims of the political classroom—political literacy (learning about politics) and political engagement (caring about politics)—but he feels that these are in tension, especially given the student demographics at Charter High School. In response, he chooses to use a curriculum that emphasizes a third aim of the political classroom: fairness. As explained in Chapter 4, aiming toward fairness encourages students to think about issues from the position of the common good and not to reason from pure self-interest. Though emphasizing fairness could look to some as being "one-sided," these commitments help him, as a White teacher, to connect with his students, who are nearly all African American and Latino. Further, he hopes this will motivate them to get politically engaged.

Insofar as students can recognize that the curriculum tilts ideologically to the political left, this could be viewed as a type of teacher disclosure, though in this case we found no evidence that students were aware of this. Perhaps one reason curricular disclosure went unnoticed is that while Mr. Dunn prioritized issues that press students to think about fairness and the tension between the common good and self-interest, once the issue was selected, he presented it as a controversial political issue. Mr. Dunn explained that in classroom deliberations he saw his role as trying to shape "intellectual conflicts," "spark disagreements," and create "a catalyst" for students' thinking. Students reported, and we observed, that Mr. Dunn did not attempt to steer the students toward a particular point of view in class discussions.

Mr. Dunn also noted that context matters when thinking about his pedagogical decisions. Prior to coming to Charter, Mr. Dunn taught in a politically diverse public high school where he felt he did not have to work as hard to spark discussions "because there was already a healthy sense of disagreement in the room, and so that could play itself out in a way that would help me achieve my educational goals for my students." At Charter, the students' views fell within a "much narrower [political] spectrum" because the students were all "minorities from poor neighborhoods" in the city. As a result, he played the devil's advocate and impartial facilitator because "it is my role to present them with both sides." Mr. Dunn explained that he often draws on this technique as a way to promote critical thinking and generally avoided inserting his opinion into the discussion.

The story of Mr. Dunn and Erica illustrates the complex interactions happening within all classrooms and especially in the political classroom. In 2005, Mr. Dunn chose to introduce the question of whether same-sex couples should receive the same legal standing as heterosexual couples as a controversial issue. As explained in the previous chapter, the decision to do so was not obvious and required professional judgment. In Mr. Dunn's classroom, Erica was a new student who held views that were more conservative than those being voiced by her peers and felt unsure about expressing her religious views—for her, this was a sensitive issue. Mr. Dunn chose to withhold his actual views and instead, defended the views typically expressed by people opposed to same-sex marriage. Most students recognized this as a familiar move by Mr. Dunn to stir the pot and get them to think deeply, and they enjoyed this pedagogical strategy. Erica, on the other hand, heard this as teacher disclosure and concluded that Mr. Dunn was a supportive teacher. In the classroom, teachers are negotiating many relationships—as are the students—and sorting through these dynamics makes teaching both exciting and tremendously difficult. One read of Erica's response is that she wanted the teacher to agree with her, but we suspect that even if Erica understood that Mr. Dunn was playing devil's advocate (and withholding his actual views), what she appreciated the most was hearing her views defended and treated with respect. Teachers cannot know how their every decision will be interpreted, but as John Dewey suggests in the epigraph to this chapter, teachers can and should be conscious, deliberate, and observant about their practice. Good professional judgment requires that teachers act with intention, and this requires attention to evidence and ethics.

Evidence and Ethical Reasoning

There is limited social science research available to help high school teachers make decisions about sharing views.[1] In a study of 12 middle and high school teachers, Jonathan Miller-Lane, Elissa Denton, and Andrew May (2006) found that the middle school teachers all withheld their views and the high school teachers made different decisions, with some disclosing views and others withholding. The age of the students was one reason that high school teachers felt more comfortable sharing. In Northern Ireland, Alan McCully (2006) studied community educators engaging students in discussions of "The Troubles" and found that 19 out of 20 facilitators disclosed their views to the participants. In a society trying to reconcile after a period of violence, they believed disclosure was necessary to build the trust necessary for meaningful discussions. Wayne Journell (2011) and Nancy Niemi and Richard Niemi (2007) each observed high school social studies teachers during presidential elections. In both studies, the researchers found teachers who claimed to be "neutral" and not disclosing their views were nevertheless communicating partisan leanings through sarcasm, humor, name calling, and material selection. While these studies are important, there is still much to learn about when and how teachers share their views and what effects differing practices have on students.

In our study, we were interested in the interaction between what students thought, what teachers did, and how both affected the classroom dynamic. On the post-surveys, students were asked 11 questions using a Likert scale about whether and how teachers communicated their views to students (e.g., "My social studies teacher only shares his or her opinion about issues when asked directly by a student in class"). Teachers were asked a similar set of questions regarding their own practice. In their interviews, students were asked whether they knew their teacher's views; if a student said she did know, we asked how she knew and what she thought about this practice. If students reported the teacher did not share, we asked how they felt about that policy. We also asked teachers about their policies and what motivated their choices. Finally, in the follow-up phone surveys, students were asked the open-ended question "Do you remember if your teacher shared his or her personal views on political issues during class?" Related questions probed students' opinions of their teacher's practice (see the Appendix).

One of the most salient aspects of this research was how much disagreement we encountered among students in the same classroom about whether their teacher was sharing personal political views. Of the 25 teachers in the study whose students were surveyed about their views on this issue, 15 had students who were in at least 70% agreement about whether their teacher withheld or disclosed their views. Of those, two were Mr. Hempstead and Ms. Matthews at Adams High (recall that in Chapter 4 we reported that Ms. Heller's ELLs were confused by devil's advocacy), reporting 100% agreement that they withheld their views. Mr. Kushner's students were in 75% agreement that he did not share, and 78% of Mr. Walters's students felt that he did. In the other classes, students were quite divided about the teacher's policy. The differing perceptions among students in the other classes were likely caused by the fact that there are many ways in which a teacher's views come into the classroom, and students are not always able to pick up on these more subtle communications, or, as was clear in Mr. Dunn's case, they might misinterpret what a teacher is trying to do. Elsewhere, we have described in detail the qualitative and quantitative findings from the study regarding disclosure and withholding (Hess, 2009). We summarize this evidence below.

The Teachers' Views

1. Teachers were divided about whether it is appropriate to share their views with their students, with 50% saying sharing is appropriate and 50% saying it is not.
2. The teachers who opposed sharing were most often concerned about influencing students' views about the issues being discussed. There are two worries with "influencing." First, sharing a view will cause students to adopt that view. Second, students could feel coerced to express agreement with the teacher—perhaps to get a better grade.
3. Teachers in favor of sharing identified some educational value in letting students know where they stand. For example, a teacher who explained in detail how he came to hold his views by explaining what evidence and values he found most convincing could model for students how to reason through a complex issue. Most teachers who found value in sharing also felt they were able to present competing views fairly. Others who valued sharing felt that it was more respectful to students to reveal a bias than try to hide it.

Evidence in Favor of Sharing

1. When asked about their social studies teacher during the post-survey at the end of the course, 79% of students thought it was fine for teachers to share personal views. About 77% did not think sharing would cause them to adopt the teacher's view.
2. We did not find evidence that classes of students were moving to align with their teacher's ideological views, though we note that students and teachers in Like-Minded Schools were largely aligned from the beginning of the course. This suggests that alignment between ethos of the school and the community in which one is coming of age can effectively shape the political orientations of young people.
3. Students were supportive of teachers who "share," but they did not support teachers who "push," "preach," or "force" their opinions onto students. That is, students were not in favor of teachers who use the classroom for political proselytizing.
4. High-SES students were significantly less likely to believe that knowing the teacher's views would cause them to change their minds.

Evidence Against Sharing

1. A total of 41% of students suspected that when a teacher shares, *other* students will change their minds.
2. The 23% of students who thought that they were likely to change their views to align with those of the teacher were more likely to be low-SES students and students with low scores on our measure of political knowledge.[2]
3. Students in classrooms in which the teacher did not share enjoyed feeling like they have to "think more" about the issues and work harder to figure out the issues "for ourselves."
4. Students were significantly more likely to believe that they had a responsibility to participate in classes when the teacher did not share her views.

Evidence That Points in Both Directions

1. Students were overwhelmingly supportive of their own teacher's policy related to sharing—whatever it was—and they remained supportive in the longitudinal follow-ups. In the first follow-up survey, for example, 297 students agreed with their teacher's policy, 12 disagreed, and 23 were not sure.
2. Students wanted to feel that they were figuring out what they think about issues; some felt that knowing the teacher's view helped with this process, while others thought it interfered.
3. There was no clear consensus in teacher practice. About 48% of teachers reported that they did share their opinions. About 54% of the students said their teacher shared, while 37% said their teacher did so only when directly asked by students.[3]

We find that the teacher's pedagogy has some bearing on this issue. As explained in Chapter 3, we sorted teachers' pedagogies into three categories: Discussion, Best Practice Discussion, and Lecture. Students in Discussion and Best Practice Discussion classes were significantly less likely than students in Lecture classes to think they would be persuaded by their teacher's views, probably because students in such classes were given plenty of opportunity to voice their own opinions. In the interviews, this was often expressed as an issue of free speech: these students felt that the teacher should be allowed to participate in the discussion too. In addition, we found that students in Best Practice Discussion classes were more likely to report that their teacher presented multiple points of view. In contrast, students in Lecture classes were more likely to report that their teacher shared views without being asked; these students were more in favor of teachers sharing than students in Best Practice Discussion classes. We suspect that this difference may be attributable to the fact that lectures are more interesting when they are infused with opinions and not simply a recitation of factual information. It could also be that a lecturer who is clear about what is and is not his view helps students process the material. We note, however, that lecturing about controversial issues without giving students the opportunity to discuss and deliberate the topics being presented is not in line with the aims of the political classroom.

Ethical Considerations

When we presented these findings to teachers attending professional-development programs, there was considerable disagreement about how to interpret the evidence. One contingent held that an instructor who uses Best Practice methods and shares without imposing his views is doing no harm; it appears that if the teacher is careful about when and how to share, students are likely to be supportive. Others, however, were concerned about the minority of students who stated that they are susceptible to their teacher's views. This contingent felt the views of these students should carry more weight, especially since they are significantly more likely to be low SES and to score lower on the measure of political knowledge, a combination that might leave them less prepared to critically evaluate the teacher's views. Further, if teachers want students to engage in deliberation, it appears that serving as an impartial facilitator is the better way to get students to take ownership of trying to figure out which view or views they want to defend.

Other teachers objected to the framing of the debate: "Wait," they argued. "It doesn't matter what students say they want; disclosure is still *wrong*." These teachers were arguing that sharing political views with students is an ethical question and there are principles of professional practice that are violated when a teacher uses the classroom to" impose" her opinion on her students. Recall that in Chapter 1 we recounted the objections that Horace Mann raised when Samuel May took a class of students to an abolitionist meeting in 1843. This was an early articulation of the idea that public schools should be "neutral" to the political debates happening in the larger community. If the state was going to make schooling compulsory, then the institution must respect the autonomy of students and the authority of parents; to do otherwise, Mann cautioned, was a "violation of State trust" (Mann, 1865, p. 170). Many teachers and students that we interviewed and spoke with in workshops also appealed to the principle of "neutrality" when defending a commitment to withholding. Because teachers are in a position of authority, the worry is that disclosing can easily turn into imposing views on students; this was commonly expressed as a concern that teachers could unfairly "influence" students. Further, promoters of neutrality argue that this practice could violate the development of a student's autonomy if the teacher's sharing results in less critical thinking among members of the class; this is a particular concern in lecture-only classrooms if students are not being presented with multiple points of view and not given the opportunity to hear from anyone other than the teacher. Another set of teachers argued the opposite. They believed that transparency, not neutrality, was the most important value. In their view, because neutrality is not possible, the most defensible position is to be explicit about one's views. This approach, they argued, encourages the development of autonomy, because students will be better equipped to evaluate the teacher's practice and openly disagree with the teacher's views.

In these discussions of the evidence, two different ethical frames are being applied. The first set of teachers was thinking about disclosing and withholding as what we term "pedagogical tools" that should be used with good judgment. These teachers were often open to the possibility of changing their minds based on the evidence but also considered their context, their values about what "good" teaching requires, and the arguments of their peers. The second set of teachers, those concerned about neutrality, argued that disclosure was an issue for which there was a single correct answer: It is categorically wrong. The teachers who rejected neutrality and made an appeal for transparency also believed that there was one right answer: Withholding was categorically wrong.

To make our case for why we believe the "pedagogical tools" approach is stronger, we first discuss why we reject both the categorical appeal to the principle of neutrality and the categorical appeal to the principle of transparency. Neither of these views, we argue, is adequately focused on the aims of the political classroom.

Neutrality, Transparency, and Mutual Respect

It is often assumed that teachers should not discuss their own views with their students. This is typically motivated by a fear that teachers over-share and violate the public's trust and student autonomy. In fact, a recent survey found that nearly half the public feels that "too many social studies teachers use their classes as a 'soap box' for their personal point of view" (Lautzenheiser et al., 2011, p. 4). This concern leads some to express the view that teachers should always be "neutral." In this understanding of neutrality, the teacher should "strive to insure that students have the opportunity to consider all relevant positions on the issue" and "teachers should remain silent about their own views" (Kelly, 1986, p. 228). Neutrality is often justified for two reasons. First, democratic theorists argue that the state ought to be neutral to the plurality of values, religions, and cultural beliefs that citizens choose to endorse. That is, the state should not use its power to endorse, privilege, or persecute particular beliefs. As a public institution, the school must adhere to the same principle of neutrality and allow young people to explore and express competing beliefs and values. A second justification is that withholding views and assuming a position of neutrality promotes the autonomous development of young people; eliminating the potentially coercive power of the teacher's voice allows students to make their own decisions. There is some merit to both of these rationales. Teachers ought to be conscious of the fact that schools are institutions that compel students to attend and ought to be cautious about when and how competing views are silenced or privileged. Further, the development of autonomy is one of several important aims for schools generally and for democratic education in particular. That said, using the principle of neutrality as a guide for teacher practice is problematic.

First, as we argued in Chapter 4, the classroom is not "neutral." Teachers have particular aims for what it means to be educated and what it means to be a good citizen; these aims inform their practice, and educating toward these ends is inherently value-laden.[4] Proponents of the political classroom seek to develop within students a set of dispositions grounded in deliberative democratic theory; these dispositions include political equality, tolerance, autonomy, fairness, engagement, and political literacy. These values are nonpartisan, but they also are justified by a theory of democracy that is less individualistic and more oriented toward thinking about the "common good" than other conceptions of democracy.[5] The aims we identified are sufficiently open to competing perspectives to make them appropriate for schooling in a democratic society. They will certainly be controversial to some, but the point here is that valuing "neutrality" ignores the ways in which schools are and should be institutions committed to democratic values.

Second, the pedagogical argument for neutrality concludes that withholding is required for teachers to respect student autonomy. This is not necessarily the case. We have seen many teachers who are able to occasionally express their political views in ways that are fair and in line with the aim of autonomy (noting, of course, that autonomy is *one of several* important aims). Mr. Elliot of Central High explains it this way:

> [If students] know my opinions . . . I can still approach the issue from the opposite side . . . or discuss it or deliberate it very intelligently. And I can back it up with facts. And I can back it up with good information even if I don't . . . agree with what is going on.

This teacher's approach shows that he values *fairness* and models *respect* for competing points of view. In this way, his practice promotes political tolerance and autonomy by showing students that while he has his own opinions, he also is able to engage respectfully with other points of view. At times, this sort of engagement may be appropriate and valuable. Aiming toward a classroom culture that is fair and models mutual respect is more in line with the aims of the political classroom than an absolute commitment to the principle of neutrality. Still, it requires professional judgment to know when sharing a view furthers these aims and when it might detract. We return to this issue in the next section.

As noted earlier, one response to recognizing that neutrality is not possible or ideal is to conclude that the most justifiable policy for teachers is to consistently and explicitly disclose their views to students. Like neutrality, this commitment to transparency is seen as categorically the right thing to do. Recall that in Chapter 4 we introduced Ms. Potter at St. John's High School and described her lesson on the unequal distribution of the world's resources. In her interview, Ms. Potter explained that during her teaching career, she changed her mind about sharing her political views with students. When she started teaching, she believed that she "would always stay objective and neutral" and "never reveal my personal opinion on things." She later concluded, "That is a total fantasy," and decided to alter her policy to explain to her students at the beginning of a term that she would share her views but would make clear to them what is fact and what is "my personal opinion." Another teacher in the study subscribed to the view that because neutrality is impossible, it is better to be transparent about one's views, and we have encountered numerous other teachers who support this position. There are two ways that we have seen transparency play out in the classroom; we will identify these as the practices of Teacher A and Teacher B.

Teacher A reasons, "I want to be explicit about my political views, so that my students can better identify when I fail to uphold the principle of neutrality." In practice, this teacher aims toward fairly representing multiple perspectives in the classroom and encouraging students to come to their own autonomous decisions, but she might begin the term by explaining what her general political views are so that students can be better judges of her practice. She might also feel obligated to insert her views into class discussions so that students are clear about where she stands. Thomas Kelly (1986) defends this practice, which he labels "committed impartiality," on the grounds that it respects students' autonomy by making transparent the ways in which the teacher's view may be tilting the scales, by inviting disagreement, and by modeling a person who has political commitments (p. 234). This is a compelling argument, especially because it was clear that students in our study who did not know their teacher's views were often unaware of the ways in which the curriculum and the instructor were subtly tipping the scales. But notice that while Teacher A is still primarily concerned with being fair to competing views, she doubts that she be sufficiently neutral. We have evidence—the Adams High teachers being the best example—of teachers who do not share their views but are able nevertheless to create a classroom that promotes fairness and mutual respect. If we concede that neutrality is not possible and agree that fairness and mutual respect are the principles that matter, then a *commitment* to transparency seems less necessary because it is possible to be fair and respectful and to teach students to disagree with each other. Further, we believe that context matters. Recall that Mr. Kushner at Academy High—a Like-Minded School—decided to withhold his views for the good of the few conservative students in the classroom. He felt that not sharing his views invited more participation from the students who were most likely to be silenced. Our primary worry is that a blanket commitment to transparency foregrounds the teacher's voice, and the political classroom aims to get students talking to each other. Our evidence suggests that too much of the teacher's view undermines classroom deliberation: Some students feel less motivated to participate and to examine the issue being discussed when everyone knows what the teacher thinks. It is clear that, at times, students would like to hear from the teacher, but they also want the opportunity to discuss the issues themselves and to feel as if they are puzzling over an issue. While Teacher A's policy might on the surface seem reasonable, in practice it may interfere with student engagement because it puts the rule "I should always share" above what is best for creating a vibrant classroom discussion.

Alternatively, Teacher B reasons, "I believe neutrality is impossible, so I will make it my practice to teach my views in a straightforward manner." This teacher fully abandons the principles of fairness and mutual respect and is not just sharing but advocating her own views about controversial political issues. Students may be invited to disagree, but the teacher makes no attempt at showing the reasonableness of competing views, though she may respectfully argue with students who disagree. This is likely the teacher imagined when people say they believe teachers use the classroom as a soapbox. At times, Ms. Potter came quite close to being this teacher. She is one of the only teachers in the study for which a student said that she occasionally "forced" her view on students and "sometimes she kind of goes at the other side of the issue so hard, and if someone in the class disagrees with it, then . . . [it is] like a shock." To be clear, this student, and others in Ms. Potter's class, was supportive of Ms. Potter "voicing her opinion" but felt that at times she crossed the line. In her follow-up phone survey, this student recalled that the discussions were "very biased" and Ms. Potter "should not have been so open with her personal views."

A teacher whose response to the impossibility of neutrality is to freely advocate her views about controversial political issues violates students' autonomy by denying them the opportunity to evaluate the reasonableness of views for themselves. Further, the aims of fairness, political tolerance, and political equality are undermined if students are not introduced to the complexity of an issue and asked to consider that reasonable people disagree about open policy issues. With regard to political controversies, Teacher B is reasoning that advocacy is good practice because its presumed opposite—neutrality—is not possible. We agree that neutrality is not possible, but it is also not the most important value if the aim is to engage students in discussions of political controversies. Teachers can and should teach political controversies by giving a best-case fair hearing to competing points of view while modeling mutual respect.

Sharing as a Pedagogical Tool

While doing this research, it became clear to us that to expect teachers never to share a personal political view was an unrealistic and occasionally undesirable standard, but to take the position that teachers should *always* share their views also was problematic. That left us with the murky answer "it depends" when faced with the question "When, if ever, should teachers share their views with students?" In this section, we apply our model for professional judgment to this issue. We present several cases of teacher practice to show how careful consideration of context, evidence, and the aims of the political classroom will help teachers make better judgments about sharing personal views.

Adams High: Purposeful Withholding

In Chapter 5, we introduced the teaching team at Adams High and the legislative simulation that is the foundation for their required Government course. These three teachers were unusual for several reasons. First, the teachers have collectively agreed to hold themselves to a common policy: We will never share our views. This is such a tightly adhered-to rule that they will not even put up political yard signs in front of their own homes during election season. We did not encounter any other set of teachers who had decided to abide by a common policy. The team at Adams High also is unusual because their students were in nearly unanimous agreement that the teachers always withheld their opinions about political issues. We explained in Chapter 5 that the exception to this was in Ms. Heller's ESL class, in which some students were misinterpreting devil's advocacy as Ms. Heller's actual views. Again, she has since made it her policy to wear devil's horns to signal to students that she has taken on that role.

The team at Adams is incredibly disciplined in adhering to this policy, and each teacher explains it to the students at the beginning of the course—a practice that contributes to why their students are in agreement about what is happening. Ms. Heller's student explains, "She made it clear to us that she has her own opinions, but she wasn't going to state them. So that was good." One effect of this policy was that it seemed to pique the students' curiosity about the teachers' views. In their interviews, students made comments such as "It killed us because we wanted to know" and "I asked him all the time." Students also reported looking for clues that would reveal their teachers' views on issues. One student described an example when students were taking turns practicing their speeches for the Full Session. Ms. Heller voiced arguments that a Republican might use against a Democratic speaker, and the class said, "Oh, you are a Republican!" But then "the next person would go," and in response, Ms. Heller would "speak like a Democrat." This student concluded, "It was hard to figure it out" Ms. Heller's personal views, because "she is very good at hiding [them]."

The teachers reason that this policy is important for the success of the simulation. First, the instructors worry that disclosing will negatively influence students' views, and they do not want members of the class to "brown-nose and take our opinion," nor do they "want kids to feel rejected if they have an opposite opinion." Overall, students supported the policy, even if they wanted to know what the teachers thought. One of Mr. Hempstead's students explained, "I wish he had [revealed his opinions]", but went on to say that he supported the policy because "I guess it is better for the class." The other reason that teachers point to for their purposeful withholding is that it communicates to students that the instructors are training class members to run the simulation; the teachers are not participants in the simulation. As Mr. Hempstead put it, "It is not about us. It is about them, and I think the minute that we get involved, it stops being about them." Students are expected to do most of the intellectual work of developing their own arguments, forming political parties, and running their own meetings. Taking on the role of impartial facilitators communicates to students early on that the teachers will be coaches but not participants who provide answers. We suspect that students would likely not be overly influenced if the teachers shared views occasionally, but in the context of the simulation, the policy of withholding is in line with their aims of promoting engagement and modeling for students that teachers will support them as they develop strong arguments for whatever policy they are advancing. Finally, because there is a competitive aspect to the simulation, this policy helps create the deliberative spirit the teachers try to cultivate and tempers, to some extent, the partisan politics at play. One of Mr. Hempstead's students supported the policy because

> I think [their policy] is good because obviously peer pressure is already so heavy in that class. . . . So if [students] were to know a teacher felt a certain way, like if Mr. Hempstead had said he was a . . . hardcore Republican, it would have given the Republicans a feeling that they had an edge over the Democrats, because they had the teacher's support, and it would have made the Democrats feel like, "Okay, well can I actually speak my mind knowing that the teacher is going to disagree with me?" So I just think the fact that Mr. Hempstead didn't reveal or even lead on to what kind of political party he was affiliated with was really good.

One could argue, however, that political tolerance and political equality might be better taught if teachers revealed their political views. Doing so—particularly if they were still able to create a classroom norm of fairness and mutual respect—would reinforce the point that members of a democracy can still like and support each other, while also disagreeing. We suspect that the trade-off to this potentially positive outcome is that it would heighten the partisan aspect of the simulation. If a Republican teacher were, for example, to be seen as the coach for the Republican Party and a Democrat were to become the lead Democrat, this could extend the "winner-take-all" mentality to a new level. Further, if the teaching team were all members of one party, it could feel to some students that they have no role models on their side or that their views lack merit. The teachers' policy is an indication that they have clear aims for what they want students to get out of the course, and they have concluded that sharing their views would detract more than it would add to the experience.

A total of eight teachers, including the three at Adams High, reported in their interviews that they did not share their views with students and typically assumed the role of impartial facilitator. Even though these five teachers were not conducting an elaborate simulation, their reasoning was quite similar to those articulated by the team at Adams High. As one teacher put it, "My job is to get them to think," which is another way of saying, "It is not about me." Mr. Murphy of Riverdale High, for example, reports,

> [I don't insert my opinion] because I don't think it is important to the process. One of the reasons is that it allows [students] to really think about

the issues on their own and make their own judgment and form their own opinions. And if I put my two cents in, I don't see them accomplishing that. It just doesn't serve any purpose.

As at Adams High, students at other schools appreciate this approach:

> I would say Mr. Murphy is probably one of the best teachers I have ever had. He is really understanding of the students. He really takes more of a neutral position on issues. And I think that the most redeeming quality of him as a teacher is that he really makes you understand what you say. A lot of people have uninformed opinions. . . . So I would say he really understands History, International Relations. He is a very well-educated man. He really knows what he is talking about.

Before moving on to teachers who do occasionally share their personal views, we ask, "Is it ever bad professional judgment to remain in the role of impartial facilitator?" We do not have a case from the study in which we observed a teacher who we felt made a bad decision to withhold a view, but we think that such a scenario is possible. Imagine, for example, that a teacher asks a class to deliberate the DREAM Act, which would create a pathway to permanent residency for young people who were brought to the United States as minors and without legal documentation. As it happens, the class is nearly unanimously opposed to the act, while one student, Saul—who is an immigrant to the United States—sets out to defend the bill but is being dismissed by the other side. The teacher sees that she has presented a controversial political issue that is also sensitive to one of her students. The instructor then makes the following statement to the majority, who are convinced that this would encourage further border crossings, "Listen, I actually agree with Saul, and I don't think that you are really hearing him, or taking his views seriously. I'm going to side with Saul right now and give you what I think are the best reasons against your position. I'm doing this so that you will be forced to think more deeply about your position—maybe you'll end up agreeing with us, but even if you don't, I want you to reexamine why you hold the views that you do." This teacher could have just chosen to play devil's advocate at this moment, but that would not have communicated to Saul that he had a genuine ally in the room. It also might have allowed other students to conclude, "She's just doing that to be nice to Saul; I bet she really agrees with us." The teacher's decision to share her personal views motivates the other students to take the situation more seriously. Notice that the teacher in this case is a) articulating the reason that she is disclosing her views; b) motivated by the desire to prompt students to reexamine their views (autonomy); and c) committed to encouraging students to think about this policy question from a position of fairness. She is also expressing her views in order to provide support to Saul.

The context certainly matters in this case. We assume that the teacher has a good rapport with the students in her class and has already established the norms of fair play. We also recognize that this teacher is taking a risk, especially if the community is one that would strongly object to her views. We further assume that the teacher agrees with Saul and is supportive of the DREAM Act. If the teacher did not, she should still feel that it is her responsibility to help Saul by playing the devil's advocate on his behalf. We would not expect a teacher to lie to the class about her own views; but she put Saul in this situation, and, if she is treating immigration policy as an open question, she should want her students to confront the best views. Recall that we saw something similar occur in Mr. Dunn's class when no students stood to defend traditional marriage; Mr. Dunn defended those views despite the fact that he disagreed with everything he said.

Mr. Walters: Occasional Disclosure

Thirteen of the teachers we interviewed reported that they sometimes share their views with students. Three said that they "try" to keep their views out of classroom discussions but admitted that they occasionally "slip." The other ten had a variety of policies that ranged from answering honestly when asked by a student to believing that modeling how they came to a view was important for helping students understand how to develop their own arguments. We are not able to discuss all their practices, but we argue that an important difference between sharing that reflects good judgment and sharing that is problematic is whether the teacher values the principles of fairness and mutual respect and the aims of the political classroom.

Recall that in Chapter 7, we introduced Mr. Walters, who teaches at King High, an evangelical Christian school. As we explained, Mr. Walters does occasionally share his political views with his students, but he also makes sure that students know they can disagree:

> [W]hile I would never balk at sharing with a student how I felt about these certain political and social issues and why I felt it, I wouldn't say, "This is also how you should feel." Now there is a little different dynamic here, because certainly when we are trying to train our students to have a Christian worldview, I am going to say this is how I think one would think Christianly about this issue. . . . But I am still not going to say that you are going to hell if you don't think this way.

Mr. Walters seems to have effectively communicated this intention to his students, who report that he "has always been unbiased in presenting things" and that he encourages students to "openly discuss."

Recall also that Mr. Walters is politically to the left of his students and he tries to promote political autonomy by asking them to question the conservative views they have come to hold, while also encouraging them to adhere to Christian views—an aim we labeled "bounded autonomy." In this context, Mr. Walters's occasional sharing allows him to acquire enough trust from the community so that he is able to ask students to question their (and often their parents') views. Given that King High was one of the most conservative schools in the study, we note that it would be very easy for Mr. Walters to capitalize on the like-mindedness of his students and simply encourage them to hold more deeply to their conservatism. This would likely result in students developing more ideologically polarized views. Ideological polarization correlates with becoming a member of the "engaged public" (Abramowitz, 2010), but Mr. Walters rightly prioritizes political fairness and autonomy over engagement, a value that his students already embrace as a result of their like-minded upbringing. It is not that he discourages political participation, but in a climate in which students are already prone to dismissing views from the left, Mr. Walters's occasional sharing helps him develop tolerance and critical thinking among students.

Other teachers who were able to share with good effect were similarly committed to making sure that multiple and competing views were treated with respect. For the most part, these teachers play the role of impartial facilitator but feel that when a student asks about a teacher's political views, there is no harm in answering honestly. As Mr. Allen put it, "I think it is natural for them to want to make that connection with you . . . and have a good idea why you believe what you believe."

Insofar as these teachers are, in fact, able to create classroom community based on fairness and mutual respect and choose to share at moments when doing so furthers educational aims as well as the aims of the political classroom, they are exercising good judgment. It is when teachers no longer play fair that their judgment becomes questionable. For example, a student in Ms. Gardner's class explained that "at the beginning of the year," Ms. Gardner stated that her policy was not "to mix in my views" and that she would act instead as an impartial facilitator. The student went on to say, "by the [end of the] semester, the jig [was] up. She [was] not even pretending to be that equally balanced anymore . . . you can obviously tell that she's liberal . . . she really pounds on [President] Bush." Another student reflected:

> She doesn't yell at us or anything. She really yells at the government and things she doesn't agree with. And she will tell us stories and she gets really, really angry at the president or the governor, really easily. But she is not mean to us.

Even though students also reported that Ms. Gardner resorted to name calling—on occasion referring to President Bush as an "idiot"—the students we interviewed were for the most part supportive of Ms. Gardner and did not object to these practices, because they tended to agree with many of her views, though one noted that there were some closeted Republican students in the class. Perhaps most importantly, students described off-the-cuff discussions in which they were invited to react to Ms. Gardner's views, but they did not report being prepared to engage in deliberation with each other or to seriously consider divergent points of view. The variety of "soapbox" sharing that Ms. Gardner engaged in does not further, and likely undermines, the aims of the political classroom. Students are not learning how to deliberate across difference or digging into the complexity of issues; those who agree with Ms. Gardner are not asked to reflect on their views and instead found that their opinions are reaffirmed in a way that reduces issues to a battle between those who are "idiots" and those who are not. This is the type of pedagogical practice that reinforces the divisiveness of polarization.

Political Seepage

The last type of sharing we discuss is what we term "political seepage." By this we refer to teachers who believe that they should not explicitly state their views to students but whose political opinions nevertheless "seep" or "spill" into the classroom. Seepage is not always a problem. Mr. Kushner, for example, offered this comment toward the end of a class discussion about the documentary film *The 11th Hour,* which depicts the ways in which human activity is causing environmental disasters. The left-leaning Academy High students had been discussing why sparking action is so difficult, arguing that it is because people will not give up modern conveniences. Mr. Kushner had been mostly quiet during the discussion but then stepped in with this thought:

> We often talk about [the possible solutions] as if this is all about sacrifice, when many of these changes—living closer to grocery stores, eating healthy, etc.—might improve our quality of life. Also, as we become more aware, consumers will want more green products, then we create demand, and these [green] companies become more profitable. I just don't like all this sacrifice talk—that's my two cents.

He then turned to cue up the next part of the film, and students discussed whether buying green would really have much effect. This is a very subtle moment of seepage. Here, Mr. Kushner revealed some of his own views about environmental issues, but most students likely did not even pick up on the opinions embedded in his comment. Nevertheless, the remark inserted something new to the discussion, which the students then addressed. Moments such as this make some students say that even though Mr. Kushner is "objective," they can "guess that he's liberal" because of "a little wink-wink now and then." As one girl explained:

> Well, it is interesting because he doesn't give us his opinion on anything, which I like. But it is not like he is cold. He is not standing there like this blank slate of emptiness that is a completely unhuggable [or] unapproachable . . . guy.

At times teachers do—and likely should—reveal some genuine concern about particular issues and perhaps share that they have political commitments upon which they act. Modeling engagement and concern are important qualities of citizenship, and teachers should express these when appropriate.

The negative side of seepage is when the effect becomes divisive and/or confusing for students who are not sure where the teacher's views begin and end. Ms. Brown has this problem. Ms. Brown teaches a year-long, senior-level American Government course at Washington High School, located in a wealthy suburb of a major Midwestern city. Our observations found her to be a dynamic teacher who often uses humor to illustrate her points and has a friendly rapport with young people. Students describe the class and the teacher as active and engaging, with some type of discussion or interactive lecture happening nearly every day. Students further report that a lot of discussion of current events occurs when Ms. Brown "throws out a topic," and students react without much preparation. On the whole, students report "learning a lot" and find the class "useful and interesting."

We interviewed nine students during the study semester; they experienced a great deal of confusion about whether Ms. Brown was sharing her views. Three said that the teacher does share but usually at the end of a discussion. Two of these students felt this is fine because Ms. Brown is open to all points of view. One of the three found Ms. Brown biased against the Republican Party and speculated that a conservative student in this classroom would "not be completely open to say what she wants." Three other students said that the teacher does disclose her views, and all three agreed that this is the right thing to do because it makes for better discussions and allows class members to make up their own minds. However, one of these students also said she had been "confused all year" because "I don't know when she's joking." This student guessed that Ms. Brown voted for George W. Bush, but "honestly . . . [has] no idea"—she based her guess on knowing where Ms. Brown lives and believing that it is a conservative neighborhood. This student stated that Ms. Brown's policy of withholding is a good approach because it prevents teachers from playing favorites. Finally, three students reported that Ms. Brown implicitly reveals her views through the use of sarcasm and other indirect forms of communication that conveyed she is anti-Bush and anti-Republican. Only one of these three gave an opinion about implicit disclosure; she felt it was fine because it only happened "sometimes" and because students did not feel intimidated.

There are several salient points to note in Ms. Brown's case. First, her implicit sharing slips past many students, some of whom identified her as a Democrat and others who concluded she voted for Republican George Bush. In the follow-up surveys, nine students recalled that Ms. Brown never shared, while six made reference to the implicit ways she revealed her views. In the second follow-up survey, we asked respondents if their teacher was more or less biased than other social studies teachers they had had in high school. Ms. Brown stood out as eliciting a wide range of responses, with some students saying she was "much more neutral" and others saying she was "much more biased" than her colleagues in the social studies department. Finally, like Ms. Potter, Ms. Brown is unusual in that some students did not support how she communicated her views. The longitudinal surveys asked students whether they agreed with what they believe to be their teacher's policy regarding sharing of political views. As noted at the beginning of this chapter, only 12 respondents in the first follow-up survey reported that they disagreed with their teacher's policy around sharing political views; three of these were in Ms. Brown's class, and all three were against what they saw as implicit sharing. These students viewed her practice as unintentional teaching and reported that she, "didn't realize what she was doing," and "I don't think she tried to let us know, but in her explanations of Democrats and Republicans, she would make the Republicans seem worse." All three felt she should have been more even-handed.

Ms. Brown's political seepage is problematic. She intends to withhold her views, but they seep out in indirect ways through her use of humor and sarcasm, in the way she presents course material, and in casual interactions with students. This is a problem for several reasons. First, we find that this type of humor is particularly confusing to students, especially those with low political knowledge or who cannot recognize sarcasm. Using partisan humor also is annoying to students who are not politically aligned with the teacher. Two students who identified as members of the Republican Party reported that they learned "very little" from Ms. Brown's class, and they were not in favor of the tone that she set in the classroom. It can also make these students feel like they are the butt of the joke. Finally, seepage is a problem because it undermines the aims of the political classroom. As was the case with Ms. Gardner, partisan humor that makes one side look laudable and the other side laughable invites the divisive culture of polarization into the classroom. Further, this does not encourage students to seriously interrogate competing points of view (tolerance), nor does it model treating one another as political equals.

Most importantly, seepage is a problem because it does not reflect judgment; these "slips" often get a laugh but are not made with a consideration of the likely effect they will have on students in the classroom. Recent studies have found that these behaviors are not that unusual (Journell, 2011; Niemi & Niemi, 2007). In a study of six 11th- and 12th-grade social studies teachers, Niemi and Niemi (2007) were surprised by the amount of cynicism and partisan name-calling that they observed among the instructors. Many of these teachers withheld their views about particular issues but used insulting language about political leaders. In one case, a school superintendent popped into a civics class and referred to Hillary Rodham Clinton as "Hillary Rotten Clinton" (p. 43). Yet "few teachers remembered that they had even made the remarks" when researchers asked about them (p. 54). Journell (2011) found similar practices in a study of social studies teachers' treatment of the 2008 presidential election: It was often the teachers who thought they were "neutral" who expressed the most cynical and divisive views. Niemi and Neimi (2007) were further troubled by the fact that these teachers "simply did not discuss any really controversial subjects" and, as a result, "students have no choice but to hear the name-calling and the opinions that teachers use and to digest them, somehow, in interpreting the political world" (p. 54).

Throughout this book, we have emphasized that context, evidence, and the aims of the political classroom ought to be considered when teachers make decisions about how to include politics in the classroom. One of the relevant contextual details that matters for the students and teachers we studied is the highly polarized political climate outside of school, the norms of which are neither fair nor respectful. Engaging students in discussions of political controversies requires some discipline on the part of the teacher, who ought to act with intention in the classroom. Ideally, classrooms are places in which students are encouraged to think about the complexity of issues. This is difficult and rigorous work for both students and teachers; when teachers grossly oversimplify the political sphere through the use of off-handed comments, they rob students of the opportunity to experience the disciplined thinking that is necessary to discuss and reflect on how we want to live together.

Conclusion

The questions of whether, when, and how a teacher is using good judgment about withholding or disclosing views is clearly ethically complicated. It is our hope that by examining the conceptual terrain and considering what good professional judgment looks like in multiple contexts, teachers will be better equipped to think through these questions for themselves and with their colleagues. In this chapter we have made the case that teachers should think about disclosing and withholding their views as pedagogical tools that can have a profound effect on classroom dynamics. For the most part, teachers who make good decisions about when and how to share their political views are first and foremost setting a tone of fairness and mutual respect in the classroom. They welcome the diverse views of their students, and they deliberately resist the values of the polarized political sphere. Relatedly, these teachers strive to create a classroom community engaged in inquiry about the focal question of the political classroom, "How should we live together?" And, to that end, they structure learning so that students do much of the intellectual work. These teachers remind students that discussions benefit dramatically when participants cite solid evidence, employ logical reasoning, consider issues with concern for fairness and not pure self-interest, and, most importantly, engage with one another. We notice also that teachers who make explicit to students what their policies are around withholding and disclosing and, when appropriate, explain why they are making a different choice at a particular moment help alleviate some of the student confusion about this issue. Finally, teachers who share in ways that are unintentional or that simply take up air time are not furthering the aims of the political classroom. Instead, they are diverting students from articulating their own views and creating an atmosphere that diminishes, rather than enhances, the power of discussion.

Notes

1 At the university level, in a study of 24 undergraduate political science courses at 24 different colleges and universities, Matthew Woessner and April Kelly-Woessner (2009) found that while the students moved slightly toward support for the Democratic Party from the beginning to the end of the course, that movement was not correlated with the political views of the professors, suggesting that factors beyond the classroom were motivating partisan shifts. It is important to note that 75% of the professors in this study said that they "rarely" or "never" discuss their partisan affiliation in class, but two-thirds of students were able to correctly identify their professor's party affiliation at the end of the course (p. 346). Students who reported regularly following politics were more likely to correctly identify the professor's party. In earlier studies, Kelly-Woessner and Woessner (2006, 2008) found that students who held views opposed to the professors' views were more likely to be critical of the course, reporting in their evaluations that they had learned little from the course.

2 Testing for whether students become significantly more in line with their teacher's ideology, we found no evidence that these students who felt they were likely to change their minds were becoming more like their teacher. However, we cannot say whether students adopted their teacher's views on particular issues, because we cannot say precisely which views a teacher shared.

3 As part of a national Teacher Survey the Commission on Youth Voting and Civic Knowledge (2013) distributed for the report *All together now: Collaboration and innovation for youth engagement*, the commission found that 65% of teachers try to keep their views to themselves. This finding did not appear in the report.

4 We recognize that many, many scholars have argued and observed that schools are not and should not be neutral. Our point here is to note the particular values promoted in the political classroom.

5 Chantal Mouffe (2000), for example, critiques deliberative democracy and argues for "agonistic democracy," which conceives of democracy as a struggle for power among competing ideologies.

10

SUPPORTING THE POLITICAL CLASSROOM

The Discussion of Controversial Issues Study was developed with advice from high school teachers, professors, and leaders of organizations that design and run programs to support civic learning in schools. These experts provided concrete and highly valuable guidance about what we should seek to learn from the study in light of our overarching goal: to improve both the quality and quantity of democratic education during a political era marked by rapid change and significant challenges. Our readers will be the judges of how well we have met that goal.

In this conclusion, we look to the future and address the question, "What should be done to make it more likely that young people will receive a high-quality democratic education?" Specifically, we aim for an education in which young people are actively engaged in the project of figuring out the central question of the political classroom, "How should we live together?" Throughout the book, we have shown—vividly, we hope—many examples of what such an approach to democratic education looks like in practice. We also have concentrated on some of the most important ethical issues that arise for teachers in the political classroom and have contended that the best professional judgments about such issues will be made by thoughtful consideration of aims, context, and evidence.

In Chapter 1, we addressed a paradox about political education that undergirds much of what makes this enterprise so difficult. This paradox can be simply described, but it is by no means simple. On the one hand, we need to provide students with a nonpartisan political education; at the same time, we seek to teach young people how to participate in the highly partisan arena of real-world politics. And we are undertaking this enterprise in schools that mirror many of the political, economic, and social dynamics that permeate the communities in which they are situated.

One of the effects of increasing political polarization in the United States is that the public lacks trust in many core institutions of democracy, including schools.

Recall that one recent study reported that 50% of Americans think that social studies teachers use their classrooms as political soapboxes (Lautzenheiser, Kelly, & Miller, 2011). When we observed what the teachers in this study actually did in their classrooms we find little evidence for the public's concern. In fact, the overwhelming majority of students in our study do not think their teachers are trying to convince them to adopt particular positions on the controversial political issues that they discussed in class.

But in this time of intense political polarization, we hear concerns from some teachers that they are not as trusted as they need to be by parents or the general public to create a politically fair classroom. We especially hear this concern from students in teacher-education programs and from novice teachers, who are often surprised by the types of issues students discuss in the classrooms we have focused on in this book. As Ms. Heller reported to us, teachers at other schools are often shocked when she describes the legislative simulation that is required for all seniors at her school: "You let them talk about *what?!* You let them write a bill about *what?!* You let them express *what* opinion?!" It is hard to tell whether the teachers who react this way are concerned that students cannot handle such controversial issues or that by bringing these controversial topics into the curriculum, teachers are opening themselves (and the school more broadly) to criticism. Either way, the upshot of this line of reasoning is likely the same, which is to strip the curriculum of the very political controversies that lie at the heart of questions about how we ought to live together.

The contemporary political climate will make it more difficult for teachers to infuse their classes with discussions of controversial political issues. Consequently, in this concluding chapter we advocate actions that we hope will support and sustain the political classroom, focusing principally on what teachers can do.

It is clear to us that a teacher's knowledge, pedagogical skills, and professional judgment are critical factors in the success of the political classroom. Based on the practice of teachers in the study, we have recommendations for educators who seek to create dynamic and successful political classrooms. Even though there were important differences in the contexts in which they taught, the missions of their schools, and the backgrounds of their students, the teachers who were consistently able to engage their students in Best Practice Discussion are similar in some key respects.

First and foremost, these educators are learners themselves. They are unusually well-informed about the fast-changing content knowledge necessary to teach in the political classroom and are always on the lookout for new materials and forms of pedagogy that will engage and stimulate their students. Second, they have ambitious aims for what they want their students to learn, and they possess the pedagogical skills to realize these aims. Third, they pay close attention to their students: They make a concerted effort to create a safe environment that encourages participation, and they correct students when they make other members of the class feel uncomfortable. Fourth, they find ways to work in collaboration with other teachers.

Teachers as Professionals

In highly effective schools, teachers are viewed as professionals. What does this mean? In a new book on professionalism in education, medicine, and social services, Douglas Mitchell and Robert Ream (in press) argue that "professional work is skilled, complex, requires extensive preparation, and is grounded in the establishment of a trusting relationship between the professionals and their clients." Moreover, they note that virtually all conceptions of professionalism emphasize "a moral or ethical imperative at its core." Thus, if a school aims to treat teachers as professionals, we would expect that those they hire would be well prepared and possess considerable expertise. We would further expect that more experienced teachers and administrators would take responsibility for helping teachers with less experience develop expertise. Teachers who are treated as professionals are granted substantial authority (which should not be confused with complete autonomy), expected to work deliberatively with colleagues to make important curricular decisions, provided high-quality opportunities for professional development, and held accountable for the quality of their decisions and for what students are learning. This conception of teachers as professionals stands in contrast to the image of teachers as autonomous individuals who are able to close their classroom door and exercise free reign. While these characteristics of teacher professionalism clearly cut across grade level and subject, we learned a great deal about what they look like in the political classroom.

Teachers as Learners

Knowledge is continually being constructed; thus, all teachers need to be conversant with what is happening in their field. In social studies, this need is even more pronounced given the responsibility of social studies teachers to help students "read the world." In the political classroom, the emphasis on teaching students how to deliberate controversial issues that are authentic to the contemporary political world increases content demands even further. Since these issues are, quite literally, always changing, teachers need to focus consistently and continually on staying abreast of the issues.

The strongest teachers in our study were incredibly well-informed and devoted a significant amount of time to keeping up with contemporary issues. Recall that one of the teachers at Adams High School reported spending two to three hours *daily* consuming news in order to stay on top of the bills that students were developing for the legislative simulation. It is clear how this up-to-date content knowledge put Mr. Hempstead in a strong position to assist his students in searching for and obtaining reliable information: "I would end up researching every bill along with the kids. And [I'd] say, 'Have you seen this website? Have you checked out this argument?'"

But teachers were doing more than keeping up with current issues. We were struck by how deeply interested teachers were in *ideas* broadly defined and how conversant they were with new scholarship about the content they taught and about teaching and learning. They were also voracious readers of newspapers, blogs, and news websites. During our interviews, teachers often spoke about new books they were reading; beyond this, we frequently saw evidence of recent content being incorporated in their classes.

Clarity About Aims

The strongest teachers that we interviewed also had clearly articulated educational aims for their students. As Mr. Kushner, Mr. Walters, and the teachers at Adams High demonstrate in Part II of this book, these aims are not simply goals for covering content or developing academic skill; instead, these teachers were thoughtful about the democratic values and dispositions they were trying to develop in their students. The teacher cases also show that the teachers identified their aims with attention to their particular school contexts. Mr. Walters, for example, taught in an evangelical Christian school and he walked a fine line between developing his students' ability to think critically in the political sphere while also adhering to the religious values of the community to which both he and the students belonged. Skillful teachers are able to align their pedagogical approaches and curriculum toward the development of justifiable aims.

In Chapter 4, we identified the six aims we think ought to guide practice in the political classroom (see Table 8.1 for a summary list), and argued, throughout the book, that one aspect of professional judgment is learning how to reason well about which aims matter more in particular teaching moments and in particular school contexts. It is not the case that all six aims carry equal weight at all times. As we showed in Chapters 8 and 9, teachers need to keep these aims in mind when faced with curricular choices and ethical dilemmas that require judgment and to prioritize and reprioritize their aims in light of new evidence and with attention to the needs of their students.

We recognize that we are describing complicated intellectual work, but, if teachers are to be viewed as professionals, it is necessary work. We hope that by featuring teachers engaged in this type of professional reflection and showing moments of skill and moments of risk-taking that others will be better prepared to respond to the issues that arise in their classrooms and to engage in curricular discussions with their colleagues.

Deliberation

The image of the go-it-alone teacher is often lionized in popular films, and some teachers operate this way effectively. While some teachers are thrust into this position against their will and yearn for more direction about what the curriculum should comprise, others believe that they deserve complete authority and that anyone who tells them otherwise is improperly invading their professional space.

It is not uncommon to hear such teachers proclaim, "When I close my classroom door, I should be able to do whatever I want." The conception of the role of teachers as fully autonomous is problematic because it is based on the idea that a curriculum developed by one person is better than a course of study developed by many—an idea that we think is misguided. Professionals work in communities of practice and learn with and from their colleagues about how best to approach educational aims, content, and skills. It is even more important to engage in genuine deliberation about what and how to teach with others who have professional expertise and understand one's teaching context. Ideally, this deliberation is done with the benefit of some empirical evidence about what students are learning and in what ways.

We also find it foolish to reduce the teacher's role to one of simply enacting curriculum decisions made by others. Viewing teachers simply as "deliverers" of curriculum that others have developed is exceedingly problematic because it denigrates the root purposes of education and denies the state and students the benefit of teacher expertise and professional judgment. As students and teachers know, education differs from training. Why worry about hiring teachers with strong pedagogical skills and content expertise if they are merely delivering a script? For that role, one would need acting training, not deep knowledge of the subject and of how students learn. Moreover, stripping teachers from involvement in curriculum decision-making extracts from their role the very facet that many teachers find the most interesting about their profession because it demands their expertise and judgment. What is more, recent research indicates that when teachers lose the authority to make the decisions that their professional training prepared them to make, they are far less likely to remain in teaching.[1]

It is also unwise for teachers to think and act as if they are the only people who should influence what students learn. Instead, there are powerful reasons to vest teachers with the freedom to engage in decision-making about what and how to teach. There is a concomitant responsibility for teachers to take up that role seriously and at multiple levels. In our view, curricular decision-making is most effective when done in collaboration and by teachers who have up-to-date content and pedagogical knowledge. Teachers have a responsibility to recognize that as professionals, their expertise about content, pedagogy, and their students make it not just acceptable but essential for them to participate in decisions about what and how to teach. Thus, it is professionally irresponsible to withdraw from the frequently challenging deliberative space of curricular decision-making in decisions about what students should learn and in what ways.

Clearly, there are differences between and within states (and even school districts) about how much control individual teachers have over the curriculum in the courses they teach. In some states and districts, there are very specific standards (and often pacing guides to accompany them) and/or high-stakes exams. In those states, districts, and schools, teachers often have limited authority to determine what content their students will learn. But in all of these cases, some group is making decisions about what should be taught—and it is essential for teachers to participate in this process. Still, in many schools (including most that were in our study), teachers have quite a lot of freedom to determine what to teach and in what ways. While they may be mandated to teach a unit on civil rights movements in a history class, or on the Supreme Court in a government course, the precise nature of what they teach and how they teach it is still within their decision-making bailiwick. So for these teachers, the main challenge is not how to gain authority to influence curriculum decisions but how to best exercise the authority that they have.

The Role of School Administrators

While it is clear that teachers bear much of the responsibility for creating a political classroom that works well for all students, others have a role to play in the process as well. The support of school administrators is key. One of the reasons many teachers in our study reported so little pushback from parents and other community members when they included controversial political issues in their classes was that they had the support of their department chairs and principals— who could then serve as a front line of support. The teachers had carefully cultivated this support by making sure that administrators knew what they were doing and why. At Adams High School, for example, where teachers created a legislative simulation involving multiple course sections, there were a few days during the semester when students were pulled out of other classes to participate in the Full Sessions of the simulation. We suspect this would not be allowed in some schools because it would be seen as too disruptive to the regular schedule. But at Adams High School, administrators supported the unique approach that teachers had developed and went to great lengths to ensure that it would work. In other schools, administrators demonstrated their support by allocating funds so that students could attend multi-school deliberations or by providing release time and substitute teachers so that instructors could attend professional-development workshops and conferences.

The Role of Intermediary Organizations

One strategy used by teachers to ensure that their students were exposed to many different perspectives was to take students to multi-school deliberative events. As noted previously, we studied numerous classes in Illinois and Indiana that were participating in either the Illinois Youth Summit or the Indiana or Illinois Capitol Forum. Of the 35 teachers and 1,001 students in the sample, nine teachers and 49 students attended one of these statewide deliberations, and 188 students experienced the classroom curriculum that is part of each program.

The teachers' primary motivation for involving their students in these events was to provide an opportunity for students to engage with points of view that were not always represented in the student body of their school. For example, students from a range of strikingly different schools and communities attended the Illinois Capitol Forum: these included an evangelical Christian school, a small school in a farming community, an urban all-girls Catholic school, a comprehensive high school in a university community, and another school in an upper-middle-class suburb. While it is crucial to note that there was ideological diversity within the classes we studied, there were striking differences from class to class and from school to school that were especially important for students (and their teachers) to be exposed to and to consider thoughtfully and respectfully. Mr. Walters, whose classes in a religious school are the focus of Chapter 4, said he took his students to the Capitol Forum as a way to help prepare them for the broader secular world they were likely to encounter in college and the workplace. Mr. Dunn, one of the teachers discussed in Chapters 8 and 9, felt that interacting with different types of people was one of the most powerful aspects of the Youth Summit. He explained,

> What I think they get out of it is realizing that there are other people their age in the area and in the city who are smart and curious and care about these issues. So . . . it is almost like the creation of a new context for peer pressure, for peer pressure in a positive way, for handling teenagers and talking about political issues. [I]t sets up the examples and this is a good thing. It is interesting and worthwhile for them to do.

Similarly, students who participated in the forums and summits wanted to hear the views of other young people and appreciated realizing that there are multiple and competing ways to frame and resolve issues. Often the very simple realization that their views are not the "only" or even the "best" views was important to students. For example, a college senior who had participated in the Choices program as a high school student reflected in a follow-up phone interview,

> We would, by chance, have to assume different roles, so even if you didn't necessarily agree with one side it was a neat and fun challenge to think in the other person's perspective, and through that you gain a sense of empathy, which becomes extremely important as you go on to college and encounter people with different views. It also helps your argument if you're debating and have to see an argument from both sides.

Another student reported that she was not used to airing and interrogating multiple opinions within a discussion. "In my family," she explained, "we don't do multiple perspectives." She went on to say that the Choices session enabled her to feel comfortable speaking and listening. Another student extended this point:

> It was just really nice to hear different perspectives. Like, definitely the kids from the inner city and the kids from out in the country [had] totally different

worldviews from here in the suburbs. There is something in the middle, I guess. It was just interesting to talk to people who were genuinely interested in these issues.

When young people were asked to reflect upon their experiences at the Summit, the most common reaction was that they appreciated the diversity of participants. Students enjoyed having the opportunity to discuss controversial issues with peers from different backgrounds and who hold opinions different from their own. As one student from a charter school described it,

> I met some really cool suburban kids. I didn't know there were so many out there . . . you know, because I am an inner-city youth. And I really don't get exposed to those suburban kids or anything. So it was really cool to see how, well, they were primarily White—that was really cool to see how I can relate in some ways to White students that are not from the city.

Another student from a suburban school expressed similar views: "It was a lot of fun to go there with other schools and to see their viewpoints on certain things. Because I think a lot of it has to do with where your school is located and the type of people you are going to school with on how you are going to have an opinion about something."

These experiences are clearly powerful for the students, but we note that they are equally valuable for teachers. The educators who participate expand their professional networks to teachers across the state, and they acquire new pedagogical strategies and current resources that influence their practice. Gaining access to these resources is one reason that teachers chose to participate. Further, preparing students to engage in large-scale deliberations about political issues often required the teachers to collaborate about curricular planning and to deliberate about how best to represent competing political views and make sure that all voices were being heard, and these are the types of deliberations we would hope teachers also have in their schools. Last, the connections made during these events are important for improving pedagogical skills and for developing a professional identity.

To Close

The goal of the political classroom is to be as authentic as possible to the real-world political environment in which we hope young people will engage without contributing to the many problems that mark contemporary democracy. Meeting this challenge is difficult in all the venues in which young people are learning how to take their place on the democratic stage. But as we have seen throughout the book, schools provide both unique and positive opportunities for democratic education, as well as some significant challenges.

At a moment when teaching is often conceptualized as short-term missionary work, it is striking to us that the teachers we studied were not passing through on the way to another career. Instead, they had invested considerable time and money in their initial preparation and ongoing professional education, and they worked continually to improve their practice—even as some of the supports in their schools dwindled and the needs of their students increased. Why did these educators make this commitment? Quite simply, because they *like* teaching and recognize that their work is important. They take pride in their professional expertise. We do not want to give the impression that the teachers we studied were unaware of or unaffected by the challenges that are commonplace in the daily lives of educators. In fact, a number were activists in their schools and communities. But the most effective teachers in our study did not see themselves as martyrs or victims. Quite the opposite—they viewed themselves as dedicated professionals doing an important job that they found interesting and challenging. They respected and believed in their students, and their students respected and believed in them. In an era when the challenges to self-government are steep and mounting, the teachers in these political classrooms had not given up on the power of education or on the promise of democracy. Neither should we.

Note

1 See Hess, D. (2010). Teachers and academic freedom: Gaining right defacto. *Social Education, 74*(2), 316–321.

AFTERWORD

Teaching is a profession without a well-articulated ethic. This is not entirely a bad thing. Professional ethics can never be fine-grained enough to guide action in every circumstance a practitioner finds herself in, and rough-grained statements can often be unhelpful: Does the "do no harm" clause of the Hippocratic Oath require a doctor who has no anesthetic available to allow a patient to die slowly and agonizingly when she could, instead, administer a lethal injection? This is a question that at least requires rigorous exploration. But the medical profession has, over the past 50 years, developed a rich set of intellectual and institutional resources for exploring the moral questions left unanswered by their formal ethic. Journals of medical ethics abound, and professional magazines and journals routinely take up ethical debates in a way that is informed by contributions to those journals; classes in medical ethics form part of the training of almost all physicians and nurses; all hospitals have Ethics Boards that inform both hospital policy and individual practice. The National Bioethics Advisory Commission in 1996 was replaced by the President's Council on Bioethics in 2001, which was, in turn, replaced by the Presidential Commission for the Study of Bioethical Issues in 2009.

Educational professionals have fewer resources and, in particular, far fewer institutions charged with bringing the expertise of practitioners and scholars together. Philosophy of education as a field has been conducted at an unhealthy distance from the problems of professional practice; there are no analogues of ethics boards; and no president has authorized a commission on educational ethics.

Teachers rarely face life-and-death issues, it is true. But the work of the teacher involves constant, and consequential, decision-making. *The Political Classroom* is an essential contribution to the development for educators of intellectual resources as rich as those the medical profession has for considering ethical issues of practice.

It focuses our attention on three of these questions that social studies teachers all face: how to decide which topics to present as controversial political issues; how teachers should balance the tension between engaging students in authentic political controversies and creating a classroom climate that is fair and welcoming to all students; and whether teachers should share their own political views about the issues that they introduce as controversial.

The Political Classroom is exemplary in its combination of philosophical thinking and careful empirical social science. Moral problems are fundamentally philosophical. We cannot derive an "ought" from an "is": Empirical social science cannot decide fundamentally moral questions. One way to think about philosophy is as the systematic exploration of questions for which neither empirical science nor mathematics can provide answers. If teachers are to develop a well-articulated professional ethic, they will need to use philosophical reasoning.

Now, one parodic picture of philosophical reasoning is exemplified by Rodin's *The Thinker:* a single, solitary person consulting reason without regard to the experiences or perspectives of anyone else, and without attention to evidence about the world, and coming up with a rational framework that can cover all cases.

The picture, however pervasive (and maybe flattering), is quite wrong. While scientific evidence cannot *decide* moral questions, individuals unequipped with knowledge of the world, and drawing only on their own experiences and perspectives, cannot make much progress, however smart, and however rational, they are. In fact, philosophizing about moral matters requires extensive collaboration and careful attention to the detail and contexts of decisions. Progress is achieved through careful, interpersonal deliberation in much the way that we go about developing frameworks for scientific understanding. Each of us has different experiences which both give us different insights into the moral truth as well as creating different blind spots; the hope is that through a process of what philosophers call "wide reflective equilibrium" of offering reasons among diverse but reasonable interlocutors, we can get closer to the truth. We consider specific cases where choices have to be made and offer one another reasons for making one choice rather than the other; those reasons are refined, or countered, and we see whether they generalize to be able to help us with different kinds of cases. The best evidence we can get for claims about what we ought to do are the reasons that survive careful scrutiny through this process. Even in collaboration this process is limited if the participants are all alike—all White, or male, or atheist, or working in an elite university setting. The more diverse the participants in terms of their sex, race, ethnicity, religion, professional life, and personal experience, the more reason we have to accept the reasons that survive it.

A striking feature of the interviews in *The Political Classroom* is that, with the exception of the Adams High teachers, the teachers seem to have done much of their thinking about the framework they bring to their decisions about, for example, whether to disclose their views and whether to advocate, in a fairly solitary way. They have arrived at quite different conclusions, and in some cases it is easy to imagine that, had they been able to converse with the *other* subjects over the course of their professional development, they might have drawn somewhat different conclusions and engaged in somewhat different practice.

This is not a criticism of the teachers. Individual teachers are not to blame for the lacunae in their profession's practices. I have spent 22 years teaching undergraduates about controversial moral issues, and, like the teachers portrayed in the preceding pages, most of my own reflection about the difficult moral decisions I make about issues like disclosure has been solitary, and that is precisely because the profession to which I belong lacks an ethic and a practice of collaborative discussion of instructional matters. When Diana Hess and Paula McAvoy were first working on the book, they designed three day-long deliberations, each concerned with one of the specific normative questions of the book, and recruited distinguished scholars and teachers from a range of related disciplines to deliberate about the questions in the light of the research they had done. For me, involvement in these unusual and outstandingly helpful discussions was the first time I had thought systematically about these issues with anyone other than my own students; the discussions were a perfect model of how to conduct careful collaborative normative investigation.

The Political Classroom provides two key resources that educators and scholars need in order to think well about the ethical questions the book addresses. First, it provides rich empirical research. We learn how different teachers have struggled with the ethical questions they face and see how they have resolved those questions, often by reference to contingent features of their particular context. We also learn what the students think about the issues; what they think teachers are doing; what they think the effects of those actions are; and what they think teachers should be doing. We see, plainly, the reasoning teachers give for making exceptions to the rules they give themselves and, sometimes, see how well their practice and their ethics match up. The reader is, therefore, brought inevitably into conversation with the teachers; and that conversation is informed, on the reader's side, by the perceptions of the students.

The second essential resource is the elaboration of the ethical concepts framed in terms of the purposes, or aims, of education. *The Political Classroom* treats the ethical questions it addresses not as matters of whim or personal preference but offers us a set of values to use when exploring the questions. Now, it does not attempt to *settle* the questions; and rightly so, because the book opens up debates that no two authors can expect to settle alone without extended conversation with a diverse set of interlocutors. Educators need a professional ethic, but that professional ethic cannot be stipulated early in the conversation; it must arise from the process that *The Political Classroom* makes possible, a process that must involve a wide range of stakeholders, including, crucially, teachers themselves. The book is a service to the profession; a service performed with respect for the essential contribution teachers will make to the necessary debates.

I have two hopes for *The Political Classroom*. Good philosophical scholarship about education needs to be attentive to empirical detail in order to ask the right questions; and good empirical work, if it seeks to be valuable for practitioners, needs to pertain to the right ethical questions. The authors know what ethical questions to ask, and they understand what resources we need to make progress on those questions. My first hope, then, is that both empirical social scientists and philosophers concerned with education will emulate the kind of work being done here. My second is that it will be widely read by educators and that they will see it as the valuable resource that it is and use it in a process of collaborative reflection through which the profession *itself* can develop the kind of ethic it needs and the society it serves needs to have.

Harry Brighouse

APPENDIX

Methodology

In this appendix, we provide greater detail about the methods used in the Discussing Controversial Issues Study. We have also made more data displays available at: http://www.routledge.com/political_classroom/.

This is a mixed methods study, and at each stage of analysis, quantitative and qualitative data and analytic techniques were used to interpret findings and inform further data collection. In the discussion below, we separate the quantitative from the qualitative to clarify how each data set was developed and analyzed. Ethical reasoning also became an important part of our methodology and focus of this book. It was used in all parts of the analysis, but we include a separate section to clarify how we approached this part of the project.

Research Questions

1. How do high school students experience and learn from participating in social studies courses that emphasize the discussion of controversial international and/or domestic issues?
2. Do such discussions influence students' political and civic participation after they leave high school? If so, what are the pathways to participation?

Points of Contact

1. Baseline: This survey was administered during the spring of 2005 to 250 students. This point-in-time survey was given toward the end of the course and contained 86 questions.
2. Pre-course survey: Based on the findings from the baseline survey and the first round of student interviews, the team developed pre- and post-course surveys

that were used during the 2005–2006 school year and again in 2008. The pre-course survey was administered during the first two weeks of the course and contained 86 questions from the Baseline and an additional 22 questions that asked about views on international policy, Hurricane Katrina, classroom discussion (including items about teacher disclosure), and plans after high school. A total of 749 students took the pre-course survey.

3. Post-course survey: This survey was administered in the last two weeks of the course and consisted of 114 questions. In addition to the pre-course survey questions, it included measures of open classroom climate, and a series of teacher disclosure items. A total of 525 students took the post-course survey.

4. Teacher survey: Teachers were given a single survey that included 72 questions. Nearly all questions aligned with questions on the student surveys. Surveys asked about views on particular political issues, opinions about disclosure, levels of political participation, and attitudes toward classroom discussion. All 35 teachers completed a teacher survey, though the survey was expanded after the baseline year to include disclosure items and other questions added to the student survey.

5. Follow-up phone interviews: We contracted with the University of Wisconsin Survey Center to conduct two rounds of telephone interviews. The first was completed in 2007 with 401 participants. The second was completed in 2009 with 369 participants. These interviews lasted about 20 minutes and consisted of closed questions and several open-ended questions asking about what they remembered about the course. The closed questions asked about their political views, levels of civic and political engagement, news consumption, electoral behaviors, engagement with social media and gaming, and party affiliations. Of these participants, 95% had completed high school. We were able to obtain parent and student consent for participation in the follow-up interviews from just over 600 students from the first two years of data collection. Consequently, while our overall response rate of 401 follow-up interviews (after high school) was roughly 40% of the total sample at that time, it was more than 70% the portion of the sample that we could have drawn from, given the consent situation.

Constructing the Sample

In the spring semester of 2005, we selected schools in Illinois and Indiana, where at least one social studies teacher in each school was participating in a deliberation project coordinated by one of two democracy education non-profit organizations: The Constitutional Rights Foundation Chicago's Illinois Youth Summit and the Choices for the 21st Century Education Program's Capitol Forum. Both of these programs provide professional development for teachers, written curricula on international (Choices for the 21st Century) or domestic (Constitutional Rights Foundation Chicago) issues that utilize deliberation as a primary pedagogical strategy, and provide opportunities for students to deliberate with peers from other schools at statewide events. In order to create a comparison group, we also recruited teachers in the same school who primarily taught using lectures.

During the 2005–06 school year, we retained some of the teachers from the first year, but broadened our sample to a third state (Wisconsin). We recruited additional teachers in Wisconsin and Illinois who reported engaging their students in issues discussions using other curricula or materials they developed. We decided to broaden the sample to capture a wider range of how teachers design and execute discussions of controversial political issues. As in the year before, we also recruited a comparison groups of teachers who lecture.

During the 2007–08 year, we returned to Academy High for more data collection, because it had become clear that this was a particularly interesting case of Best Practice Discussion teaching in what we call a Like-Minded School. We also added another evangelical Christian school to increase our private school sample, and as it turned out, this school also contributed to the like-minded findings that we described in Chapter 7.

Limitations of the Data Set

There are at several important limitations in our study that relate to our sample. The first is that a range of 50–90% of students in each class participated in the study. We made every effort to assess whether the students from each class who elected to participate were roughly representative of the gender, race, ethnicity, and political ideology of the class as a whole. The sample, in fact, was very similar to the classes from which it was drawn, with a slight overrepresentation of females and European Whites. We lost a slightly higher percentage of students of color from the pre- to post-course surveys and from the post survey to the follow-up survey than was the case with European/White students. Table A.1 shows the race and ethnicity of the sample at each point of contact.

As the study progressed, there was selective attrition of students of immigrant origin, students of color, and those who came from less affluent families. That is, significantly fewer students who were in one or more of these categories either had a consent/assent to be interviewed in the follow-up phase or were not interviewed for other reasons (such as unavailability of most recent contact information, refusal to be interviewed upon contact). The selective attrition was higher among students of lower socioeconomic status (SES), many of whom were also students of immigrant origin and/or of color. As a result, the follow-up sample is skewed toward students of high SES who were also born in the United States. Table A.2 summarizes the mean and median socioeconomic index score of participants and portion of students who reported that they were not born in the United States.

The selective attrition by students' immigrant origin, race, and SES indirectly affected how students from different types of classrooms were retained in the study. Although there were no significant differences in average SES between

TABLE A.1 Race and Ethnicity of Students at Each Wave

Wave	White, Non-Hispanic (%)	Latino/ Hispanic (%)	African American, Non-Hispanic (%)	Asian American, Non-Hispanic (%)	American Indian, Non-Hispanic (%)	Other, Non-Hispanic (%)	Total
Baseline	77.9	6.8	2.8	7.2	0.4	4.8	249
Pre-Survey	76.2	9.7	4.3	3.1	1.4	4.5	845
Post-Survey	79.6	8.3	4.6	2.3	1.5	3.7	520
Follow-Up 1	83.2	5.5	2.5	2.8	1.3	3.8	395
Follow-Up 2	87.1	4.9	1.1	2.7	0.8	3.3	365

Note: The values in parentheses are percentages. The Baseline is the point-in-time survey administered in the Spring of 2005.

TABLE A.2 Socioeconomic Characteristics of Students By Wave

Wave	Mean SES	Median SES	Born Outside of the U.S. (%)
Baseline	.18	.23	6.0
Pre-Survey	−01	.04	8.1
Post-Survey	.01	.05	6.9
Follow-up 1	.18	.25	5.3
Follow-up 2	.20	.32	5.2

Note: The Baseline is the point-in-time survey administered in the Spring of 2005.

classroom practices as a group, the Best Practice Discussion classroom students were significantly more likely to be students of color and/or not born in the United States. Thus, the selective attrition in this group resulted in uneven attrition from different types of classrooms. That is, Best Practice classrooms lost many members who were either students of color or of immigrant origin, and who also had relatively low socioeconomic status as a subgroup. This attrition resulted in even more selective retention in the Best Practice Discussion classrooms, and to a certain extent, Lecture classrooms than Discussion classrooms. Thus, the selective attrition by socioeconomic status in the follow-up sample is further confounded by classroom practice type.

Analysis of Classroom Effects

In order to assess the effect of learning in a specific environment, such as a classroom that is rated Best Practice Discussion or school that is like-minded, we chose to use multiple linear regression. For each model, we entered the independent variable of interest (e.g., classroom practice) as a dummy-coded variable and entered control variables (socioeconomic status, gender, citizenship status, race, and prior-civic exposure). We reported the major findings of the multiple linear regressions in Chapter 3, Table 3.2. Tables A.3, A.4, A.5, and A.6 report the outputs of this analysis. In each case, Best Practice Discussion and Discussion courses were compared to post-course survey changes in the Lecture classes.

TABLE A.3 Post-Course Survey Comparison: Classroom Discussion

	Deliberative values	Discussion efficacy	Good at group work	Share ideas in class
Dep. variable name	sdiscscr_2	pdiscrs_2	q33_2	q35_2
Classroom practice				
Best Practice Discussion	0.15	0.18	−0.05	0.1
	[0.11]	[0.10]+	[0.09]	[0.10]
Discussion	0.08	0.15	−0.07	−0.01
	[0.12]	[0.11]	[0.10]	[0.10]
Demographics				
SES	0.15	0.04	0.05	0.07
	[0.06]*	[0.06]	[0.05]	[0.06]
Black	−0.14	0.27	0.19	0.21
	[0.17]	[0.16]+	[0.15]	[0.15]
Hispanic	0.06	0.03	0.14	0.08
	[0.16]	[0.15]	[0.14]	[0.14]
Female	0.03	−0.24	0.04	−0.13
	[0.08]	[0.07]**	[0.07]	[0.07]
Noncitizen	0.01	0.1	−0.07	0.29
	[0.17]	[0.16]	[0.14]	[0.15]
Other characteristics				
Ideological Scale	−0.12	−0.07	<0.01	0.02
	[0.06]*	[0.05]	[0.05]	[0.05]
Prior-Civic Exposure Index	0.14	0.47	0.04	0.4
	[0.06]*	[0.06]**	[0.05]	[0.06]**
Age	−0.11	−0.09	0.04	−0.01
	[0.06]*	[0.05]	[0.05]	[0.05]
Constant	6.655	5.26	2.54	3.06
	[0.77]**	[0.91]**	[0.83]**	[0.87]**
R^2	0.07	0.19	0.02	0.15
N	445	462	455	451

Note: +p < 0.10; * p < 0.05; ** p < 0.01

TABLE A.4 Post-Course Survey Comparison: News & Political Talk Outcomes

Dependent variable	Frequency of news discussion	Frequency follow news	Total news consumption: breadth and frequency	Political talk with friends	Political talk with parents	Political disagreement in conversation	Listen when disagree
Dep. var. name	disnewsfreq_2	snewsfreq_2	sgrandsumnews.2	q40_2	q41_2	q42_2	q43_2
Classroom Practice							
Best Practice Discussion	0.21	0.22	0.34	0.18	0.01	0.34	0.32
	[0.12]	[0.12]+	[0.24]	[0.14]	[0.15]	[0.15]*	[0.16]*
Discussion	0.23	0.21	0.34	0.18	0.13	0.34	0.24
	[0.13]	[0.13]	[0.26]	[0.15]	[0.16]	[0.16]*	[0.17]
Demographics							
SES	0.17	0.16	0.32	0.26	0.24	0.17	0
	[0.07]*	[0.07]*	[0.14]*	[0.08]**	[0.09]**	[0.09]+	[0.09]
Black	0	0	0.03	-0.49	0.43	0.27	-0.03
	[0.19]	[0.19]	[0.37]	[0.22]*	[0.24]+	[0.24]	[0.25]
Hispanic	-0.08	-0.01	0.2	-0.03	-0.1	-0.22	0.1
	[0.18]	[0.17]	[0.35]	[0.21]	[0.22]	[0.22]	[0.23]
Female	-0.15	-0.09	-0.21	-0.28	0.02	-0.2	-0.21
	[0.09]	[0.09]	[0.18]	[0.10]**	[0.11]	[0.11]+	[0.12]+
Noncitizen	0.35	0.13	0.18	0.57	0.7	0.24	0
	[0.19]	[0.18]	[0.37]	[0.22]**	[0.23]**	[0.23]	[0.24]

Other Characteristics

Ideological Scale	-0.09	-0.05	-0.11	-0.1	-0.12	-0.04	-0.06
	[0.07]	[0.06]	[0.13]	[0.08]	[0.08]	[0.08]	[0.08]
Prior-Civic Exposure Index	0.42	0.25	0.52	0.47	0.47	0.43	0.49
	[0.07]**	[0.06]**	[0.14]**	[0.08]**	[0.09]**	[0.08]**	[0.09]**
Age	-0.08	-0.13	-0.3	-0.01	-0.19	-0.02	-0.08
	[0.07]	[0.06]*	[0.12]*	[0.07]	[0.08]*	[0.08]	[0.08]
Constant	2.93	4.44	8.63	2.13	5.42	2.13	3.26
	[0.87]**	[1.06]**	[2.15]**	[1.27]+	[1.37]**	[1.37]	[1.42]**
R²	0.16	0.08	0.08	0.18	0.14	0.12	0.1
N	459	453	453	453	452	451	444

Note: +p < 0.10; * p < 0.05; ** p < 0.01

TABLE A.5 Post-Course Survey Comparison: Knowledge & Interest

Dependent variable	General knowledge score	Democracy knowledge score	Interesting issues	More interest in politics because of class
Dep.var. name	gknow_2rev	dknow_2rev	q1_2rc	q14_2
Classroom Practice				
Best Practice Discussion	0.23	0.02	−0.07	0.38
	[0.14]+	[0.15]	[0.11]	[0.10]**
Discussion	0.16	0.49	−0.39	0.17
	[0.15]	[0.17]**	[0.12]**	[0.11]
Demographics				
SES	0.22	0.47	0.07	0.05
	[0.08]**	[0.09]**	[0.07]	[0.06]
Black	−0.46	−0.48	0.43	0.13
	[0.22]*	[0.24]*	[0.17]*	[0.16]
Hispanic	−0.44	−0.29	0.39	0.16
	[0.20]*	[0.22]	[0.16]*	[0.15]
Female	−0.14	−0.01	−0.19	−0.1
	[0.10]	[0.11]	[0.08]*	[0.07]
Noncitizen	−0.38	−0.14	−0.17	−0.35
	[0.21]+	[0.23]	[0.17]	[0.15]*
Other Characteristics				
Ideological Scale	0.15	−0.32	0.02	0.04
	[0.07]*	[0.08]**	[0.06]	[0.05]
Prior-Civic Exposure Index	0.24	0.33	0.34	0.11
	[0.05]**	[0.08]**	[0.06]**	[0.05]*
Age	0.24	0.01	0.31	0.09
	[0.08]**	[0.09]	[0.07]**	[0.06]
Constant	0.64	5.28	0.7	1.67
	[1.24]	[1.08]**	[0.80]	[0.71]*
R^2	0.11	0.23	0.17	0.08
N	453	458	460	458

Note: +$p < 0.10$; * $p < 0.05$; ** $p < 0.01$

Measures of Students' Ideology and Coherency

To address our questions about ideology, we included eight items on the student and teacher surveys about important controversial political issues, such as taxation, civil unions for gay people, and the death penalty. We also asked for whom they would have voted in the 2004 presidential election had they been legally eligible.

TABLE A.6 Post-Course Survey Comparison: Political Participation

	Willing to volunteer	Political efficacy	Expect to vote	Vote every election
Dep. var. name	pvol_2	pefficy_2	q24_2	q66_2
Classroom Practice				
Best Practice Discussion	0.11	0.21	0.14	0.27
	[0.09]	[0.13]	[0.11]	[0.09]**
Discussion	0.04	0.26	−0.03	0.1
	[0.10]	[0.14]+	[0.12]	[0.10]
Demographics				
SES	0.23	0.06	−0.02	0.03
	[0.06]**	[0.08]	[0.06]	[0.06]
Black	0.32	0.41	0.08	0.27
	[0.15]*	[0.21]*	[0.17]	[0.15]+
Hispanic	0.13	0.47	−0.12	0.13
	[0.14]	[0.19]*	[0.16]	[0.14]
Female	0.25	−0.05	0.06	0.14
	[0.07]**	[0.10]	[0.08]	[0.07]*
Noncitizen	−0.06	−0.01	−0.14	0.03
	[0.15]	[0.20]	[0.16]	[0.15]
Other Characteristics				
Ideological Scale	−0.01	0.2	0.03	−0.03
	[0.05]	[0.07]*	[0.06]	[0.05]
Prior-Civic Exposure Index	0.37	0.36	0.28	0.21
	[0.05]**	[0.08]**	[0.06]**	[0.05]**
Age	−0.01	−0.14	−0.08	−0.08
	[0.05]	[0.07]*	[0.06]	[0.05]
Constant	4.15	4.46	4.76	4.59
	[0.85]**	[1.19]**	[0.97]**	[0.85]**
R^2	0.24	0.1	0.07	0.1
N	454	455	455	453

Note: +$p < 0.10$, * $p < 0.05$; ** $p < 0.01$

The teacher survey also contained the same issues questions, but we did not ask for their presidential preference.

We used the eight questions about important controversial political issues to create a political orientation scale. The items were structured as statements that implied a particular orientation based on responses that ranged on a five-point scale from Strongly Disagree (1) to Strongly Agree (5), with Undecided/Don't Know serving as the mid-point (3). The scale we constructed can be used to assess an individual's, or, if averaged across a classroom of individuals, a class's political orientation, described on a spectrum of strong-left to strong-right in terms of political orientation: 1 = Strong left, 2 = Left, 3 = Undecided/Independent, 4 = Right, and 5 = Strong Right. On this spectrum, the mean of the spectrum of the student population in year two was 2.6, suggesting a somewhat left-leaning population of students. For the sample, classroom averages ranged from 1.75 (1 = Political Left) to 3.63 (5 = Political Right).

These Political Ideology scores provide only a cursory view of the political orientations of students, with inadequate information on the extent to which a class consists of a fairly homogeneous group of students (all hold similar opinions, or express similar political orientations), or heterogeneous (a wide range of opinions are represented in the class). For example, it would be theoretically possible to have a class mean of 3.00, which could indicate that the students were undecided or did not know, or that there was more diversity, such as a class with half holding strong left views, half with strong right views. Some indication of the range of political orientations expressed within a class can be derived from including the range, along with the mean response for a given class. For additional information, we turned to intra-student political orientation as another way to flesh out the diversity that existed in each class. We examined how consistent (politically speaking) a student's own opinions were across a variety of politically-charged issues. That is, did individual students tend to consistently respond across issues with the same political orientation, or did students express more politically incoherent thinking, leaning right on some issues and leaning left on others?

The measures of Ideological Coherence we used gauge the consistency of political orientation expressed by a student across a variety of controversial political issues. A measure of zero indicates perfect consistency in terms of the political orientation expressed by the student across all controversial political issues reported. The mean of the standard deviation for students' ideology scores was 1.22 (compared to their more politically coherent teachers, with a mean of 0.87), and the majority of students in the sample scored between 1 and about 1.75 on the Ideological Coherence scale. Measures above 1.5 indicate that the student responses across the controversial political issues spanned two or more categories on the five-point Likert scale for political orientation, e.g. from Strongly Disagree to Undecided, or from Agree to Disagree.[1] While students did tend to lean to the "right" or "left," most were not very coherent ideologically, and this often manifested in two ways. First, students were undecided about many issues (a mean of 2.6 per student of the eight issues included in the ideology scale). Second, when students did have views on issues, they were rarely politically coherent in those views.

Analysis of Like-Minded Schools (LMS)

When doing the analysis of students' political views, we used the eight questions on the survey that asked their opinions about the controversial political issues. We noticed that several classes were clearly "red" classes, in which lots

TABLE A.7 Like-Minded and Politically Diverse School Sample By Wave

School Type	Pre-Survey	Post-Survey	Follow-Up 1	Follow-Up 2
Like-Minded	158	113	56	76
Politically Diverse	841	412	345	293

of the students had conservative views and others as "blue" classes, in which lots of students had liberal views. Further, in the interviews with students in these classes, it was common for them to refer to their school in partisan/ideological terms. We began a study of this subset of students by first defining a Like-Minded School as one in which (1) at least 80% of the surveyed students reported that that they would have voted for the same presidential candidate had they been able to vote in 2004; (2) they had average Political Orientation and Ideological Coherence scores that showed the class's views leaned heavily to the political right or left; and (3) interviewed students, without prompting, described their schools as places where "everyone" is ideologically alike. Chapter 7, Table 7.1, shows that we had four teachers in three schools that were labeled a LMS.

For this analysis, we investigated whether students in LMS had different levels of political participation than students growing up in politically diverse communities. To do this, we divided the sample into two groups and compared their answers at each of the four points of data collection. Table A.7 compares each type of school at each time point.

Chapters 6 and 7 discuss these findings in more detail. In all cases, the analysis was conducted holding SES, gender, race/ethnicity, and prior-civic exposure constant. We have made the output tables for this analysis available at: http://www.routledge.com/political_classroom/

Analysis of Disclosure and Withholding

The major findings around teacher disclosure are discussed in Chapter 9. Initially, disclosure and withholding were not planned to be such a major focus of the study, but during the student interviews in the first year, students were asked if they knew their teacher's views about issues and what they felt about their teacher's policy. There was such a variety of views among students in the same classroom that we wanted to better understand what was happening in classes and what students felt about their teacher's practice. To that end, in the second year we added a series of questions to the post-course survey (questions were based on a Likert-scale from Strongly Agree to Strongly Disagree). See Table A.8 for the frequencies from the post-course survey.

The pre-course survey disclosure data was based on one question that asked students to what extent they felt that "The teacher should not voice his or her

TABLE A.8 Teacher and Student Views on Disclosure

	Teachers (n=22)		Students (n=518)	
	Disagree (%)	Agree (%)	Disagree (%)	Agree (%)
1. I wish my social studies teacher would share his or her opinions on issues more often.	N/A	N/A	46.61	50.39
2. I think it is fine for social studies teachers to share their opinions about the issues in class.	45.46	54.55	20.74	79.26
3. I would prefer that social studies teachers not share their opinions about the issues discussed in class.	47.83	52.17	78.21	21.60
4. I feel like I need to have the same opinion on issues as my students do/as the rest of the class.	91.30	8.70	88.78	11.22
5. Most of the students in this class have similar opinions on the issues we are discussing.	82.61	17.39	45.81	54.19
6. I feel that when a social studies teacher shares his or her opinions on the issues we are discussing in class **that students** are more likely to adopt those same opinions.	54.55	45.45	58.80	41.20
7. I feel that when my social studies teacher shares his or her opinions on key issues we are discussing in class **that I** am more likely to adopt those same opinions.	N/A	N/A	76.94	23.06
8. I feel like my students want me to have the same opinion on issues as they do / I feel like my teacher wants students to have the same opinion on issues as he or she has.	65.22	34.78	90.35	9.65
9. Students do not know / I do not know my teacher's opinions on the issues we are discussing in class.	47.83	52.17	56.56	43.44
10. I do not share my / My social studies teacher does not share his or her opinions about issues we are discussing in class.	47.83	52.17	53.82	46.18
11. I only share my / My social studies teacher only shares his or her opinions about issues when asked directly by a student in class.	52.17	47.83	62.50	37.50
12. I do not think it is a good idea for social studies teachers to tell students his or her opinions about the issues they are discussing in class.	50.00	50.00	72.76	27.24

opinion" during class discussions (measured on a Likert-scale). This item was used to measure changes in support for disclosure over time.

In the longitudinal phone interviews, respondents were asked an open-ended question about teacher disclosure, "Do you remember if your teacher shared his or her personal views on political issues during the class?" If respondents answered "yes" to the first prompt, they were asked, "Did that influence you?" If respondents answered "Yes, disclosure did influence me," then they were asked to explain how it influenced them. Codes were induced from these responses and quantified so that they could be merged into the survey data set. In addition to these descriptive statistics, we also ran multiple analyses to investigate what factors predict whether students are in favor of disclosure (such as, race, class, gender, type of classroom). These and other findings about disclosure are discussed in Chapter 9.

Qualitative Data

The qualitative data consists of student and teacher interviews, classroom observations, and open-ended questions from the follow-up surveys.

Teacher Interviews

We interviewed 27 of the 35 teachers who participated in the study. Five teachers (the Adams team, Mr. Walters, and Mr. Dunn) were interviewed twice, because they participated in the study for more than one year. Mr. Kushner was interviewed in 2005, 2006, and 2008 for a total of three times. These were semi-structured interviews of about 45–60 minutes that asked about their professional biographies, teaching philosophies, and their reasoning about pedagogical choices. Mr. Kushner, Ms. Heller, Ms. Potter, and Mr. Walters all read and gave feedback on the chapters that focused on their classroom practices.

Student Interviews

To select which students to interview, we analyzed the survey results to get a sense of the nature of the diversity that existed in each class and then selected students to represent that range. We paid particular attention to diversity related to four factors: gender, race, class, and political views. For example, in one class more than 80% of the students marked President George W. Bush as the candidate they would have voted for in the 2004 election. In that class, we interviewed four students— three George Bush supporters and one John Kerry supporter. Student interviews were conducted during the last two weeks of the term and usually lasted 20–30 minutes. During these semi-structured interviews participants were asked how much of class time was devoted to various types of activities (lecture, small group discussion, large group discussion, individual work, and films), their interest in the course, how much they participated, how they thought the course would influence them, the extent to which people in the class disagreed about issues, which issues were discussed, and their experiences and opinions about disclosure.

Observations

Each of the 35 participating teachers was observed at least once, and some twice or more, in each course that participated in the study. If they participated for more than one year, their courses were observed again. There were also several teachers for whom we chose to collect more in-depth observational data. At Adams High each of the three teachers was observed one to two times during each of two semesters of observation for a total of 10 observations. Researchers also observed the two-day full sessions each semester. Mr. Kushner participated for three semesters during two academic years. In the first year (2005–2006), we observed his class two times. In the second year (spring 2008) we observed two sections of his course eight times, for a total of 18 hours of observation. Mr. Walters and Mr. Dunn each participated for two years and were observed two times. Their students also participated in a statewide deliberation and were observed in this setting as well. Observers took detailed field notes and recorded thoughts in post-observation memos.

Evidence-Based Philosophic Deliberations

As we moved through the data analysis and case study discussions, it became clear that there were questions that emerged from the data that could not be answered with empirical evidence alone. We identified four normative issues that are particularly relevant to the political classroom and then, using a grant from the Spencer Foundation, convened three meetings during the 2009–2010 academic year that each focused on one or more of the following:

1. What are the ethical considerations that should inform a teacher's decision about whether or not to disclose his/her political views to students?
2. What is a controversial political issue?
3. How should teachers respond to issues that are sensitive to some students?
4. What should be the teacher's aims when she/he engages students in discussions of controversial political issues?

For each convening, we invited a small group of scholars from the fields of political philosophy, philosophy of education, medical ethics, social studies education, political science, and a number of sub-fields in education. The participants are listed in the acknowledgements. We then developed case study materials that represented the evidence we had relevant to each issue, which included the quantitative data, qualitative data, and, several cases studies of teachers' practices that we developed from the data. Participants read these packets in advance of the meeting and then engaged in a series of deliberative exercises designed to attend to the evidence and promote ethical thinking about each issue. Each five-hour meeting had a note taker in the room who took detailed notes the conversations. These conversations were not used as evidence; instead, they were fantastically interesting deliberations that helped us to think more carefully about the issues we wanted to present in the book and to identify the competing points of view within each dilemma. The aims we defend in Chapter 4 and the arguments we make in Chapters 9 and 10 are our own, but are much stronger as a result of these evidence-based philosophic deliberations.

Note

1 The paragraphs in this section were excerpted from Hess (2009). Chapter 5 of that book includes a detailed discussion of the relationship between ideological diversity and classroom discussion.

REFERENCES

Abramowitz, A. (2010). *The disappearing center: Engaged citizens, polarization, and American democracy*. New Haven, CT: Yale University Press.

Abrams, S. J., & Fiorina, M. P. (2012). "The Big Sort" that wasn't: A skeptical reexamination. *PS: Political Science & Politics, 45*(2), 203–210.

Allen, D. S. (2004). *Talking to strangers: Anxieties of citizenship since* Brown v. Board of Education. Chicago, IL: The University of Chicago Press.

American Civil Liberties Union (ACLU). (2007). The death penalty: Questions and answers. Retrieved from http://www.aclu.org/capital-punishment/death-penalty-questions-and-answers.

Apple, M. (2001). *Educating the "right" way: Markets, standards, God, and inequality*. New York, NY: RoutledgeFalmer.

Bailey, C. (1971). Rationality, democracy and the neutral teacher. *Cambridge Journal of Education, 1*(2), 68–76.

Barbaro, M. (2012, May 6). A scramble as Biden backs same-sex marriage. *The New York Times*. Retrieved from http://www.nytimes.com.

Barber, B. R. (1984). *Strong democracy: Participatory politics for a new age*. Berkeley, CA: University of California Press.

Barr, A. (2009, September). Newt Gingrich: 'Every child' should read speech. *Politico*. Retrieved from http://www.politico.com/news/stories/0909/26865.html.

Beck, T. A. (2013). Identity, discourse, and safety in a high school discussion of same-sex marriage. *Theory & Research in Social Education, 41*(1), 1–32.

Bishop, B. (2008). *The big sort: Why the clustering of like-minded America is tearing us apart*. New York, NY: Houghton Mifflin.

Blum, L. (2012). *High schools, race, and America's future: What students can teach us about morality, diversity, and community*. Cambridge, MA: Harvard Education Press.

Bollier, S. (2014, May 20). How gay marriage is winning in America. *Aljazeera*. Retrieved from http://www.aljazeera.com/indepth/features/2014/05/how-gay-marriage-winning-america-20145683396325.html.

Bowden, M. (2009, October). The story behind the story. *Atlantic Monthly.* Retrieved from http://www.theatlantic.com/magazine/archive/2009/10/the-story-behind-the-story/307667/.

Brennan Center for Justice. (2012). Election 2012: Voting laws roundup. Retrieved from http://www.brennancenter.org/analysis/election-2012-voting-laws-roundup.

Bridges, D. (1997). *Education, democracy, and discussion.* Slough, UK: National Foundation.

Brighouse, H. (2006). *On education.* New York, NY: Routledge.

Brown University. (n.d). The Choices program. Retrieved from http://www.choices.edu.

Budge, I., Crewe, I., & Farlie, D. (1976/2010). *Party identification and beyond: Representations of voting and party competition.* Wivenhoe Park, Colchester: European Consortium for Political Research Press.

Callan, E. (1997). *Creating citizens: Political education and liberal democracy.* New York, NY: Clarendon Press.

Campbell, D. E. (2004). Acts of faith: Churches and political engagement. *Political Behavior, 26*(2): 155–180.

Center for Information & Research on Civic Learning (CIRCLE). (n.d). Trends by race, ethnicity, and gender. Retrieved from http://www.civicyouth.org/quick-facts/235–2/.

Center for Information & Research on Civic Learning (CIRCLE). (2008). *2004 youth voter turnout rates among citizens, ranked by state.* Retrieved from the Center for Information & Research on Civic Learning website: http://www.civicyouth.org/PopUps/FactSheets/FS08_2004_state_turnout.pdf.

Center for Information & Research on Civic Learning (CIRCLE). (2012a). *Young voters in the 2012 presidential election.* Retrieved from the Center for Information & Research on Civic Learning website: http://www.civicyouth.org/wp-content/uploads/2012/11/CIRCLE_2012Election_ExitPoll_OverviewFactSheet.pdf.

Center for Information & Research on Civic Learning (CIRCLE). (2012b). Youth voting. Retrieved from http://www.civicyouth.org/quick-facts/youth-voting/.

Citizens United v. Federal Election Commission, 558 U. S. _____ (2010).

Clayton, M. (2012). Debate: The case against the comprehensive enrollment of children. *Journal of Political Philosophy, 20*(3), 353–364.

CNN (2008). Election center 2008: Exit polls [Data Set]. Retrieved from http://www.cnn.com/ELECTION/2008/results/polls.main/.

Cohen, C. J., & Kahne, J. (2012). *Participatory politics: New media and youth political action.* Retrieved from the Youth Participatory Politics Research Network website: http://ypp.dmlcentral.net/sites/all/files/publications/YPP_Survey_Report_FULL.pdf.

College Board. (2005). Student grade distributions. Retrieved from http://media.collegeboard.com/digitalServices/pdf/research/studentgradedistribut_47038.pdf.

College Board. (2011a). Annual AP program participation, 1956–2011. Retrieved from http://media.collegeboard.com/digitalServices/pdf/research/AP-Annual-Participation-2011.pdf.

College Board. (2011b). Program summary report. Retrieved from http://media.collegeboard.com/digitalServices/pdf/research/AP-Program-Summary-Report-2011.pdf.

Commission on Youth Voting and Civic Knowledge. (2013). *All together now: Collaboration and innovation for youth engagement.* Retrieved from the Center for Information & Research on Civic Learning and Engagement website http://www.civicyouth.org/wp-content/uploads/2013/09/CIRCLE-youthvoting-individualPages.pdf.

Constitutional Rights Foundation Chicago (CRFC). (n.d). Illinois Youth Summit. Retrieved from http://www.crfc.org/student-programs/illinois-youth-summit.

Cooper, K. J. &. Pianin, E. (1991, October 3). Funding of Bush speech draws fire. *The Washington Post,* p. A14.

Dahl, R. A. (1998). *On democracy.* New Haven, CT: Yale University Press.

Dearden, R. F. (1981). Controversial issues in the curriculum. *Journal of Curriculum Studies, 13*(1): 37–44.

Dershowitz, A. M. (2002). The case for torture warrants. Retrieved from http://www.alandershowitz.com/publications/docs/torturewarrants.html.

Dewey, J. (1916/2004). *Democracy and education.* Mineola, NY: Dover Publications.

Dreher, R. (2006). *Crunchy cons: The new conservative counterculture.* New York, NY: Three Rivers Press.

Dwyer, J. G. (1998). *Religious schools v. children's rights.* Ithaca, NY: Cornell University Press.

Feinberg, J. (1980). The child's right to an open future. In W. Aiken & J. LaFollette (Eds.), *Whose child? Children's rights, parental authority, and state power* (pp. 124–153). Totowa, NJ: Littlefield, Adams, & Co.

Flanagan, C. A. (2013). *Teenage citizens: The political theories of the young.* Cambridge, MA: Harvard University Press.

Frankenberg, E. (2012). Understanding suburban school district transformation. In E. Frankenberg, & G. Orfield, (Eds.), *The resegregation of suburban schools: A hidden crisis in American education* (pp. 27–44). Cambridge, MA: Harvard Education Press.

Frankenberg, E., & Lee, C. (2002). *Race in American public schools: Rapidly resegregating school districts.* Cambridge, MA: The Civil Rights Project, Harvard University.

Freeman v. Pitts, 503 U.S. 467 (1992).

Ganzler, L. M. (2010). *Simulated citizen: How students experienced a semester length legislative simulation* (Doctoral dissertation). Retrieved from ProQuest Dissertations & Theses Full Text database (UMI No. 3448866).

Gauchat, G. (2012). Politicization of science in the public sphere: A study of public trust in the United States, 1974 to 2010. *American Sociological Review, 77*(2), 167–187.

Gereluk, D. (2013). The democratic imperative to address sexual equality rights in schools. *Educational Theory, 36*(5), 511–523.

Gerson, M. (2014, May 19). The Holocaust is not a he-said, she-said debate. *The Washington Post.* Retrieved from http://www.washingtonpost.com.

Gratz v. Bollinger, 539 U.S. 244 (2003).

Green, D., Palmquist, B., & Schickler, E. (2002). *Partisan hearts and minds.* New Haven, CT: Yale University Press.

Gutmann, A., & Thompson, D. F. (1996). *Democracy and disagreement.* Cambridge, MA: Harvard University Press.

Gutmann, A., & Thompson, D. F. (2012). *The spirit of compromise: Why governing demands it and campaigning undermines it.* Princeton, NJ: Princeton University Press.

Hahn, C. (1998). *Becoming political: Comparative perspectives on citizenship education.* Albany, NY: State University of New York Press.

Hahn, C. L. (1999). Citizenship education: An empirical study of policy, practices, and outcomes. *Oxford Review of Education, 25*(1–2), 231–250.

Haidt, J., & Hetherington, J. M. (2012, September 17). Look how far we've come apart [Web blog post]. Retrieved from http://campaignstops.blogs.nytimes.com/author/jonathan-haidt/.

Hand, M. (2007) Should we teach homosexuality as a controversial issue? *Theory and Research in Education, 5*(1): 69–86.

Hand, M. (2008). What should we teach as controversial? A defense of the epistemic criterion. *Educational Theory, 58*(2), 213–228.

Hand, M. (2013). Framing classroom discussion of same-sex marriage. *Educational Theory, 63*(5), 497–510.

Hess, D. (2010). Teachers and academic freedom: Gaining right defacto. *Social Education*, 74(2), 316–321.

Hess, D. E. (2009). *Controversy in the classroom: The democratic power of discussion*. New York, NY: Routledge.

Hibbing, J., & Theiss-Morse, E. (2002). *Stealth democracy: Americans' beliefs about how government should work*. Cambridge, MA: Cambridge University Press.

Jones, J. M. (2014, January 14). Congress job approval starts 2014 at 13%: Essentially unchanged since December [Poll]. Retrieved from http://www.gallup.com/poll/166838/congress-job-approval-starts-2014.aspx.

Journell, W. (2011). The disclosure dilemma in action: A qualitative look at the effect of teacher disclosure on classroom instruction. *Journal of Social Studies Research, 35*(2), 217–244.

Kahne, J., Crow, D., and Lee, N. (2013). Different pedagogy, different politics: High school learning opportunities and youth political engagement. *Political Psychology, 34*(3), 419–441.

Kahne, J., Lee, N. J., & Feezell, J. T. (2012). Digital media literacy education and online civic and political participation. *International Journal of Communication, 6*, 1–24.

Kahne, J., & Middaugh, E. (2008). Democracy for some: The civic opportunity gap in high school. Working paper #59. Retrieved from the Center of Information & Research on Civic Learning and Engagement website: http://www.civicyouth.org/PopUps/WorkingPapers/WP59Kahne.pdf.

Kahne, J., Rodriguez, M., Smith, B., & Thiede, K. (2000). Developing citizens for democracy? Assessing opportunities to learn in Chicago's social studies classrooms. *Theory and Research in Social Education, 28*(3), 311–338.

Kahne, J. E., & Sporte, S. E. (2008). Developing citizens: The impact of civic learning opportunities on students' commitment to civic participation. *American Educational Research Journal, 45*(3), 738–766.

Katz, M. B. (2001). *The irony of early school reform: Educational innovation in mid-nineteenth century Massachusetts*. New York, NY: Teachers College Press.

Kelly, T. E. (1986). Discussing controversial issues: Four perspectives on the teacher's role. *Theory & Research in Social Education* 14(2): 113–138.

Kelly, T. E. (1989). Leading class discussions of controversial issues. *Social Education, 53*(6), 368–370.

Kelly-Woessner, A., & Woessner, M. C. (2006). My professor is a partisan hack: How perceptions of a professor's political views affect student course evaluations. *PS: Political Science & Politics, 39*(3), 495–501.

Kelly-Woessner, A., & Woessner, M. (2008). Conflict in the classroom: Considering the effects of partisan difference on political education. *Journal of Political Science Education, 4*(3), 265–285.

Keys, M. (2011). *What should we teach as controversial? A critique of the epistemic criterion*. Paper presented at the Philosophy of Education Society of Great Britain Annual Conference, Oxford, UK.

Kirby, E. H., & Marcelo, K. B. (2006). *Young voters in the 2006 elections*. Retrieved from The Center for Information & Research on Civic Learning & Engagement website: http://www.civicyouth.org/PopUps/FactSheets/FS-Midterm06.pdf.

Lareau, A. (2003). *Unequal childhoods: Class, race, and family life*. Berkeley, CA: University of California Press.

Lautzenheiser, D. K., Kelly, A. P., Miller, C. (2011). *Contested curriculum: How teachers and citizens view civics education* [Policy Brief]. Retrieved from the American Enterprise

Institute (AEI) website: http://www.citizenship-aei.org/wp-content/uploads/Contested-Curriculum.pdf.

Lenhart, A., Kahne, J., Middaugh, E., Macgill, A. R., Evans, C., & Vitak, J. (2008). *Teens, video games, and civics: Teens' gaming experiences are diverse and include significant social interaction and civic engagement.* Retrieved from the Pew Research Center website: http://www.pewinternet.org/files/old-media//Files/Reports/2008/PIP_Teens_Games_and_Civics_Report_FINAL.pdf.pdf.

Lemon v. Kurtzman, 403 U.S. 602 (1971).

Levinson, M. (2003). Challenging deliberation. *Theory and Research in Education, 1*(1), 23–49.

Levinson, M. (2012). *No citizen left behind.* Cambridge, MA: Harvard University Press.

Levy, B. (2011). Fostering cautious political efficacy through civic advocacy projects: A mixed methods case study of an innovative high school class. *Theory and Research in Social Education, 39*(2), 238–277.

Lopez, M. H., Levine, P., Both, D., Kiesa, A., Kirby, E., & Marcelo, K. (2006). *The 2006 civic and political health of the nation: A detailed look at how youth participate in politics and communities.* Retrieved from Center for Information and Research on Civic Learning and Engagement (CIRCLE) website: http://www.civicyouth.org/PopUps/2006_CPHS_Report_update.pdf.

Lupu, N. (2014). *Party polarization and mass partisanship: A comparative perspective.* Unpublished manuscript, University of Wisconsin-Madison, Madison, Wisconsin. Retrieved from http://www.noamlupu.com/polarization.pdf.

Mann, M.T.P. (1865). *Life of Horace Mann.* Boston, MA: Walker, Fuller, and Company.

Mann, T. E., & Ornstein, N. J. (2012). *It's even worse than it looks: How the American constitutional system collided with the new politics of extremism.* New York, NY: Basic Books.

Mansbridge, J. J. (1983). *Beyond adversary democracy.* Chicago, IL: University of Chicago Press.

Mansbridge, J. J. (1991). Democracy, deliberation, and the experience of women. In B. Murchland (Ed.), *Higher education and the practice of democratic politics: A political education reader* (pp. 122–135). Dayton, OH: Kettering Foundation.

Mansbridge, J. J, Bohman, J., Chambers, S., Estlund, D., Føllesdal, A., Fung, A., . . . Martí, J. l. (2010). The place of self-interest and the role of power in deliberative democracy. *Journal of Political Philosophy, 18*(1), 64–100.

Marquis, D. (1989). Why abortion is immoral. *Journal of Philosophy, 86*(4), 183–202.

Maxwell, B., Waddington, D. I., McDonough, K., Cormier, A.-A., & Schwimmer, M. (2012). Interculturalism, multiculturalism, and the state funding and regulation of conservative religious schools. *Educational Theory, 62*(4), 427–447.

McAvoy, P., & Hess, D. (2013). Classroom deliberation in an era of political polarization. *Curriculum Inquiry, 43*(1), 14–47.

McAvoy, P., Hess, D., & Kawashima-Ginsberg, K. (in press). The pedagogical challenge of teaching politics in like-minded schools. In T. Misco (Ed.), *Cross-cultural case studies of teaching controversial issues: Pathways and challenges to democratic citizenship education.* Tilburg, The Netherlands: Legal Wolf Publishers.

McCarty, N. M., Poole, K. T., & Rosenthal, H. (2006). *Polarized America: The dance of ideology and unequal riches.* Cambridge, MA: MIT Press.

McClure, W. (1916). *State constitution-making, with especial reference to Tennessee.* Nashville, TN: Marshall & Bruce Company.

McCully, A. (2006). Practitioner perceptions of their role in facilitating the handling of controversial issues in contested societies: A Northern Irish experience. *Educational Review, 58*(1), 51–65.

McDonald, M. (2006). 2006 general election turnout rates. Retrieved from http://elections. gmu.edu/Turnout_2006G.html.

McKinley, J. C., & Dillon, S. (2009, September 3). Some parents oppose Obama school speech. *The New York Times*. Retrieved from http://www.nytimes.com.

Meehan, C.R. (2012). *Global warming in schools: An inquiry about the competing conceptions of high school social studies and science curricula and teachers* (Doctoral dissertation). Retrieved from ProQuest Dissertations & Theses Full Text database (UMI No. 3547783).

Miller-Lane, J., Denton, E., & May, A. (2006). Social studies teachers' views on committed impartiality and discussion. *Social Studies Research and Practice, 1*(1), 30–44.

Missouri v. Jenkins, 515 U.S. 70 (1995).

Mitchell, D. E., & Ream, R. K. (Eds.) (in press). A brief introduction to the problem of professional responsibility. In *Professional responsibility: The fundamental issue in education and health care reform*. New York, NY: Springer.

Morrell, M. E. (2005). Deliberation, democratic decision-making and internal political efficacy. *Political Behavior, 27*(1), 49–69.

Moss, H. J. (2009). *Schooling citizens: The struggle for African American education in antebellum America*. Chicago, IL: University of Chicago Press.

Mouffe, C. (2000). Deliberative democracy or agnostic pluralism. *Political Science Series, Institute for Advanced Studies, 72,* 1–17.

Mutz, D. C. (2006). *Hearing the other side: Deliberative versus participatory democracy.* New York, NY: Cambridge University Press.

National Center for Education Statistics. Common Core of Data (CCD). (2007–2008). Public Elementary/Secondary School Universe Survey Elementary/secondary information system (ELSi) [Table Generator]. Retrieved from http://nces.ed.gov/ccd/.

National Conference on Citizenship. (2009). *American's civic health index: Civic health in hard times*. Retrieved from the National Conference on Citizenship website: http://www. ncoc.net/2gp78.

Niemi, N. S., & Niemi, R. G. (2007). Partisanship, participation, and political trust as taught (or not) in high school history and government classes. *Theory and Research in Social Education, 35*(1), 32–61.

Nocera, A. (2013). Teaching controversy in moral education: A critique of the epistemic criterion. In C. Mayo (Ed.), *Philosophy of Education Society Yearbook* (pp. 67–75). Urbana, IL: Philosophy of Education Society.

Noll, M. A. (2002). *The old religion in a new world: The history of North American Christianity.* Grand Rapids, MI: Eerdmans.

Nystrand, M., Gamoran, A., & Carbonaro, W. (2001). On the ecology of classroom instruction: The case of writing in high school English and social studies. In P. Tynjälä, L. Mason & K. Lonka (Eds.), *Writing as a learning tool: Integrating theory and practice* (pp. 57–81). Dordrecht, Netherlands: Kluwer Academic Publishers.

Nystrand, M., Wu, L. L., Gamoran, A., Zeiser, S., & Long, D. A. (2003). Questions in time: Investigating the structure and dynamics of unfolding classroom discourse. *Discourse Processes, 35*(2): 135–198.

Oakes, J. (1985). *Keeping track: How schools structure inequality.* New Haven, CT: Yale University Press.

Oakes, J., & Wells, A.S. (2004). The comprehensive high school, de-tracking and the persistence of social stratification. In F. M. Hammack (Ed.), *The comprehensive high school today* (pp. 87–113). New York, NY: Teachers College Press.

Ochoa, G., & Pineda, D. (2008). Deconstructing power, privilege, and silence in the classroom. *Radical History Review, 102,* 45–62.

Okin, S. (2002). Mistresses of their own destiny. In K. McDonough and W. Feinberg (Eds.), *Citizenship and education in liberal-democratic societies* (pp. 325–351). New York: Oxford University Press.

Orfield, G., Kucsera, J., & Siegel-Hawley, G. (2012). *E pluribus . . . separation: Deepening double segregation for more students.* Los Angeles, CA: Civil Rights Project.

Parents Involved in Community Schools v. Seattle Public Schools, 551 U.S. 701(2007).

Parker, W. (2003). *Teaching democracy: Unity and diversity in public life.* New York, NY: Teacher's College Press.

Parker, W. (2006). Public discourses in schools: Purposes, problems, possibilities. *Educational Researcher, 35*(8), 11–18.

Parker, W. (2011). Feel free to change your mind: A response to "The Potential for Deliberative Democratic Civic Education," *Democracy & Education, 19*(2): 1–4.

Parker, W., Mosborg, S., Bransford, J., Vye, N., Wilkerson, J., & Abbott, R. (2011). Rethinking advanced high school coursework: Tackling the depth/breadth tension in the AP US Government and Politics Course. *Journal of Curriculum Studies, 43*(4), 533–559.

Parker, W. C. (2010). *Social studies today: Research & practice.* New York, NY: Routledge.

Parker, W. C., & Hess, D. (2001). Teaching with and for discussion. *Teaching and Teacher Education, 17*(3), 273–289.

Peters, R. S. (1966). *Ethics and education.* London, UK: Allen & Unwin.

Petrovic, J. E. (2013). Reason, liberalism, and democratic education: A Deweyan approach to teaching about homosexuality. *Educational Theory, 63*(5), 525–541.

Pew Research Center. (2011). *Angry silents, disengaged millennials: The generation gap and the 2012 election.* Retrieved from the Pew Research Center website: http://www.people-press.org/files/legacy-pdf/11-3-11%20Generations%20Release.pdf.

Pew Research Center. (2012). *Trends in American values: 1987–2012: Partisan polarization surges in Bush, Obama years.* Retrieved from the Pew Research Center website: http://www.people-press.org/files/legacy-pdf/06-04-12%20Values%20Release.pdf.

Pew Research Center, (2013a). *Growing support for gay marriage: Changed minds and changing demographics.* Retrieved from the Pew Research Center website: http://www.people-press.org/files/legacy-pdf/3-20-13%20Gay%20Marriage%20Release.pdf.

Pew Research Center. (2013b). *GOP deeply divided over climate change.* Retrieved from the Pew Research Center website: http://www.people-press.org/files/legacy-pdf/11-1-13%20Global%20Warming%20Release.pdf.

Pew Research Center. (2014). *Millennials in adulthood: Detached from institutions, networked with friends.* Retrieved from the Pew Research Center website http://www.pewsocialtrends.org/files/2014/03/2014-03-07_generations-report-version-for-web.pdf.

Prensky, M. (2001). Digital natives, digital immigrants part 1. *On The Horizon, 9*(5): 1–6.

Putnam, R. D. (2000). *Bowling alone: The collapse and revival of American community.* New York, NY: Simon & Schuster.

Putnam, R. D, & Campbell, D. E. (2010). *American grace: How religion divides and unites us.* New York, NY: Simon & Schuster.

Reich, R. (2002). *Bridging liberalism and multiculturalism in American education.* Chicago, IL: University of Chicago Press.

Rocha, V. (2014, May 7). Rialto school officials apologize for Holocaust assignment, *Los Angeles Times.* Retrieved from http://www.latimes.com.

Rosenblum, N. L. (2008). *On the other side of the angels: An appreciation of parties and partisanship.* Princeton, NY: Princeton University Press.

Sanders, L. M. (1997). Against deliberation. *Political Theory, 25*(3), 347–376.

Schkade, D., Sunstein, C. R., & Hastie, R. (2007). What happened on deliberation day? *California Law Review, 95*(3), 915–940.

Schlozman, K. L., Verba, S., & Brady, H. E. (2012). *The unheavenly chorus: Unequal political voice and the broken promise of American democracy.* Princeton, NJ: Princeton University Press.

Schwab, J. J. (1978). Eros and education: A discussion of one aspect of discussion. In I. Westbury & N. J. Wilkof (Eds.), *Science, curriculum, and liberal education: Selected essays* (pp. 105–132). Chicago, IL: University of Chicago Press.

Silver, N. (2012, July 15). Measuring the effects of voter identification laws [Web log post]. Retrieved from http://fivethirtyeight.blogs.nytimes.com/2012/07/15/measuring-the-effects-of-voter-identification-laws/?_php=true&_type=blogs&_r=0.

Smith, A. (2009). *The internet's role in campaign 2008: A majority of American adults went online in 2008 to keep informed about political developments and to get involved with the election.* Retrieved from the Pew Research Center website: http://www.pewinternet.org/files/old-media//Files/Reports/2009/The_Internets_Role_in_Campaign_2008.pdf.

Smith, A., Schlozman, K. L., Verba, S., & Brady, H. (2009). *The internet and civic engagement.* Retrieved from the Pew Research Center website: http://www.pewinternet.org/files/old-media//Files/Reports/2009/The%20Internet%20and%20Civic%20Engagement.pdf.

Stanley, W. (2010). Social studies and the social order: Transmission or transformation? In W. Parker (Ed.), *Social studies today: Research and practice* (pp. 17–24). New York, NY: Routledge.

Sunstein, C. R. (2001). *Republic.com.* Princeton, NJ: Princeton University Press.

Sunstein, C. R. (2009). *Going to extremes: How like minds unite and divide.* Oxford, UK: Oxford University Press.

Theriault, S. M. (2013). *The Gingrich senators: The roots of partisan warfare in Congress.* New York, NY: Oxford University Press.

Torney-Purta, J., Lehmann, R., Oswald, H., & Schulz, W. (2001). *Citizenship and education in twenty-eight countries: Civic knowledge and engagement at age fourteen.* Amsterdam, Netherlands: International Association for the Evaluation of Educational Achievement. Retrieved from the International Association for the Evaluation of Educational Achievement website: http://www.iea.nl/fileadmin/user_upload/Publications/Electronic_versions/CIVED_Phase2_Age_Fourteen.pdf.

United States v. Windsor, 570 U.S. 12 (2013).

U.S. Census Bureau, American Community Survey. (2005). Sex by age by citizenship status. Retrieved from http://factfinder2.census.gov/faces/tableservices/jsf/pages/productview.xhtml?pid=ACS_05_EST_B05003&prodType=table.

U.S. Department of Education. (2009). President Barack Obama makes historic speech to America's students. Retrieved from http://www2.ed.gov/admins/lead/academic/bts.html.

Valenzuela, A. (1999). *Subtractive schooling: U.S.-Mexican youth and the politics of caring.* Albany, NY: State University of New York Press.

Van Orden v. Perry, 545 U.S. 677 (2005).

Williamson, V., Skocpol, T., Coggin, J. (2011). The Tea Party and the remaking of Republican conservatism. *Perspectives on Politics, 9*(1), 25–43.

Wineburg, S. (2001). *Historical thinking and other unnatural acts: Charting the future of teaching the past.* Philadelphia, PA: Temple University Press.

Woessner, M., & Kelly-Woessner, A. (2009). I think my professor is a Democrat: Considering whether students recognize and react to faculty politics. *PS: Political Science & Politics, 42*(2), 343–352.

Wright, R. (1940). *Native son.* New York, NY: Harper & Brothers.

INDEX

abolitionism 2–3, 189

abortion 21, 31, 32t, 137

Abramowitz, Alan 22, 24, 146

Academy High 4, 17, 51, 109, 110, 136t, 137, 146, 150, 156, 173, 175, 192, 199; and conditions of social inequality 118–23; moving from "me" to "we" 128–9; political friendship at 110–13; race and distrust 123–8; student reflections 118–19; students of color at 115; teaching for political tolerance at 115–18

achievement gaps 28

Adams High School 14, 52–3, 69n6, 156, 173, 175, 177–8, 186, 192, 194–7, 206, 207, 214; American Government course at 85–6; changing school culture at 99–100; civil discourse at 88, 91, 93–6, 105; culture of political talk at 96–8; inclusive participation at 87–90; legislative simulation at 85–6, 88, 90t, 90–1; lessons in democracy at 100–5; low SES students at 69n6; party affiliation at 96, 100–2; regulated public space at 91; role of teachers at 92–3, 98–9

administrators, role of 209

affirmative action 25, 123–7

Affordable Health Care Act 1, 20, 23, 31, 32t, 33t

Afghanistan, war in 19

African Americans: as study participants 37; voting rate of 34; see also students, African American

aims: clarifying 207; of course 141–4; educational 74–7; of political classroom 77–81, 156–7; prioritization of 75

Allen, Danielle 8, 110, 111, 119–20, 122, 127, 129

Allen, Mr. 198

American Government AP class 29–30, 54, 56, 89; course design in 44n7

Asian Americans: as study participants 37; voting rate of 34; see also students, Asian American

authenticity 173–9

autonomy 78, 149, 150, 156; bounded 134, 139–41, 156, 198; minimalist vs. bounded 151n4; and religion 133–6; vs. multiculturalism 151n3

avoidance 174–6

Baby Boom generation, demographic and ideological differences 31t, 32t

Bailey, Charles 166

Barber, Benjamin 27, 102

Biden, Joe 32

Big Sort: Why Clustering of Like-Minded America Is Tearing Us Apart, The (Bishop) 26

Bishop, Bill 26

Blackboard 93–4

Blum, Lawrence 179

Bowden, Mark 26

Brady, Henry 24

Bridges, David 172

Brighouse, Harry 149
Brown, Ms. 54–5, 200–1
Bush, George H. W. 1–2, 3
Bush, George W. 19, 37, 39, 54, 70–1, 87, 136, 150, 200

Capitol Forum 34, 139, 144, 145, 150, 209–10, 219
Central High School 191
Charter High School 183–5
Choices for the 21st Century Education Program 34, 53, 54, 139, 210, 218
Church High 136*t*, 137, 146
Citizens United v. Federal Election Commission 24
citizens: democratic 53, 76–7; digital 40–1; education of 5, 76, 129, 133; engaged 24–5, 63, 75, 146; informed 43; role of 4, 77, 79, 87; students' development as 6, 43, 46, 53, 56–7, 63, 68, 75, 145, 151
civic engagement: and news awareness 41–2; predictions and outcomes 62–3
civic participation 60; five clusters of 64–6
civil discourse 58, 88, 91, 93–6, 105
civil rights 21, 28, 119
civility 93–4, 106, 118, 176, 180
classroom types 47–8, 69n3; Best Practice Discussion class 47–58, 59*t*, 60–1, 63, 66–8, 69n6, 188, 236; and classroom diversity 54–7, 68–9; differences in engagement and learning 49–52, 67–8; Discussion class 47–52, 58, 59*t*, 60–1, 63, 66–8, 71, 188, 236; impact of social class on 60–1; increased interest in political discussion 57–8, 60; Interactive Lecture class 140; Lecture class 48–52, 56–7, 59*t*, 60–1, 66–8, 129, 188, 236; multiple perspectives in 52–4, 68–9; post survey observations 59*t*; *see also* classrooms; political classrooms
classrooms: culture in 7; as deliberative space 159; dynamic of 186; environment in 173–4; fostering climate of respect 122–7, 129; heterogeneous 81; homogenous 87–8, 148; importance of demographics in 87–8; majority-White 115, 121–2, 125–6, 128; minority-dominant 185; non-tracked 14, 52, 88, 98, 101, 107, 109, 121; politics in 4–5; as political space 122; practice effects 59*t*; *see also* classroom types; political classrooms

climate change 164–5
Clinton, Hillary 113
cluster analysis: classroom experience as predictors 66; follow-up cluster labels and profiles 64*t* ; cluster mean scores for outcomes used in clustering 65*t* ; on political and civic participation 64–6, 69n7; and political ideology 67
Coggin, John 23
collaboration 74, 205, 208, 214, 236
College Board 29–30
Common Core Standards 163
Common School Movement 2–3
communities, ideologically homogeneous 26, 67, 69
Congress, polarization in 21–3
conservatives 67, 137; class political orientation 136*t*; degree of trust in scientific community 27; in LMS 137; Republicans as 20–1, 23; students as 14, 37, 57, 67, 70, 96, 130, 137–8, 192, 198, 200, 229; teachers as 138
Constitution Party 146, 152n7
Constitutional Rights Foundation Chicago (CRFC) Youth Summit Program 34, 210–11, 218–19
Contemporary Controversies class 109–11, 114
context: and classroom discussions 185, 197, 202; of lessons 74; significance of 12; social and political 13; *see also* polarization
controversies: avoidance of 8, 15, 172; definition of 168; ethical 14–15, 158–60; live 161, 163, 165, 171; over Obama's speech 1–2; political 8–9, 15, 73, 77, 159, 168; racial 123; over role of schools 3
Controversy in the Classroom (Hess) 4–5, 38, 171
Crunchy Cons: The New Conservative Counterculture and Its Return to Roots (Dreher) 138
culture wars 21
curriculum: AP Government 30, 89; in government classes 54, 76, 88–90, 93, 97, 116, 136, 141, 149, 157, 160, 164, 171, 184, 192, 207–9, 236; inclusion of political issues in 4, 6, 13–15, 34, 74, 158–6, 170–3, 179, 180, 205; *see also* Choices for the 21st Century Education Program; Street Law
Curtis, Brett 1

Dahl, Robert 77, 79, 82n8
Dearden, Robert 166–7
death penalty 37, 49, 52, 56, 70, 86–7, 98, 105, 107n3,
debate, on current issues 4, 51, 58, 76, 86–7, 91–5, 98–101, 105, 129; see also deliberation; discussion and discussions
Defense of Marriage Act 159
deliberation 176–8, 207–9, 219; vs. discussion 5–7; see also debate; discussion and discussions
democracy 101–2; agonistic 203n5; deliberative 102, 104, 203n5; ideal version of 79–80; lessons in 100–5; requirements for 79–80, 82n8; role of citizens in 4, 77, 79, 87; and sacrifice 119–20; see also democratic society
democratic society 2, 4, 5, 6, 75, 80, 112, 114, 134, 191; see also democracy
Democrats 20–2; as liberals 21; Millennials as 33t; Southern 21
demographic factors: for beliefs and values 25; cohort 31t; differences by generation 31t; of study participants 36t, 37–8
Denton, Elixa 185
devil's advocate 92, 115, 117, 149–50, 185, 196–7
Dewey, John 5, 12, 16n2, 82n4
digital citizens 40–1
digital immigrants 40
digital natives 40
Disappearing Center: Engaged Citizens, Polarization, and American Democracy, The (Abramowitz) 24, 146
Discussing Controversial Issues Study 204; analysis 236–7; analysis of classroom effects 222–3t; analysis of disclosure and withholding 233–4; analysis of Like-Minded Schools (LMS) 229; data collection process 9–11, 34–6, 218–19; description of 34–6; evidence-based philosophic deliberations 237; findings of 13; framework 11; limitations of the data set 219–21; and the measures of social class 221; measures of students' ideology and coherency 226–9; observations 235–6; participants as digital natives 40–1; participation and study stages 35t; political engagement and the study sample 38; political views of participants 38–40; post-survey phone interviews with students 63; qualitative analysis 23; race and ethnicity

of students by wave 220t; research questions 217; school communities of participants 37–8; the sample 36, 217–18; scope and focus of 45–7; socioeconomic characteristics of students by wave 200t; study sample by state 35t; teacher and student views on disclosure 233–4t; teacher interviews 235; the teachers 38; teachers, students and schools by classroom type 48t; typology for class instruction styles 47–9; see also Discussing Controversial Issues Study post-survey comparisons
Discussing Controversial Issues Study post-survey comparisons: classroom discussion 223t; Like-Minded and Politically Diverse School sample by wave 229t; news and political talk outcomes 224–5t; political participation 227t; student interviews 218–19, 235
discussion and discussions: clarifying the aims of 207; in Contemporary Controversies class 114; vs. deliberation 5; dynamics of 126, 129; maintaining civility in 94–6; mitigating negative effects 179–80; political 57–60; of political controversy 155; scarcity of in social studies classes 47; selection of issues for 14, 160–9; "steering" in 172; student participation in 54–6; teachers sharing views in 186–9; teaching with and for 93, 114; see also debate; deliberation; issues for discussion
diversity 88, 114, 117, 179; at Academy High 110–11; at Adams High 87; in classrooms 54–7; in private religious schools 135; at St. John's High School 70
Dobson, James 136, 152n5
DREAM Act 196–7
Dunn, Mr. 158–60, 183–5, 197, 210

E Pluribus . . . Separation: Deepening Double Segregation for More Students (Orfield, Kucsera, & Siegel-Hawley) 28
education: aims of 74–7; civic 62–3; democratic 4–5, 11, 20; philosophy of 78; process of 11
Egan, Patrick 32
electoral participation 33–4, 67
11th Hour, The (film) 199
Elliot (Mr.) 191
engagement, political 79, 146–8, 156, 184

English language learners (ELLs) 89, 93, 98, 173, 186, 194
Equal Protection Clause (14th Amendment) 124
equality 7, 75–7, 80, 123, 156, 176, 184, 191, 193, 195; *see also* inequality
ESL class *see* English language learners (ELLs)
Establishment Clause 113–14

Facebook 42
Facing History and Ourselves 184
fairness 78, 112, 121, 156, 184, 191
families: influence of 31; political discussions with 63; values of 134, 135
First Amendment 113
Flanagan, Constance 60
flourishing 75, 82n5
Focus on the Family 136
Framework for Professional Judgment 12*f*
Frank, Barney 20

Ganzler, Louis 9, 107n1
Gardner, Ms. 198, 199
Gauchat, Gordon 27
gay rights 31–2; *see also* marriage, same-sex
Generation X, demographic and ideological differences 31*t*, 32*t*
Gephart, Richard 2
Gilbert, Joanne 163
Gingrich, Newt 2, 21–2
global poverty 71–2, 80–1
government: representative 101–2; role of 31, 32*t*, 33*t*, 79
Gratz v. Bollinger 123, 124
Green, Mr. 49
guest speakers 117, 131n5, 150
gun control 21, 31, 32*t*
Gutmann, Amy 5, 24

Hand, Michael 167–8, 172
Hearing the Other Side (Mutz) 148
Heller, Eileen 14, 49, 52, 53, 86–90, 92–5, 98–100, 104, 177, 186, 194, 205
Hempstead, Andrew 14, 52, 86–8, 91–2, 94–5, 97–8, 102–3, 194–5
Mr. Hempstead. (Mr.) 186
Hess, Diana 4, 5, 9, 45, 93, 107n1, 114, 171, 215
Hibbing, John 57
hierarchical linear modeling (HLM) 222
Hispanic/Latino/a Americans: as study participants 37; voting rate of 34; *see also* students, Latino/a

Holocaust 163–4
humanism 21, 117, 144
humor 50; partisan 201
Hurricane Katrina 19

ideological differences, by generation 32*t*
Illinois Youth Summit program 34, 44n9, 209
immigration 23, 88, 139–40
inclusive participation 14
inclusivity 173–9
Independents 25; Millennials as 31, 33*t*
inequality: of access 88; economic 21–4, 43, 60, 106; of outcomes 14; resource 72; social 7–9, 15, 54, 80, 110, 119, 126; *see also* equality
Ingles, Ms. 49–50
Interactive Lecture 140
intermediary organizations, role of 209–11
International Relations course 53
Internet, as news source 26
interviews: follow-up telephone 10, 35, 41, 46, 51, 63–5, 94–5, 105, 117–18, 128, 145, 210, 218–19, 234; student 10, 34–6, 46–9, 54–7, 67, 69n3, 74, 82n2, 94–5, 99, 101, 105, 111, 112, 116, 126, 136, 140–2, 144, 148, 158, 174, 179–80, 183, 186, 188–9, 194, 197, 200, 214, 220, 229, 233–6; teacher 10, 34, 38, 47, 49, 72, 92, 104, 120–1, 130, 159, 169, 171, 175, 183, 189, 191, 195, 207, 234–6; *see also* surveys
intolerance 81, 235; and tolerance 148–50; *see also* tolerance
Iraq, war in 19, 72, 74, 82n3, 97, 169–70
issues for discussion: balancing authenticity and inclusivity 173–9; behavioral criterion for 166–7; and the case of torture 169–73; empirical 163–6; empirical vs. policy 161, 162*t*; epistemic criterion for 167–8; ethical considerations 215; framing 163–6; mitigating negative effects 179–81; political 14, 166; political authenticity in 168–9; settled vs. open 161–3, 162*t*, 163*t*; types of 161*t*; *see also* discussion and discussions

journalism, changes in 26–7

Kahne, Joe 60, 62
Kelly, Thomas 192
Kerry, John 37, 39, 54, 70, 87

King High School 14, 111, 132, 136, 136*t*, 137, 146, 150, 156, 197–8
Kucsera, John 28
Kuehl (Mr.) 50, 51, 111, 129, 136*t*, 137
Kushner, Joel 14, 51, 109–31, 136*t*, 137, 138–9, 148, 149*t*, 150–1, 156, 175, 178, 186, 192, 199, 207; and the discussion on torture 169–73

Lareau, Annette 16n4, 63
Latinos/as *see* students, Latino/a
Legislative Simulation *see* Adams High School
Lemon Test 114
Levinson, Meira 121
Liberals 44n1, 79; class political orientation 136*t*; degree of trust in scientific community 27; Democrats as 20–1; in LMS 137; Millennials as 32; students as 37, 57, 62, 111–12, 114–15, 117, 119, 156, 229; teachers as 138, 198
Libertarians 23, 79
Lincoln, Mr. 56–7
literacy, political 79–81, 156, 184

Mann, Horace 2–3, 189
Mann, Mary Tyler Peabody 3
MANOVA (Multivariate Analysis of Variance) 69n5, 222
Mansbridge, J. J. 102
marijuana, legalization of 31, 32*t*, 33*t*
marriage, same-sex 19–20, 31, 32*t*, 33*t*, 137, 158–60, 178, 183–5
Matthew Effect 61–2
Matthews, Julie 14, 52, 86–7, 104, 186
May, Andrew 185
May, Samuel J. 2–3, 189
McAvoy, Paula 9, 215
McCain, John 39, 148
McCarty, Nolan 21, 22–3, 27
McCully, Alan 186
Medicare 23
Meehan, Casey 165
Millennial generation 30–4; demographic and ideological differences 31*t*, 32*t*; ideological variance among 33*t*; as news consumers 41–2; as political producers 42–3; racial diversity of 32; views correlated with race 32
Miller-Lane, Jonathan 185
Mitchell, Douglas 206
moderates *see* conservatives
moot court activities 112, 121

"A More Perfect Union" (Obama speech) 123
multiculturalism: and autonomy 151n3; at Academy High 109; at Adams High 87; at St. John's High School 70
Multivariate Analysis of Variance (MANOVA) 69n5, 222
Murphy, Mr. 53, 196
Mutz, Diana 26, 110, 148

Nader, Ralph 37, 39
National Bioethics Advisory Commission 213
neutrality 189–93
news awareness, and civic engagement 41–2
news media 26
Niemi, N. S. 201
Niemi, R. G. 201

Obama, Barack 1, 3, 4, 20, 33, 37, 39, 42, 113, 123, 129, 148; demographics of supporters 33, support of Millennials for 32, 33*t*
O'Brien, Ms. 53
On Education (Brighouse) 149
open-mindedness 53–4
Orfield, Gary 28
organizations, intermediary 209–11

Parker, Walter 5, 47, 93, 114, 160
parliamentary procedure 91
partisan gap 25; *see also* polarization
Peters, Richard Stanley 11
polarization: divisiveness of 199; history of 22; ideological-partisan 24; increase in 21; political 3, 6, 8–9, 20, 54, 80, 110, 143, 204–5, in the political classroom 28; of the public 24–6
political activities, online 42–3
political affiliation, by generation 31*t*
political classrooms 4; aims of 77–81, 156–7; conservation and support of 15, 204; ethical question in 14; goals of 211; in practice 81; policies working against 28–30; values of 80–1
political friendship 14, 81, 110–12, 120, 122, 128
political ideology: and cluster membership 67; at St. John's High School 70
political literacy 79–81, 156, 184
political participation: demographic variables affecting 46; five clusters of 64–6

Poole, Keith 21
Potter, Ms. 70–4, 80–1, 191, 193
poverty, global 71–2, 80–1
Prensky, Marc 40
President's Council on Bioethics 213
Presidential Commission for the Study of
    Bioethical Issues 213
presidential speeches to schools 1–4
Prior Civic Exposure Index 60–2, 68, 146,
    221–2
professional development 34, 158–9
professional judgment 11, 14, 72–4, 73*f*,
    205; framework for 12*f*, 155
public *see* citizens

race and ethnicity: and the test data 220*t*;
    and trust/distrust 122–8
racial segregation 28
Ream, Robert 206
recession, economic 20
Reich, Rob 133–4
religion: and autonomy 133–6; Catholic
    70; Christian 37, 113, 135–6, 139;
    evangelical Christian 21, 133, 134, 136,
    143; influence of 31, 150–1
Republicans 20–2; and evangelical
    Christianity 136; Millennials as 33*t*;
    platform of 137; student identification
    with 145; younger members 31–2
resegregation 30; *see also* racial segregation
resources, distribution of 71–2, 80–1
respect 7, 8, 13, 48, 53, 58, 70, 76–7, 93–4,
    96, 111, 113–14, 117–18, 125, 127, 141,
    165, 171–2, 177, 185, 187, 189–93, 195,
    197–8, 202, 210, 212
Rodriguez, M. 60
Rosenthal, Howard 21
roundtable discussions 124

Sanders, Lynn 7, 121
Schlozman, Kay Lehman 24
school administrators, role of 209
schools: all-girls 210; Catholic 12, 191, 210;
    changing culture of 99–110; charter
    9, 12, 36, 38, 158, 183, 211; Christian
    12, 14, 35, 81, 132–3, 137–8, 142, 144,
    197, 207, 210, 219; homogeneous
    146; Like-Minded 14, 111–12, 133,
    146–8, 149*t*, 152n8, 192, 222; Politically
    Diverse 146–7; politically like-minded
    136–9; prayer in 21; relationship with
    democratic society 4; suburban 211
Schwab, Joseph 13

scientific community, issue of trust in 27
secular humanism 21, 117, 144
segregation 7–8, 15n3
self-government 78
Siegel-Hawley, Genevieve 28
Silent Generation, demographic and
    ideological differences 31*t*, 32*t*
Skocpol, Theda 23
Smith, B. 60
social class 221; *see also* socioeconomic
    status (SES)
social networking 42
social policy, redistributive 23
social science 185
Social Security 23
socioeconomic status (SES) 29, 44n10, 54,
    124–5; at Adams High 87; and civic
    engagement 146; determination of
    221; effect on civic participation 66–7;
    impact of 60–1, 68; and the test data 220*t*
Socratic dialogue 50, 140
Stanley, William 6
St. John's High School 70, 191
Street Law 124
students: at Academy High 110–11; at
    Adams High 87; African American
    30, 37, 70, 87, 104, 111, 122–6, 173,
    178, 184; Asian American 27, 70, 87,
    111, 126, 132, 140; of color 102–3,
    115; conservative 67; as "engaged and
    learning" 48, 49–52; immigrant 87,
    103, 108n6, 173; impact of prior civic
    experiences 61–2; inclusive participation
    of 87–90; increased interest in politics
    57–8, 60, Latino/a 30, 37, 87, 103, 111,
    122, 173, 175, 184; LBGTQ 176; lessons
    learned by 145; level of classroom
    participation 49–52, 54–6; low-SES
    173; middle-class 7, 16n4; Native
    American 111; perceptions of teachers
    sharing views 186–7; post-survey
    phone interviews with 63; prediction
    and outcomes on civic engagement 62;
    voting choices of 39–40; White 25, 28,
    36*t*, 37, 87–8, 102, 121, 122, 124–7, 220;
    working-class 7, 16n4
Supreme Court 28, 113
surveys: baseline 34, 218, 220*t*; pre- and
    post-course 9, 34, 37, 41, 46, 48, 51,
    53, 58, 59*t*, 60–3, 66, 69n4, 87, 93,
    111–12, 129, 136–7, 146–8, 159, 173,
    180, 186–8, 201, 218, 220*t*, 220–3, 224*t*,
    227*t*, 229*t*, 233, 234; phone 35, 37, 42,

46, 47, 64, 68, 186, 193, 200, 218, 219; teacher 38, 143, 218, 220*t*, 226; *see also* interviews

Tea Party movement 20, 23, 164
teachers: and the Adams High American Government course 92–3, 98–9; aims of 72–4; avoidance of controversy by 8, 15, 172; commitment of 212; as conservatives 138; content knowledge of 180; deliberation by 207–9; differences among 10; different teaching styles of 49–52; effect of on teaching discussion skills 45; good judgment of 13; ideological diversity of 38; influence of pedagogy on view-sharing 188–9; as learners 206–7; as liberals 138, 198; opinion on sharing views with students 187; professional ethics of 213–16; professional judgment of 11, 12*f*, 14, 72–4, 73*f*, 155, 205; as professionals 206
teachers' views: ethical considerations on sharing 189–90, 202, 237; evidence against sharing 188; evidence for both directions 188; evidence in favor of sharing 187–8; example of teacher sharing 183; occasional disclosure 197–9; personal views of 155; political 199–202; public perception of 205; purposeful withholding 194–7; sharing as pedagogical tool 193; student opinions on 186–7; teacher opinion on 187; teachers' decisions to share 186
Teenage Citizens: The Political Theories of the Young (Flanagan) 60
Theiss-Morse, Elizabeth 57
Theriault, Sean 22
Thompson, Dennis 5, 24
Thiede, K. 60
tolerance 13, 77–9, 112, 115–19, 156, 178–9, 191, 193, 195, 198, 201; vs. intolerance 148–50

torture, as discussion topic 169–73
tracking 28–9, 30, 43, 76, 82n2, 88, 102, 106, 121
transparency 189–93
trust 3, 8, 20, 23, 45, 80, 86, 110, 122, 189, 190, 198; as cause of polarization 8; public 27; in the scientific community 27
Twitter 42

undocumented workers, legal status of 31, 32*t*; *see also* immigration

values: American 25; Christian 132, 134–6, 142–3, 150, 156, 197; of family 134, 135; of political classroom 80; of school community 70, 74, 135
Van Orden v. Perry 113, 114
Verba, Sydney 24
Voigt, Mr. 43, 52
volunteering 43, 61, 64–7, 221
voters: demographic variables in 33–4; misperceptions of 57; students from Like-Minded Schools as 147–8

Walters, Tom 14, 111, 132–51, 149*t*, 156, 186, 197–8, 207, 210
war: in Afghanistan and Iraq 19, 72, 74, 82n3, 97, 169–70; culture 21; justification for 76; use of torture in 169
Washington High School 28–9, 29*t*, 200
wealth, distribution of 22–3
White Americans: as study participants 37; voting rate of 34; at Washington High School 28; *see also* students, White
Whitman (Mr.) 139
Williamson, Vanessa 23
Wright, Jeremiah 123

Xander (Mr.) 50, 136*t*, 137

young people *see* Millennial generation
Youth Summit 34, 210–11, 218–19

Made in the USA
Middletown, DE
02 October 2018